Memory and Dread

Memory and Dread
Or
The Memory of Childhood

Néstor A. Braunstein

Translation by Peter Kahn

Jorge Pinto Books Inc.
New York

Concerning the English edition

I am pleased to present the English version of the first volume of a trilogy on memory. Julio Cortázar once stated, with the security of one promulgating a law, "Memory starts with dread." Following that clue I found the traces of that banal and terrible "first recollection" not only in the work of this Argentine novelist but also in Freud's entire theory of psychoanalysis; in certain sonnets of Shakespeare and Sor Juana; in Borges's whole literary output; in Jean Piaget's "genetic epistemology"; in the plan of "living to tell the tale" of writers like Gabriel Garcia Márquez, Elias Canetti, Georges Perec, Vladimir Nabokov, Michel Leiris; in the painful encounters with the mirror recounted by prominent women writers; in the history of the development of the suspicious literary genre known as "autobiography." I wish my reader to travel through this book as if on a safari hunting for first memories—her/his own included.

I gave the title of *La memoria, la inventora* (*Memory, the inventor*) to the second volume, already published in Spanish in Mexico by Siglo XXI Editores, because the narrative of a memory is always a compromise between what happened and what was registered as happening; with the way one remembers it happening and with the way one retells it; by the manner in which it is received by the listener or reader and his reaction to it. In that second book I evoke some of the countless ideas, metaphors and tales about memory written by poets, physicians, philosophers and scientists. The third and last volume, soon to come out, deals with a subject that borders on the dramatic: the relationship between personal memory, collective memory and documented history, that nightmare from which James Joyce could not wake up. The title: *La memoria del uno y la memoria del Otro* (*One's memory and the memory of the Other*).

The outline followed in the trilogy is kept the same throughout the three books: to articulate the knowledge of psychoanalysis, history, philosophy, literary critique and the neurosciences around a subject that bears the same name but receives different meanings; it is homonymy that makes the vague semantic kinship for the word "memory" seem identical for each of the five disciplines involved. The childhood recollection is a privileged province where the five threads converge and exhibit their differences: this is the reason I chose it as a first laboratory for my research on memory. The rest, rests in the hands of the reader . . . as it is meant to be . . . as it always happens.

Contents

12: MICHEL LEIRIS: THE FORTUNATE FAILURE OF AUTOBIOGRAPHY (. . . *TUNATELY!*)

13: AUTOBIOGRAPHIES AND SELF-PORTRAITS

14: PROSOPOPEIA: APPROACHES TO AUTOBIOGRAPHY

15: HETEROTHANATOPHONIA

Dedication

TAMARA

One of the most sublime, imaginative works of the century now rushing into the past is the voyage taken by Italo Calvino in "Invisible Cities." On pages 13 and 14 of the English translation, the traveler, Marco Polo, makes his way toward the city of Tamara. As he approaches it he feels that all he sees corresponds to the reality of things: "a print in the sand indicates the tiger's passage"; the cloud indicates the possibility of rain; the fruit implicates the tree that bore it, and the seed hidden within the fruit signals another tree that shall emerge.

But upon entering the city of Tamara he is astonished to see that everything suggests something different and arbitrary, something demanding interpretation. The relationships are indirect: a tankard is the sign for a tavern; pincers for a dentist; the order and size of the houses and gardens reflect the opulence of their owners; the thinness of the jackass, the poverty of its owner; the smile of the child corresponds to the love of his parents; the elegance of a young woman, the good taste of her suitor. Nothing is as it appears: the city is not toured, it is read, for it contains nothing that does not symbolize something else, every detail must be translated because it dictates what must be thought. After living for a time in Tamara the traveler moves on, without knowing for certain what the true nature of the city is, what is hidden beneath the avalanche of signs . . . and then he discovers that the clouds are no longer clouds nor do they presage rain but rather they appear to be dancers, the marks in the sand are the writing of a drunk calligrapher, fruits are emblems for masculine or feminine anatomy.

Certainly some might say that the pre-Tamara traveler was better prepared for reality and did not complicate his life searching for inscrutable meanings, getting lost in doubtful interpretations. Certainly some might affirm that being in that confounding city he was overcome by an inclination toward suspicion, a tendency to investigate simple things in order to decipher them as if they were cryptograms, an unrest, a feeling of ignorance, a necessity to assure himself of what seemed so natural to the city's inhabitants. But it would be better not to suggest this to the traveler passing through Tamara: he would respond that his world is now infinitely richer than before, that his uncertainty over the meaning of what he sees and hears has sharpened his eyes and ears, that his sense of touch now receives testimonies heretofore unsuspected, sublime, subliminal vibrations, imperceptible nuances, microtonalities, unfathomable subtleties of mood and humor, bizarre messages of the inaudible.

Nietzsche and Heidegger, Kandinsky and Francis Bacon, Schoenberg and Ligeti, Musil and Eliot, Freud and Lacan, Resnais and Greenaway. These are some of the authors that have represented Tamara. One does not pass through their work with impunity. The subject who submits himself to them has to remove all blinders and prepare to see the world in another way. They are not consumed: one is consumed by them. And one cannot say what they say. Who could "retell" a sculpture by Brancusi, a page by Beckett, a sequence by Berio? And this is not because these productions contain a certain "mystery." It is because they border upon what is truly worth expressing, what is indeed inexpressible.

(From *Ficcionario de psicoanálisis*. México: Siglo Veintiuno, 2001. pp. 68–70.)

INTROIT: PAPER SCRAPS

In every analytic work on a life-history it is always possible
to explain the meaning of the earliest memories along these
lines. Indeed, it usually happens that the very recollection to
which the patient gives precedence, that he relates first, with
which he introduces his confession, proves to be the most
important, the very one that holds the key to his mental life.[1]

1. From the Book of Life Whose Pages Are Memories

Where, when and how is the memory machine set in motion?
What degree of fidelity—of authenticity—does our first memory
contain? Is it something that really happened or is it a foundational
myth that we appeal to, recovering it from a dark and unknowable
past in response to our current needs? What significance does it
have, what meaning can be retroactively given to the moment at
which the movie of memory begins? How does that first island
emerge, protruding from the ocean of infantile amnesia? How can
there be a first episode if, in order to narrate it, one has to say: "I
remember that . . ." and, necessarily, there must be a supposed "I,"

---

1. Freud, Sigmund [1917]. "A Childhood Recollection from " '*Dichtung und
   Wahrheit*,' " in *Character and Culture: Psychoanalysis applied to anthropology,
   mythology, folklore, literature, and culture in general.* Editor, Philip Rieff.
   New York: Collier Books, 1963, p. 193.

a "subject" for which the evoked would be a "predicate?" Is that "I" not already the result of a previous and established memory, of an agreement between oneself and one's self-image, already an effect of memory? Or is it possible to suppose that first there is the memory—the embryo of the self—and later, like a keloid scar of the memory, the person emerges capable of evoking it? In this case, we might say: "I remember, therefore (ergo, then) I exist." "I" am the person to whom at one time "that" happened and, if it were not for "that" I would not be who I am; I would be someone else. I am only a block of memories (and forgotten memories) that I presume belong to "me." I am the consequence of certain uncertain reminiscences.

Do I *have* a memory archive or *am* I an archive of memories and forgotten memories? Is it not in the memory (or in the fantasy of "having a memory") that my enigmatic "identity" resides?

Let us explore this idea: memory comes first. It is prior to being. Each of us becomes the person we believe ourselves to be by organizing the facts of our experiences with a singular mold and without instructors to teach us how to remember. Clearly stated: we are not "who we are" because "that happened to us" but rather because we have registered and understood what happened to us in a certain way, selecting, mending and patching traces of personal experiences with other people's narratives. Memory is not an archive of documents but rather a construct enriched by the imagination. Let us consider a non-fictional example: "I must have been three years old when there was a fire in the neighbor's tire repair shop. That is my first memory: the night, the heat, the sirens, the asphyxiation, the smell of burnt rubber, my father wrapping me in damp sheets. We were forced to live in my grandparents' house for two weeks . . ."

Certain *impressions* are *recorded*, more or less vividly, with greater or lesser exactitude, in a child's "soul." The girl—who certainly already exists, already speaks, already counts herself as "one" of the family—has an experience. Is it the first that she can remember? It is difficult to verify, to establish a precise chronology in the memory banks. In this case, without a doubt it is a *traumatic* event. Surrounding the events of that chaotic night of the fire, that distant memory, she organizes in reverse—in retrospect—all the information that she has about herself and that she has garnered from the network of relations in which she is immersed. From that confusion she can extract a representation of who she is in the eyes of others, which expands with the image of her face as reflected in the mirror and with the recognition of her own name and of her position in the network of family relationships. The incipient self adds coherence to the whole of her knowledge, bringing together the disperse fragments. The girl (or the boy) has, from then on, a starting point for a narrative that she will be able to continue in first person; the traumatism of the night marked by the sirens of the fire trucks begins a certain historicization, a story in which she is the protagonist and not just someone who repeats what others have told her. *Life Is a Novel* (Title in French: *La Vie Est Un Roman*; Title in English: *Life Is a Bed of Roses*) is the title of a film by Alain Resnais, and "life is a novel" is the underlying motto of all the *Bildungsroman* (formational novels) that have inundated us thanks to the romantic movement and subsequent traditions. "Life is a novel," ours, hers, the one we narrate and that our patients narrate, session after session, throughout their psychoanalysis, written in diaries, notebooks and autobiographies. In the text of that novel there is always a foundational myth, an ancestral prehistory, a story of genesis that the subject cannot remember because it has been conveyed to the subject by others. Upon the original myth and upon the remnants of unnamed experiences the house—or palace—of memory is constructed, alternating between dark caverns and dimly lit hallways. There must also be a first, basal incident that serves as an anchor to begin the narration of the peripeteias of an existence and a lifetime in exile—exile in the country of memory. *The first memory. The childhood memory.* Ghostly and mythical.

I will use the term "peripeteias" for the sudden changes, the unforeseen and, in appearance, random events, accidents and dramatic mutations that occur in the lives of everyone: the peripeteias that seem to be the work of destiny, causality or fate. They do not necessarily have to be exceptional events. Life is a novel, I have stated; it is also an unpredictable adventure. Every existence includes a variable quantity of ups and downs, of twists and turns that deviate from the ever sinuous trodden path. To begin with, the very first and undesired event is that of being born, of detaching oneself from a female body. Thereafter, all other events follow, tracing a biography full of mysterious points of silence and incomprehension which we supplant with a kind of glue so the events will not fall apart, to keep them sewn together, to assemble and affix the installments of that "volume" that we weave together with strips of memory. We are the seamstresses and bookbinders of our lives. We dress ourselves in memories . . . or we disguise ourselves.

Here the Proustian aspect of this book is manifest.[2] Every human being is like a book in which the "impressions" of one's life experiences are written or "etched." It is a pure typography, a legible and translatable text that is at the same time, in general, intricate and confusing. We decipher it the best we can through the myopic eyes of our intellect. We float among its hieroglyphics and search for the clues that have been lost to us. We sense that the book is not sealed to us once and for all; it is open to infinite rewritings, different readings, scarcely deliberate techniques that weave the past with the urgencies of the present (just as happens—as we know all too well—with the history of nations, the lies written by the conquerors, the "collective memory" according to Halbwachs).[3] The flow of time leaves a trail of writings, of charades to be resolved, pieces of a jigsaw puzzle with an infinite number of possible solu-

2. Proust, Marcel [1913–1927], *À la recherche du temps perdu*, Paris: La Pléiade, Gallimard, 1969, v. III, pp. 877 ss.
3. Halbwachs, Maurice [1877–1945]. *Les cadres sociaux de la mémoire*, Paris: Presses Universitaires de France, 1952. *On collective Memory*. Translated by Lewis Coser. Chicago: The Chicago University Press. 1992. *La mémoire collective*, Paris: Presses Universitaires de France, 1950. *The Collective Memory*. Edited by Mary Douglas. New York: Harper and Row Colophon Books, 1980.

tions. An "instruction manual" is needed to assemble the puzzle.[4] However, it did not occur even to Georges Perec himself that the puzzle could be composed of soft, malleable, ductile parts, like Dalí's limp, melting watches. Nonetheless, such is our memory: an imbroglio inhabited by the prejudices of our personality, by the desires of those who surrounded us early on, by the pressures of our social group and the anxieties of our historical period.

So, who are we? I will venture to propose that we are memory in movement, perforated by oblivion and repression, a way of composing the charade of our precarious memories and of presenting it to the gaze of others who will have—if they are interested—a difficult mission: that of accepting or challenging it. And the pieces? Memories of fantasies, fantasies of memory. Proust,[5] who was an expert in this area, said that everyone had an obligation to fulfill: to write the book they carry within themselves. And he assembled *his* book with the blending of flavors and fragrances, mistaken and fleeting encounters, snippets of things that were seen and heard, all in an apparent temporal disorder. Proust showed that autobiographical memory does not conform to the scheme of a chronicle of successive events. It is woven like a discontinuous narrative where the threads that lead from one peripeteia to another lack premeditation and coordination. It is "involuntary memory" or, to be more precise, it is unconscious memory. The connections formed in memory are as mysterious as the associations expressed by the patient speaking from the psychoanalyst's couch. Between them there prevails a logical and semantic oxymoron: that of free linkage.

This was Freud's first discovery: *memory is discontinuous*. The subject is divided, it is multiple; among its parts, and among its memories, there are unstable borders that are always in conflict. Previously, a certain precursor had sensed the impossibility of the

---

4. Perec, Georges [1933–1992]. *La vie mode d'emploi*. Paris: Hachette, 1978. *Life: A User's Manual*. Translated by David Bellos. London: Vintage, 2002. A fascinating and essential illustration of the puzzle metaphor (See below, Chapter 11).
5. Proust, Marcel. op. cit., Vol. III, pp. 880 and 890.

autobiographical endeavor. Goethe, at the dawn of Romanticism, understood the difficulty of setting down the story of his life:

> For this seems to be the main object of biography,—to exhibit the man in relation to the features of his time [. . .] But *for this is required what is scarcely attainable*; namely, that the individual should know himself and his age,—himself, so far as he has remained the same under all circumstances; his age, as that which carries along with it, determines and fashions, both the willing and the unwilling . . . (my italics).[6]

With Freud, Proust, Virginia Woolf and other authors we will be considering, we have confirmed this "unattainable" something: no one has the privilege of remaining the same over time, no one can fully expose the self and its circumstances. Memory is torn by the impossibility of remembering, by that which was conscious and known in its moment but could not be assimilated by the subject and thus remained separate from the material of memory—the fabric (the text) of its evocations. That which does not fit into the narrative of life is "trauma"; the memory of peripeteias that cannot be reconciled with what one cannot call one's "own." Memory is egocentric and tries to be autonomous. When we are aware of what really happened, as opposed to what we would have liked to have happened, we perceive it as something "distant" and, at such a moment, we will say that we had forgotten about it. Until the advent of Freud, to forget was a valid excuse, a manifestation of innocence. After Freud, one has to justify oneself and provide explanations for what one does not remember because we suspect that there are reasons for forgetting and the act itself is guilty— amnesia is an indicator of a conflict and memory is an unfaithful servant: often it serves as an alibi, a "cover-up" for what one pre-

---

6. Goethe, Johann Wolfgang von [1811]. *The Autobiography of Goethe: (Truth and Fiction: Relating to my life)*. Translated by John Oxenford. Boston: Dana Estes & Company Publishers, 1848, p. 5.

fers not to acknowledge. With pretended sincerity, it professes to *conserve* what in fact it has *invented*.

Blanchot emphasizes the importance of the ability to forget as the trunk from which the branches of memory sprout. Similarly, he might have said that memory is a hollow pillar built around a central void constructed of forgetting and rejection:

> First to forget. To remember only where one remembers nothing. To forget: to remember everything as though by way of forgetting. There is a profoundly forgotten point from which every memory radiates. Everything is exalted in memory from something which is forgotten, infinitesimal detail, a minuscule fissure into which it passes in its entirety.[7]

An intuitive prejudice convinces us that a memory may be "in the memory" or may be "lost in oblivion." Nothing could be more false: the ability to forget is an integral part—the framework and nucleus—of memory; it is the reason for memory. It is like death: it pertains to life and, indeed, it is its essence. The aphorism cited by Bichat (1771–1802), "Life is the set of tendencies that resist death," is illuminating. If we have spoken of *"life-death"* in order to question the opposition between them and to emphasize their mutual and necessary continuity, now we might speak of "memory-oblivion" and propose a rigorous analogy between the compound terms, stating that "memory is the set of tendencies that resists forgetting." If there are drives to live that try to maintain the subject in a state of individual and collective knowledge that allows him to persevere in being, there is also a constant dissociative force that drives a movement toward the inanimate, toward the erasure of all the differences, toward the necessary forgetting implied by nights of sleeping and death. There are powerful drives behind memory and also behind its "obliteration" (*obliteration*—we take license and invent a Franco-neologism with due respect for the goddess

---

7. Blanchot, Maurice. *The Last Man.* Translated by Lydia Davis. New York: Columbia University Press, 1987, pp. 85–86.

of Etymology, half sister of Mnemosyne, the goddess of memory and mother of the Muses).

Besides, how else could a memory subsist if not for the oblivion to which it pertains and the oblivion which surrounds it? Vladimir Nabokov became lost within the immensity of a minimal memory: "How small the cosmos (a kangaroo's pouch would hold it), how paltry and puny in comparison to human consciousness, to a single individual recollection, and its expression in words!"[8] That "inaccessible something" that Goethe confessed depends on the impossibility of "truly telling a story," which Derrida also refers to,[9] and which depends on Blanchot's black light from which all memory radiates, and on the impossibility of speaking to memory, as indicated by Nabokov and all the others, on the inability of language to apprehend what is real and at the center of the minutest experience, as proclaimed by Lord Chandos in his apocryphal letter to Roger Bacon.[10] The narrative is condemned to failure; thus, as a challenge, it is tempting. Whosoever is concerned with *subjectivity*—something that is perhaps infrequent in these times that are so focused on *objectivity*—engages in a Sisyphean task, that of recording his memories both for himself and for others. It is clear that they enjoy the autobiographical endeavor; only then may it be understood how they can dedicate themselves to achieving the impossible, shuddering with emotion as they set out on the hunt for memories, experiencing the delight of venturing into a territory only they can penetrate, excited by the spiritual challenges of choosing the words to describe what they see and

8. Nabokov, Vladimir. *Speak, Memory: An Autobiography Revisited*. New York: Alfred A. Knopf, Inc., 1999, p. 13.

9. "I never learned to tell a story. And as I love above all recording and Memory—Mnemosyne—I have always felt this inability as a sad inadequacy [. . .] Why didn't I receive this gift? Based on this complaint, and probably to protect myself from it, a suspicion always arises in my thoughts: Who can truly tell a story? Is it possible to narrate?" Derrida, Jacques. *Memoires for Paul de Man*. New York: Columbia University Press, 1986, pp. 17 and 25 (my translation).

10. Hoffmanstahl, H. von [1903]. *The Lord Chandos Letter*. Translated by Russell Stockman. Marlboro, Vt.: Marlboro Press, 1986.

what they hide with the simple substitution of one adjective for another, attracted by the allure of mystification and falling into its trap, supposing—perhaps mistakenly—that it is good to know and transmit past experience. Attempting to survive the habitual death of the self. An otherwise suspicious genre: "Enter and listen, ladies and gentleman, to the passionate story of how I came to be what I am." This will be the subject of our final chapter.

There is a paradox surrounding the functioning of memory, understood as the ability to preserve the awareness of something that was, but is no longer, in the form of a recollection, the affirmation of certain knowledge of something lived, seen or heard in the past. It is better appreciated when the episode in question is distressing or shameful. One remembers . . . in spite of oneself. The recollection returns in a ghostly fashion and with it traces of anguish and shame. To avoid it, the conscious attempts to distance itself from the unwelcome guest, the intruder, and at times, but not always, it succeeds in disguising and even "forgetting" it. The unpleasant inhabitant of the spirit is condemned to ostracism. The memory wants to know nothing of the recollection that frightens or upsets it. When it can—if it can—it tolerates it. If it cannot, it plays the victim (and perhaps the accomplice?) to the attacks. Some day we will find ourselves faced with the "jouissance of the ~~sexual enjoyment~~ painful recollection."

In any case one knows—very well—what has been banished. One prefers "not to mention the rope in the house of the hanged man" (which is indeed oneself) and to flee in anguish from that which recalls the former suffering. Or to take refuge in it. We know all too well that displeasure avoided at the price of repression only returns in the form of "symptoms"—commemorative monuments of the wound. Thus, it is bad if one remembers (because one suffers) and it is bad if one forgets (because one also suffers, albeit in another way). What hurts is not the conscience; what hurts is the real force of the blow and the bruises it has left behind. What hurts are the recollections, but we must recognize that in them is hidden another reality: that of sinful and transgressive jouissance.

To have suffered—and to remember it—is a merit that demands reward. The martyr is a preferred creditor. The palm leaves open the doors to paradise.

2. Memento: The Subject of the Annunciation

Freud at first believed—excessively, according to some critics—that the recovery of forgotten memories, the lifting of repression and the overcoming of infantile amnesia, would serve to "cure" the subject. For Freud, in the beginnings of psychoanalysis, neurosis (in particular, hysteria) signified that the subject "suffered from reminiscences" and analytic treatment was a resource for the retrieval of memories expelled from the conscience. For this reason he thought it necessary to "repair" the memory, to create conditions favorable for remembering and overcoming resistance to recollection. The initial goal of psychoanalysis was "to make conscious the unconscious" at the height of the session, under favorable conditions that are created when the subject is "in transference" with a familiar person who will neither judge him nor commit indiscretions. "Here and now, with me, you can risk remembering; moreover, that's what I want and, indeed, I am commanding you: Remember!" This is what the analyst seems to be saying to the patient when he directs him to say whatever comes into his mind. "Mind," in ancient times, and particularly in Dante's time, was none other than a synonym for "memory."[11] Thus in Italian the word for "to forget" is *dimenticare*, or to "de-mind," we might say in English, taking the liberty to invent a neologism. Amnesia, preceding the creation of the term Alzheimer's, is a different phenomenon from "dementia." In distant times, the residence of the memory was the cordial organ, or the heart; thus, to preserve something in it was to "record" it (in the *cor*, from Latin). In Italian, the antonym of *ricordare*, is *scordare,* and the reflexive is *scordarsi*

---

11. Weinrich, Harald. *Lete. The art and critic of forgetting.* Translation by Stephen Randall. Ithaca (NY): Cornell University Press, 2004, p. 9.

(aria by Mozart [K. 505]: *Ch'io mi scordidi te?*), that is, to leave outside of the heart.

"Remember!" is, in Latin, an imperative that is a single signifier, "*memento.*" The most familiar construction with this form for us today is "*memento mori*" (remember death) which reminds us of one of the great lessons taught to us by Mnemosyne, daughter of Gaea and Uranus, of the sky and earth. A lesson that we tend to forget is that the memory does not proceed from the past—as we ingenuously believe—but rather from the future. What should not be forgotten is that it is from the future that all memory derives its meaning or is revealed as pertaining to the future. Death, inasmuch as it is known and foreseen, dissolves memory in advance and marks its destiny in oblivion. Like the rich man and his wealth, no one leaves this world carrying his memories, experience or accumulated knowledge.

In a narrated memory, both linguistics and psychology have distinguished the *subject of the statement* (generally "I," of someone who speaks in the present and evokes a previous experience) and the *subject of the enunciation*, falsely and incompletely represented by the "I" of the statement who is aware of the difficulty of circumscribing any recollection and of the necessary falsifications that the recollection must suffer in order to be put into words and transmitted to someone else in an unrepeatable dialogue experience. This essential distinction between the *statement* and the *enunciation* also includes, between one and the other, the *subject of the unconscious* as the focus of the discourse, hence the subject, speaking, does not know what he is saying and always says more than he believes. I will not dwell on these concepts which pertain to linguistic discourse. There is, however, a third subject I would like to add to this pair of complementary opposites—the subjects of the statement and the enunciation. I will call it the *subject of the annunciation,*[12] one that speaks of his own foreseen death, brought

---

12. I use the word annunciation in its strongest sense (*Ave Maria, gratia plena, Dominus tecum*), which indicates a promise, a messianic premonition. I will return to this idea.

into the present, anticipated in relation to the ghost of the other to whom he directs his words or writing in reference to that "inaccessible" past with which Goethe begins his autobiography. The subject of the annunciation "realizes" his memory upon articulating it in a discourse, that is, upon exhibiting it in a dialectical experience that does not reproduce nor repeat the lived past but rather constitutes it as the past upon historicizing it for an audience. The memory is constructed from the future that awaits him. Life (*bios*) is constructed as a narrative (*grafia*—as well as *fonia*) of itself (*auto*), it is a *Bildungsroman* and the novel (*roman*) does not enunciate the truth but rather offers it up for the process of deconstruction, for the dissolving erosion of the self and its transcendental pretensions that will end by reducing the biographic rocky outcrop to the powdery sands of being . . . before casting it out to its final amnesiac dissemination. We are a memory that is aware of its own inexorable destiny: oblivion.

How could we learn about a memory if someone did not tell us about it? How could we have a memory if it were not for someone else to listen to it and sanction it with agreement or disbelief? Memory is a social link. It is a demand directed at someone to receive it. It does not guarantee itself.

To remember is to re-present. It is to trap an absence and return it to the present by retelling it—or retelling it to ourselves in our "internal forum." It is *representation* in the theatrical sense of the word, a performance that is singular or repeated, but always different, changing, and subject to the whims of the actors. It is diplomatic *representation*, ambassador of a distant authority, herald of the past that speaks in representation of the future. No one denies that our mental life is formed by the interplay of representations (*Vorstellungen*) and that absence is the condition of re-presentation, not only when it has to do with words but also things. What else could memory be if not re-presentation (of a shadow of the past, on a stage, an ambassadorial secret)?

In the following chapters we will allude to the intimate and ambiguous relations that have always existed among literature, philosophy, history, psychoanalysis and, now, neurophysiology as well, with respect to the function of memory and its correlate, forgetting. We will have to begin by recognizing the fact, obvious to some, that a dream is only the memory that comes on the day of what is dreamed at night and we will duly consider the universal phenomenon of forgetting dreams and promises. Undoubtedly, forgetting has great importance; "it is altogether impossible to live at all without forgetting."[13]

Memory—a fragile pillar surrounded by forgetting, both inside and out—is life itself, even if we define it in evolutionist terms. Every organism and everything in the organism, is Darwinian memory—if not, then what is it? We formulate this conclusion and immediately we are assaulted by the sensation that the subject is overcoming and suffocating us. If all material is memory (echoes of Bergson intended), if all that is psychic is memory—inasmuch as it is a play of representations—it is all history, if all memory derives from the future, if all our works are heirs to Mnemosyne (mother of the Muses), then we find ourselves confronted with a signifier that proliferates beyond limits and thus, being omnipresent, loses significance. The disciplines we have referred to speak of the memory, and demand that the memory should speak (like Nabokov in *Speak, Memory*, cit.), but do they speak of one and the same memory? We suspect that we are dealing with a confusing homonym, one that produces a blind spot among the explorers of the past. In other words, homonymy is not synonymy, memory is not homogenous, it is necessary to dissect it in each of the different discourses and calculate its conceptual and linguistic values, recognizing the multiple "plays on language" in which the same word is used. The memory is a piece that assumes a thousand faces, confounding our attempts to assemble the jigsaw puzzles of our speculations. The memory of philosophers could well *not* be—surely it is not—the same as the memory of biologists of

13. Nietzsche, F. [1874]. *Untimely Meditations*. Translated by R.J. Hollingdale. Cambridge (UK): Cambridge University Press, 1997, p. 62.

the mind, or of those who evoke their personal memories, or of historians. Moreover, each of these groups of "memory" professionals admits the polysemy of the signifier in their own field and they surround it with epithets. If we are going to bring up proper names—which we shall do as we proceed—Platonic reminiscence is not Aristotelian *mneme*, nor the sister of Hobbesian imagination, nor the worker of Lockean identity, nor Hegelian *Gedächtnis*, nor Darwinian memory of the specie's past, nor Bergsonian memory, nor Freudian unconscious memory, nor Proustian involuntary memory, nor the complementarity between encoding and retrieval of the cognitive physiologists, nor the autobiographical memory of the writers who come to believe that they are themselves the characters they create and who speak in the first person, "I." Of signifier, there is only one: "memory"; of signified there are a thousand and one.

Even as we point out the incompatibility of so many "memories" and dissolve the monolithic aspect of the homonym, we also believe it valid to try to articulate the similarities among so many concepts. Our method shall be to reflect upon memory and forgetting theory, as well as repression, via the suspicious testimonies (what testimony is not suspicious?) of authors who have written about their first memories in order to test two hypotheses: the first—Freudian—on the fundamental importance of the first memory in the life of a human being and, the second, Cortazarian, taken from a text that was not widely promoted by the author, from which is derived the title for this book: *Memory and Dread* (*Memoria y espanto*).[14]

Concerning our method, we will need one material: the written word as testimony of the memory. We formulate two suppositions: first, that this writing on the first memory is impregnated by a de-

14. Cortázar, Julio. See epigraph. A first version of the analysis and discussion of Cortázar's hypothesis appeared under the title "Un recuerdo infantil de Julio Cortázar" (*A childhood memory from Julio Cortázar*) in N.A. Braunstein, *Ficcionario de psicoanálisis*. Mexico: Siglo Veintiuno, 2001, pp. 1–6.

sire on the part of the narrator, which is apparent in the interstices of the narrative; and, second, that this childhood evocation is in some way, phantasmatically, present throughout the entire work of the author. That the texts have reached us implies that they are letters (*cartas, lettres, Briefe*) since "a letter always reaches its destination."[15] Why cite this rather outlandish declaration when we are all aware of lost letters and e-mails that end up floating in cyberspace? Because only when they reach the addressee, even if it is the wrong person, are they truly letters, and not before. Who is the addressee? Whoever knows how to read them, whoever can decipher the signifiers, the interpreter. The desire of the letter is its interpretation. If this were not so, it would not have been written. We will concentrate on a few short pages by various authors that will demonstrate the unusual *dictum* by Julio Cortázar: *memory begins with terror.*

All of the texts to be examined share a common peculiarity: they are all early memories written decades after the event they allude to by important authors in the fields of literary creation or psychology. However, the texts we will consider are not considered "important" within the overall context of the authors' "body of work." They are, in most cases, fugitives from the volumes of "Complete Works." In some instances, they are discarded paragraphs, notes at the foot of the page, meteorites of the memory, letters that could have been "lost" or that were destined for destruction, comments that accidentally surfaced from the disorder of a magazine or televised interview, "notebooks" (like those of Valéry, which do *not* concern us here) written with nocturnal stealth, short rough drafts that found their way into the literary supplements of newspapers, or random invocations found in the middle of an autobiography. In short, these are not transcendental texts; they are, as Lacan referred to them in a text from 1958 (which has received little readership and even less commentary), "*des petits*

---

15. Lacan, Jacques [1954]. "Le Séminaire sur 'La lettre volée.'" *Écrits*, Senil, París: 1966, p. 41.

papiers," or *"paper scraps."*[16] Tomás Segovia translated (poorly) the term into Spanish as *"papeles íntimos"* (*"intimate papers"*).[17] These bits of paper are not intimate, but rather very small, thus "paper scraps." In that year (1958) Lacan was formulating the concept that he considered his greatest invention: the *objet petit a* (to be read: *object a*). A remnant, a residual of the signifier operation, a jumble of scribbles around which the characters of an event dance, just as in "The Purloined Letter" where the Minister in the story by Poe has left the letter in the most visible spot of his estate so that no one will find it and there it remains until, by audacity and genius, M. Dupin discovers it and returns it to the Queen. To find the letter and have it complete its voyage and arrive at its destination is the work of detectives. *Paper scraps* shall be the clues that will serve as evidence in our investigation.

A sought-after accident, the distant relative of chance—like the majority of accidents—has led me repeatedly towards these left-over writings starting with the first, that of Cortázar. Subsequently, following this clue, I found traces of the "first memory" in *Rayuela* (*Hopscotch*), in Freud's entire theory of psychoanalysis, in certain sonnets and running through the overall body of work by Borges (including his blindness as part of that body of work), in the "ge-netic epistemology" of Piaget, in the project of "Living to Tell the Tale" by García Márquez , in the adventure of the first encounter with a mirror as related by several acclaimed women writers, in the language of Canetti who was condemned to martyrdom and later absolved, in the dissimulation of the horror of the story in the memories of Perec, in Tolstoy's eternal struggle for freedom, and in Nabokov's beautiful and well-ordered catalogue of remi-niscences. In all cases I encountered a constant: the memory of dread as well as the dread of memory.

Such paper scraps—like those used by Jean Delay to write his remarkable psychobiography on the first twenty-five years of

---

16. Lacan, Jacques [1958]. "Jeunesse de Gide, ou la lettre et le désir." *Écrits*, cit., p. 742.
17. In the Spanish edition of this paper: *Escritos 2*, Mexico: Siglo Veintiuno, 1975, p 722.

André Gide's life[18] (drawing upon his notebooks, personal diaries, letters to his mother, travel journals)—found in Jean Delay, the seasoned psychiatrist, "their eternal destination."[19] This has been my project: to make myself the addressee and detective of the *paper scraps* [*petits papiers*] without trying to discover in them my own preconceptions or prejudices (the original sin of "applied psychoanalysis"), without producing from them the rabbit I myself had concealed in the high hat. My objective—and the reader shall decide if I have achieved it—is to produce a meaning from them that did not preexist in any inaccessible sky of pure Ideas or perfect Memories. We must never forget that these paper scraps do not reflect an experience lived with innocence at the dawn of life, but rather they are themselves literary products. They are not the "cause" of the writing: they are an effect, a manifestation of desire and the literary project. Each of them is a fiction (poetry, *Dichtung*); that is why they enjoy the status of truth (*Wahrheit*). They have reached us and we can consider ourselves their addressees because they are addressed to us. They are not the accident; we are the accident, having crossed their paths.

---

18. Delay, Jean [1956–1957]. *The Youth of André Gide*. Translated into the English and abridged by June Guicharnaud. Chicago and London: University of Chicago Press, 1963.
19. Lacan, Jacques [1958]. *Écrits*, cit., 1966, p. 744.

JULIO CORTÁZAR AND THE DREAD ROOSTER

1. On the First Memory: Foundation Stone of the Subjectivity?

On a certain occasion, outside the context of the *corpus* of his published work, Julio Cortázar described the first vital episode to leave its mark on his consciousness. It was the awakening of memory—page one, so to speak—the spark that would ignite the first-person narrative of his existence, the starting point of a narrative that no longer seemed to belong to the story of some other, the mycelium of being from which would grow the mushroom of individual history. It would confirm for us the myth of the birth of desire and the writer's vocation.

No one can determine, in this particular case, the measure to which memory responds to the "objective" truth of what really happened, as opposed to personal legend, "merely subjective" invention, or a healing bandage. Certainly, it is most logical that both hypotheses converge by diverging, like the two slopes of a roof, like the two meanings of a homonym. Be that as it may—reproduction or construction, reminiscence or myth—it is seductive to entertain the hypothesis that this first memory prefigures and contains the seeds of the existence that will follow, that it is an event in which may be read retroactively, on the basis of what the person later becomes, the seal of destiny. In the midst of the confusing void where the soul gropes for something to grasp onto, something will happen—an unexpected peripeteia—that will establish and give meaning to life. *Fiat lux*!—the urgent and fruitful imperative for a rejuvenated mind, henceforward anchored in solid bedrock.

Also seductive, albeit risky, is the hypothesis that memory is organized not on the basis of the past, nor the present, but rather the future: what a person becomes is not the result but—to the contrary—the cause of memory. In general, oracles who presage the past are more reliable than those who predict the future.

In any case, the doubt, fertile in itself, subsists: Did it really happen this way or is the memory a retroactive production for the purpose of sanctioning and confirming an already played out destiny? This is the norm for hagiographies—the biographies of saints and heroes—full of infantile anecdotes, presenting exceptional beings with marvelous attributes which will distinguish them in their adult lives. But memory does not restore what has been lost, it projects it forward. Valéry, in few words, stated: "Memory is the future of the past."[20] Lewis Carroll has the Queen of Hearts say that "It's a poor sort of memory that only works backward."[21]

How can the first memory be located in time and space if that very memory precedes all signification? It would appear to be impossible unless it is "engaged," interweaving it with subsequent memories. "Because of something that happened to me right then and at a certain age, that must have happened earlier, when . . ." "It happened at my grandfather's house . . ." The preceding implies that later—necessarily later—the narrator found out what his age was, or that the place was his grandfather's house. There are no original moments; there are only reconstructions. The suspicions accumulate on the pretensions of originality, authenticity and originariety. All beginnings are subsequent. The film of our lives (the first concern posed in this book) finds its beginning every-

---

20. Valéry, P [1936]. *Cahiers*. Paris: La Pléiade, Gallimard, 1994, vol. I, p. 1256 (my translation).
21. Carroll, Lewis [1872]. *Through the Looking-Glass*, Chapter 5.

where and, therefore, nowhere. There is no good way to begin its projection and, since all ways are bad, any option could be good.

On the other hand, we should recognize that memory is not an individual function but rather a collective construction, that the Other always interferes with it, whether by submitting extraneous information or censuring and twisting the exactitude of the narrative according to how the vague winds of interest blow, or veiling and deforming the blurry photographic images of the past on the impalpable surface of remembrance. The Other participates in the first memory if only because this numinous episode—uncertain guarantor of the continuity of existence—must be narrated in first person and because it is inconceivable as a product outside of the spoken language of a community. We know, as Wittgenstein so aptly reminds us, that language is not private.

Goethe himself discovered the following:

> When we desire to recall what happened to us in the earliest period of youth, it often happens that we confound what we have heard from others with that which we really possess from our own direct experience. Without, therefore, instituting a very close investigation into the point, *which, after all, could lead to nothing,* I am conscious that we lived in an old house . . . (Goethe, 4, my italics).[22]

It is difficult, if not impossible, to distinguish "real" memory from "induced" memory or to separate the corresponding "parts" from one another once they have intermingled.[23] The memory of one inextricably mixes with the memory of the Other. To this variable influence of the Other we obviously must add another: the autobiographical self is far from being a reliable and impartial witness. To the contrary, in the prophetic words of Rimbaud, "It

---

22. Goethe, Johann Wolfgang von. Op. cit., p. 4.
23. The most radical example is the first memory of Jean Piaget. Cf. Chapter 4.

is false to say: I think. One should say: I am thought [. . .] I is
an Other,"[24] "I" does not know and "I" does not want to know;
"I" constructs memory from heteroclitic materials; "I" works to
create and to make credible an image that is agreeable or wor-
thy of compassion, heroic or victimized, of deceptive clarity or
nebulously lacking definition of the essential elements. "I who
is an Other" participates by hurling egotistic veils over the story,
recording shreds of the past and patching them with elements
borrowed from other times and other sources. Every memory of
early childhood is a patchwork, a motivated and revealing (and
thus interesting) collection of amendments and emendations—a
collage and bricolage.

I am not concerned with finding out if the memory of childhood
is a correct mental reproduction of an event that really happened
to the child—in this investigation we shall see that it is not, nor
could it be. What is noteworthy is the knowledge that the narrative we receive is a creation of fantasy: its truth is not historic—of
what little interest it would be if it were!—but rather its truth is
directly proportional to the distortion (by the subject as well as an
Other) intromitted to the event. Christopher of the paper scraps
[*petits papiers*] carries upon his shoulders the child God of truth,
except it is another child, different from the one he believes it to be.

Memory, according to a well-used metaphor, is a tapestry: it is
subject to all the fortunes and misfortunes of a typical fabric (a
text): wear and tear, knots, holes, patches, mending, embroidery,
skillful and careless stitching, colorful and faded threads, cuts,
folds, wrinkles, frays, stains and glosses can all occur on its surface.
The moths of Alzheimer's and dementia, as well as the mending
hands of the seamstress who polishes and corrects the text, can
show by concealing (or conceal by showing) the nakedness, thus
highlighting the charms and horrors of being. As I have stated, we
are what we remember; we are also (though it may hurt) what we
forget. We are what we cannot know about ourselves. The statue

[handwritten marginal note: We are what we cannot know about ourselves]

---

24. Rimbaud, Arthur [May 13, 1871], letter to Georges Izambard. In
Poésies. Paris: Gallimard (nrf), 1984, p. 199 (my translation.)

of Mnemosyne has three faces rather than two: *memory, forgetting and repression.* Our being of forgetting and the forgetting of our being are not accidental; they are programmed.

The coordinates of time and space may be, as in the case of Cortázar (or Freud or Borges), very precise. In other cases—many other cases—the subject cannot place them in time with any precision. According to psychologists who investigate this topic, most people place their first memory between the ages of two and four. In any case, as the opening line reads in the British writer L.P. Hartley's novel, *The Go-Between* (on which Joseph Losey based his beautiful film by the same name): "The past is a foreign country: they do things differently there."[25] The investigation of the writer's first memory—whether psychological or of some other type—is therefore more than a detective-like exploration, more than a search for documents and the interrogation of suspects; it is a voyage that is analogous to Livingstone and Stanley's wanderings over the dark continent, an incursion into the past, into what has disappeared yet remains active, into the "inaccessible" (Goethe), into the abolished.[26] Into the heart of darkness.

Nevertheless, if memory is a fabric in which certain crucial threads form knots with other apparently trivial ones that may associatively lead to the former, it is also logical that they might succumb to oblivion, particularly those elements that, in themselves, do not contain any "danger" and, by themselves, are incapable of producing anxiety. It is understandable that we should erase the paths that lead us back to traumatic events—to intolerable situations—and that in their place we erect pacifying barriers from anodyne memories, from supposed trivialities that deflect the impact of the horrifying. Valéry also knew this: "Memory is

---

25. Hartley, L.P. [1953], *The Go-Between.* The quotation is the opening line of the novel. The screenplay was written by 2005 Nobel Prize winner, Harold Pinter.

26. In Latin, *abolere* is "to annul, to destroy, to cause to become forgotten" (*Le Robert. Dictionnaire historique de la langue française*). It is interesting to note the connection with *oblivisce*, from which are derived *oblio, oblivion, oubli* and *olvido.*

indelible. It is the path of memory that gets lost . . ."[27] It gets lost, yes, but it can reappear, even paved over, for example when one tastes a simple biscuit dipped in a cup of tea.

However, it is not only to ward off dread that the screening mechanisms of memory—that false witness—are activated. It may be the case—and it often is—that a distant memory is laden with unspeakable sorrow, scored by distressing and ominous features. This anxiety is unfathomable for the subject him/herself: the terror experienced in the remote past seems absurd as the surface of the memory appears innocuous to the subject. In more technical terms, there does not appear to be congruence between the intellectual representation and the affect, between the thought and the feeling. Here it is appropriate to refer to Pascal and his oft-used phrase, "The heart has its reasons, of which reason knows nothing."[28] This is certain and, in fact, the "heart" is fully involved in memory: to "re-cord" is to return to the organ of love—to what is most intimate (*Erinnerung*)—what has been taken away from it. Reason does not understand the heart . . . because the heart is unconscious, if not of memory itself, then at least of what memory implies and of the reasons for its ominous value for the subject. Dare we suggest that the mind is the organ of memory whereas the heart is the organ of recording? In that case, we might confirm the wisdom of language itself, but what umbrella would protect us from the rain of reproaches that would fall upon us from the stern sky of "science?"

Appearances are deceiving. How can we ascertain the value of a childhood memory? In principle, we should consider that if a presumably irrelevant episode escapes the usual fate of oblivion that awaits early experiences, it is because there is something particular that is preserved like an enigma and that this singularity of the first memory merits careful investigation. As it is the "first" of a series, it does not necessarily have to be important; it could

27. Valéry, Paul [1926]. Op. cit., p. 1239. In Chapter 6.2 on Gabriel García Márquez's early memory, we will see that memory scientists ardently debate this question.

28. Pascal, Blaise [1670]. *Pensées*, no. 277.

be common metal dressed up in gold by virtue of being the first, but it would be pointless to outline its every facet, to define its every detail. For its "ordinary" character, for its innocuous aspect, it might seem merely a piece of tin; nonetheless, it could also have the luster of gold once its patina of mossy nothingness has been removed. Treasure or trinket, it will have to be the analysis of the text and not its innocent countenance that will determine the answer. The decision concerning its value will be retroactive to research (*recherche*) exercised without prejudice. *We shall soon find out.*

The myth of an absolute origin of personal memory is intriguing; however, its realization in a narrative is a fantasy because . . . because there is no such origin. On the subject of origins there are only myths. However, myths always transmit some truth, though they may not contain "the" truth. They are open to interpretation. The story of Genesis serves as a good example. Fascination with the first memory, to which Freud himself subscribed, depends—it seems to me—on the *suspension of time* that is implicit in the idea of "origin." For something to be primordial (*Ur*) it must not have a past since any previous state would impugn its foundational status. Nor can there be any idea of the future—of anticipation—in this "seed," this "germinal cell," this fertilized egg of being or memory. The subject would emerge *ex nihilo* from that moment and only then could it aspire to be—to be something—to desire, to have a fantasy that is neither memory nor perception. Who amongst us is not sensitive to the incandescent light of the beginnings that radiate from the mythical instant of a present that has no past and of a future that incites no suspicion?

When one hears the first memory narrated by "its owner," the listener generally does not discover anything very unusual. If the subject himself is queried, he usually cannot provide more or better information. However, effectively and very often, upon careful analysis of the narrative, unexpected results emerge, indeed revelations that confirm Freud's assertion concerning its "fundamental importance."

2. The Auroral Dread of Julio Cortázar

It is common that, as in the precocious memory of Cortázar, it is the other, in this case the mother, who provides the precise information regarding time and space and thus "the social frameworks of memory." Although she may not provide the entire painting, she establishes the frame: Barcelona, 1917, the period of the First World War. The maternal voice, geography and history all converge at a crossroads from which the voyage of a person begins. Memory demands historiographic guarantees, presents archived information and organizes it in a cohesive narrative.

Let us return to Julio Cortázar and his narrative. We already have the setting, provided by the mother: three years of age, Cataluña. The author of *Rayuela* (*Hopscotch*) immediately delivers the categorical statement: "*Memory begins with terror.*" Let us read this carefully: he does not say "my" memory, he says "memory" and in this way he seems to assert a general law that transcends the extent of psychological, and perhaps psychoanalytic, knowledge. Is this the case for all of us? Is it always from anxiety over abandonment, from ignorance or terrible doubt over the return of the other (". . . where are you, mother, why aren't you here with me?) that a point emerges—scratching the smooth surface of nothingness—opening a crack to be filled with memories? Perhaps it has to do with terror in the face of the unknown, neglect, or the orphanhood of the child faced with what is unnameable or terrifying. The first imprint left on the fragile membrane of the self would be (or is) that of helplessness (*desamparo, Hilflosigkeit, détresse, d'êtresse*). Perhaps the first memory for all of us is our first outcry—a scream provoked by the sudden absence of our mothers. And what follows—our survival—is "living to tell the tale."[29] The spoken articulation of a scream.

---

29. García Márquez, Gabriel. *Living to Tell the Tale*. Translated by Edith Grossman. New York: Alfred A. Knopf, 2003. See Chapter 6.

Cortázar's generalization, linking memory and terror, may seem excessive. It would be easy to object that most people cannot clearly isolate a first memory among the multitude of childhood memories and there are many others whose earliest memory is not of something horrific nor does it have that quality of nightmare indicated by the Argentine writer. Certainly there are others who would sustain quite the contrary, that their first memories contain a sense of blessed tenderness and warmth, a luminous stable with straw, donkey and ox, reflecting the light emanating from the halos of the three central figures. However, resorting to the peaceful piety of origin may also lead us into error; Cortázar may be right, even if the rest of us do not agree with him, when he says that the first memory refers to the traumatic dislocation of the soul. It is possible that we have "forgotten" the initial dread, that we do not have the courage to re-present it and that we console ourselves by softening the original anguish with the image of the gifts we were given: gold, myrrh and incense.

Already in 1899 Freud revealed the "screening" character of many (or all?) infantile memories which are "seen" as a screen of intensely clear impressions and that, when these "recordings" are analyzed, they turn out not to be memories of events actually lived but rather enduring and soothing fantasies that placate the trauma of the first encounter with the dread that Cortázar addresses. Memory does not function as a clockwork mechanism; it can be—and usually is—a still for the distillation and also the adulteration of the past. In Freud's words: "these [mnemic] falsifications of memory are tendentious—that is, that they serve the purposes of the repression and replacement of objectionable or disagreeable impressions."[30] We will illustrate this—in the following chapter—with his own case. It does not seem strange to us that memory obeys the pleasure principle (such is the first Freudian theory on memory; later, approaching 1920, we find another) and that we tend to "forget,"

30. Freud, S. [1899] "Screen Memories," *The Standard Edition of the Complete Psychological Works of Sigmund Freud*. Vol. III (1893–1899). Trans. James Strachey with Anna Freud. London: The Hogarth Press and The Institute of Psycho-Analysis, 1950, p. 322.

that is, to protect ourselves by means of a kind of false forgetting, the many occasions of pain, anxiety, shame, anger and impotence that we experience with overwhelming force, without sufficient buffering mechanisms, in the early periods of life. Defenseless in the labyrinth of smallness.

The memory evoked by Julio Cortázar is as chilling as it is banal. On a morning like any other, still in possession of a virgin memory, he hears the crow of a rooster. It is a horrifying memory that will reverberate forever though the experience may be triggered by an ordinary event informed by adult knowledge. Anxiety—all anxiety—has a root cause, even though we may not know at first what it is. With the passage of time it may be revealed, retroactively, that the initial terror of the child has been displaced from a needling, "repressed," content, to another "innocent" content, apparently relieved of anxiety. This is how "screen memories" are constructed, sheltering the heart and displacing reason.

It is possible that Cortázar's account represents for the reader the source of all our memories and that all of us have suffered a similar shock, the real trauma of birth—a second birth, into language—which few of us would dare evoke, though not out of cowardice or lack of decision, a trauma that no one has known how to retell quite the way Michel Leiris does in the first pages of *Biffures*.[31] First, we should listen to Cortázar before accepting his universal assimilation of memory and terror. If it were as he describes it, we would have to search for the reasons for our forgetting in the outraged borderlands of what we can record or codify. Those precocious experiences "that are beyond our wildest imagination" that terrify as they confront us with an unbearable tension: our awakening into the unknown.

The scene that Cortázar remembers is thus described:

They made me sleep alone in a room with a disproportionately large window at the foot of the bed . . . From nothingness

---

31. Leiris, Michel. [1948]. " . . . reusement," *Biffures, La règle du jeu*," Paris: Gallimard, La Pléide, 2003, pp. 3–6. Cf., Chapter 12.

comes an awakening at dawn, I look at the gray window as if it were a sad presence, a subject for tears [. . .] a grayish rectangle of nothingness for eyes opened on the void, slipping endlessly through a vision without handholds, a child splayed on his back beneath a naked sky.[32]

And now the literary echo of this memory in Rayuela (*Hopscotch*):[33]

I woke up and I saw the light of dawn through the cracks in the Venetian blinds. It came from so deep in the night that I had a feeling like that of vomiting up myself, the terror of coming into a new day with its same presentation, its mechanical indifference of everytime: consciousness, a sensation of light, opening my eyes, blinds, dawn . . . *I am obliged to bear the daily rising of the sun.* It's monstrous. *It's inhuman* (italics in the original).

The Other has set the regulations and the body of the child must passively submit to an incomprehensible violence; there are no reasons given, simply "they made me sleep alone." It is not necessary for us to be told of whom he speaks. It could be "my parents," and perhaps not. This lack of definition of the image of the Other contributes an element of fascination to the statement, as simple and fortunate (in poetic terms) as it is bleak (in subjective terms): "They made me sleep alone." How could the large window not have been disproportionate given that there is no functional ratio to accommodate the body of a child to the house of adults? From the window comes a light piercing eyes that stare into a void, a void on the outside that flows to the inside, in a soul that is itself but a window, a window open to the exterior, as yet lacking in interiority. A window of the room and a window of the eyes—a void against a void—a child cast on his back beneath

32. Cortázar, Julio. *El perseguidor y otros textos: Antología II.* Buenos Aires: Ediciones Colihue, 1996, p. 14 (my translation).
33. Cortázar, Julio. *Hopscotch.* Trans. Gregory Rabassa. New York: Pantheon Books, 1966, p. 371.

the immensity of a sky without robes, without edges, infinite and laid bare. The *"Dasein"* (to be there) and the state of *"geworfen, Geworfenheit"* (thrown, thrownness), of which Heidegger speaks, could not be expressed better than with the simple words of this small, atomic, infantile memory.

There are no points of reference—no cracks—to grasp onto; the vision slides through a world of undifferentiated objects, in a sinister and unnameable pure reality, "in that breastfeeding stage among cats and toys that only others can remember," that is, on a stage arranged by others where things are offered with names to engage the future subject. "I" who still does not exist, can not remember: "there are only others," while I move "among cats and toys" which will become the material of my oblivion. The child's being is submerged in what is real. He does not see; he is seen by the Cyclopean eye of the immense window capable of making him sense his isolation, the precariousness of his life, the mortal condition of his infinite smallness under a desolate sky.

In this landscape where nothing means anything to anyone, on this ghostly, portentous stage, something happens that, in any case, was prepared, something that could not fail to happen and that is, nonetheless, unusual and unexpected: a deluge of awe and vertigo, the transformation of what is everyday and familiar into something terrifying and inscrutable.

Returning to the narrative: each nuance, every linguistic turn, reveals the truth of the experience, not of the event—of which we can never know anything—that is, the narrative or diegetic evocation; below, we will examine how these elements are arranged. Cortázar has still not stated, with good reason, that this infantile landscape—the room, window and sky—was that of silence. In this barren land, there was not even silence.

And then a rooster crowed, if there is a memory of this it is for this reason, but there was no notion of "rooster," there was no pacifying nomenclature, how could it have been known that this was a rooster, this horrendous shattering of the silence into a thousand pieces, this tearing up of the space that brought down on me the shrieking glass, its first and most terrible Roc.[34]

Terror is incorporated into the trivial, cloaked in the habit of the habitual. So often we have been alone in a room, we have awoken, we have seen the early light entering through the window, we have heard the roosters crowing, we have understood, sooner or later, that this is the way another day of our life begins. It seems so very normal that it may seem amazing to us that Cortázar should narrate this episode, showing its terrible nature and, deliberately or not, aspiring to—or we aspire to—erect it as a paradigm of the birth of memory.

Why should anyone be startled at awakening in the morning, seeing the light and hearing the rooster's crow? Anxiety, the writer tells us, comes from a hole, a void in our knowledge: "there was no pacifying nomenclature." The event, banal in itself, is sinister for its lack of mitigation and the absence of protective cushioning afforded by "comprehension." Absent the word, reality provides no handholds and becomes terrifying.

The birth of the spirit. Upon awakening, every morning, there is an awakening to life, an awakening of memory and of history. To evoke, as Proust did, this first and, in his case, terrifying awakening is precisely what Cortázar has done. He finishes by stating that it is the point of origin for all his memories. He wakes from the previous eternal death and enters into life. Thus he situates the instant when the child, emerging from a breastfeeding stage that belongs to the Other more than to himself, hears the rooster's crow and is bewildered by this intrusion of reality, by a scream that emanates from nature and leads him to sense his defenselessness in the face of the unknown, the unnamed.

Incapable of knowing that what he has heard is a rooster he lives the terror of "this horrendous shattering of the silence into a thousand pieces . . ." Silence was not in the foreground, silence

34. Cortázar, Julio. *El perseguidor . . .* Op. cit., p. 14 (my translation).

was the consequence of the rooster's cry, it was created by the stridency of the crowing. In the same way that a perfect crystal may surround us without our being aware of it until it is shattered by a stone and we are injured by the shards. Thus, in the wake of the destruction, the silence emerges like a dimension and capsule for existence.

The rooster's crow is not terrifying. Indeed, nothing in reality is atrocious in itself, but terror is *for itself*, it is a condition of the soul. What is devastating is ignorance, the lack of a redeeming word for the experience. Yes, the deluge of crystal shards of silence lacerates and tears as they fall, perforating the delicate epidermis of the baby's soul.

If every awakening were a reiteration of this scene, life would be intolerable. Habit and forgetting are two salvational medicines that make survival possible. We could say that there are human fates in which awakening is impossible because the self is never liberated from "the shrieking glass" that perforates the eardrum's membrane with "its first and most terrible Roc." (Roc suggests several associations: Rock'n roll, the mythical bird,[35] baby Rocamadour, roc-*coq* for a precociously bilingual child.) It is not difficult to understand the dreadful aspect of the scene; what is difficult is to understand how one can escape from the initial abandonment, how to transform every morning into one more in the workday routine. Cortázar informs us of how he was able to escape:

> My mother remembers that I screamed, they got up and came to me, it took hours to get me to sleep, that my attempt to understand was just that; the crow of a rooster beneath the window, something simple and almost ridiculous that was explained to me with words that gently and gradually broke down the immense machine of terror: a rooster, its crow prior to the

---

35. Cortázar, Julio. "Ah, si en el silencio empollara el Roc . . ." ("Oh but that the Roc could breed in silence . . .") *Rayuela*, Op. cit., Chapter 93, p. 594 (*Hopscotch*, Chapter 93, p. 427).

sunrise, cock-a-doodle-doo, sleep my child, sleep my dear.[36]

The blanket of amnesia descends upon the episode and covers it like a luminous stain on the ground, beneath the leaves, on a sunny day; patches of light and shadow remain in the fabric of memory. When the child's voice is eclipsed, another voice emerges in its place, that of the adult: "My mother remembers." As best as possible, the recollection attempts to differentiate between the memory of one from the other. Here the memory of the child was clouded by the panic that followed the shattering of silence. His anxiety is now an appeal for help, a cry, to which someone must respond. And that Other, how can he/she help? What does he/she have other than words; of what is the Other composed if not words, fragile tablets of salvation that laboriously attempt to avoid disaster, to provide handholds for the floundering self, to constitute it with subjectivity, to enable it to recognize itself as "I" with an interior and able to recognize and name the objects surrounding it in its exterior.

The rooster's crow that instills horror is followed by the lullaby that soothes and returns the child to the gentle indolence of sleep. On one hand, the invasion of an untimely reality, on the other, the reparation with a redeeming onomatopoeic device—cock-a-doodle-doo—now you can imitate the cry that upset you, now you can pretend to be the rooster that threatened you, don't be afraid anymore *my child, my dear.* The song enchants and bestows pertinence; as an object invested with the love of the Other, the child is drawn abruptly into reality, rescued from anxiety. Now he is capable of memory, albeit a memory composed of words conceded to him by the tongue of that great Other. He is now a center and a warehouse of memories, of intersections between "it happened to me" and "they told me," a book in which the present page evokes others that were already projected and forgotten in the cinematographic development of previous moments. It is, it becomes, "I."

---

36. Cortázar, Julio. *El perseguidor y otros textos: antología II.* Buenos Aires, Argentina: Ediciones Colihue, 1996, p. 14 (my translation).

Is memory, a memory, all memory born of anxiety? Am I going too far by taking Julio Cortázar's short autobiographical vignette as a model for the formation of memory and the lubricating use of the word in the genesis of the subject? I am inclined to respond that I am not being excessive and, at the same time, to suggest that this pacifying function of the word, as well as the magnitude of the preceding anxiety and the relation that exists between the fragile device of the signifiers and "the immense machine of terror," has the means and contingent characteristics that need to be defined for every person with "a good memory." The rule, which is valid for everyone, requires an investigation into the singular experience of every speaking being, one by one.

I will now give in to temptation and formulate a conjecture, an improbable and fascinating conjecture: let us suppose that the intensity of the visual and auditory sensations of this awakening, and the disproportionate aspect of the anxiety of the child, could have created an abyss from which the child was saved by the intervention of the others ("they got up and came to me, it took hours to get me to sleep"). On the edge of this abyss the vocation of the poet could have germinated, dedicated to joining and stacking words—to ensnaring the unnameable and threatening reality—in order to mitigate, with verbal incantations, the abandonment of the self. The rooster's crow, the mother's lullaby, and the verbal rhythms and cadences of the child thus initiated into poetry. He could have been driven mad, he was rescued, and he invented beautiful fictions.

The work of other writers whose work I will consult encourages me to sustain this continuity between dread and poetry—poetry that is created in order to evoke dread as well as to quell it. However I would be remiss if I did not suggest something more in relation to Cortázar's story of the rooster. What if the child had not been awakened by the rooster's cry? What if the rooster's crow functioned as a screen memory for "other sounds" emanating not from the chicken coop but from a room neighboring the one in which they "had left him alone?" Is the whole story of the rooster a screen to cover the child's panic over something else that was incomprehensible, the Freudian "primal scene" (*Urszene*), a couple's sexual activity—usually that of the parents—practicing the age-old coital custom, totally beyond the possible comprehension of the baby sleeping alone in the next room, awakened by incomprehensible sounds? Is it a violent scene unfolding a few feet away, is someone suffering, is someone feeling pleasure, what is happening among the adults that excludes him and that makes him—no matter how involuntarily—witness to a scene that beckons him though he has not beckoned it? Were the parents—acting with a vague sense of guilt—open to the pacifying interpretation . . . and did they make the child believe that all the confusion at sunrise was simply the consequence of the routine, though strident, crow of the rooster? We will never know the true explanation. I could withdraw my hypothesis since it is hypothetical, as it relies on the questionable but frequent support of "other similar clinical experiences," because perhaps it is too rash or bold.

I have started this book with an idea that is debatable: that we are what we remember; we are a book in which certain moments of our experience remain in print and the words that were spoken to us have been recorded as if they were print characters (*impressions*). We are memory. But we must remember that we are also what we have forgotten—healthy oblivion—the disappearance of the red-hot marks of the inexpressible, of those roosters that sing upon the fragile membrane of our dreams and relentlessly threaten to destroy it. We have so much to forget that, in the end, what we remember is nothing more than a small residual of the whole of our experience, a remnant that has passed through the jealous filter of our capacity to forget.

> All it actually means is that even when one remembers something one did not remember one remembered, one may have still no more than scratched the surface in regard to things one does not remember one remembers.[37]

---

37. Markson, David. *Wittgenstein's Mistress*. Chicago: Dalkey Archive Press, 1988, p. 157.

If memory begins, as Cortázar says, in terror, then it must be this same terror that produces the defense mechanism that denies memory, covering it with the pious mantle of oblivion or . . . with poetic and mystifying infantile memories.

"Mystifying," I just wrote. Why? Does this astonish the reader?

Because Cortázar's cock-a-doodle-doo memory could very well be "authentic."

I believe it is not; I believe it is a fascinating and lyrical account of the birth of memory and that it holds a truth, that of the relation between memory and terror, which will have to be sustained by *other* arguments and not only the one based in this forged episode.

And if it were not a subsequent construction? How could it be shown that there has been a poetic falsification of this "memory" which has been superimposed on the historic truth?

Easily. Simply by reading carefully, with a certain degree of distrust, playing a little bit at being word detectives. It is enough to work from one principal question: Who knew about, who spoke about, and from where came the idea that it was *the rooster* that woke the child? Certainly it was not little Julio, who claims to have suffered because he had no notion of what a rooster was nor even the pacifying nomenclature available to think about it. He could not have named the cause of his premature and distressing awakening. Nor could it have been the parents who, as hurried as they might have been to respond to the cries of their child, would have been unable to say whether it was the farmyard fowl, a stomachache, or . . . or the amorous sighs emanating from the neighboring room. If the plumed explanation given to the child was pacifying, who was being pacified? Certainly the adults introduced the idea of the rooster (were they being cocky?) and instilled a *belief* in the child. From that day forward Julio Cortázar understood what a "rooster" was: a name for his anxiety, stripped of signifiers, and he understood that to tame the source of his dread he had to form a narrative, to create a story that would serve not to help him sleep, as is commonly the case with children, but to awaken and be able to bear the weight of the dreaded dawns. In this case, as in so many others, the recollection would have been transformed into memory, into *Deckerinnerung*, a screen memory. *Later, with the passage of time, the story would become (edgar allan) poetic. Dreadful and, and at the same time, soothing. To the greater glory of oblivion.*

MEMORY IS A WARDROBE BRIMMING WITH GHOSTS

1. Freud and the Origins of Memory

No one hesitates to attribute to Freud certain essential discoveries regarding the enigmas of child psychology. Our topic—the beginnings of personal memory—is almost coessential to the birth of psychoanalysis. It is not an exaggeration to say that Freud's research was exhaustive, focusing on his patients and himself as well as studying whatever testimonies he could obtain by his colleagues and literary figures who had written on the subject. Closely related to the exploration of the origins of *memory,* and equally tenacious, are his studies on the reasons for the inverse and apparently negative phenomenon: that of *forgetting.* At first, for Freud at the end of the nineteenth century, it was certain that we forget in order to gain distance from painful memories just as we remember in a disguised (screen memory) way in order to maintain control over other memories that we prefer to expel from the conscious. We remember in order to better forget or disregard.[38] Memory, from the perspective of psychoanalysis, is a patchwork: the fragmentary

---

38. The obligatory references are Freud's works "Screen Memories" (1899), "Childhood memories and screen memories," in *The Psychopathology of Everyday Life* (1901), *Leonardo da Vinci: A Memory of his Childhood* (1910), and "A Childhood Recollection from *Dichtung und Wahrheit* [on Goethe]." (1917).

and selective aspects of the work of memory (indeed, memory is work) derives from its obedience to the pleasure principle. The subjective economy, according to the early Freud, tends to avoid displeasure and, to this end, prefers repression over remembering so as not to violate this sovereign principle. It is better to forget pain . . . if one can. The later Freud, after 1921, discovered that on many occasions the opposite occurs, that—*beyond the pleasure principle*—traumatic memory exercises a fatal attraction and the subject *enjoys* remembering humiliations, embarrassments and irrecoverable losses.

Freud continues and will continue to be relevant on this topic. The most detailed research into the cerebral mechanisms of memory and forgetting—welcome as it necessarily is—does exactly as it promises: it provides knowledge of the mechanisms and the nuclei of cells and chemical neurotransmitters involved. Even with advanced technological resources we cannot enter into the question of why we remember one thing in particular while forgetting something else. To be more precise in order to preempt objections: this opinion is not universally accepted. In the field of neuroscience there is a "reductionist" current that asserts that the perpetuation of "psychological" theses in the twenty-first century is only the consequence of a temporary lack of natural-scientific knowledge. This agenda, also maintained by extreme cognitive psychologists, aspires to a total "naturalization" of the mind, to a landscape of dualism (Cartesian or not), to a simplified ontology of a radical monism. From this perspective, the brain once researched will reveal all the keys to explain psychological functions and the individual's mental life.[39]

---

39. Kandel, E.R. *In Search of Memory. The Emergence of a New Science of Mind.* New York: Norton, 2006. Noteworthy work: the author, a Jew born in Vienna in 1931, admirer of Freud, Nobel Prize winner for Medicine (2000), narrates the beginnings of his training as a psychoanalyst and his later dedication to a "science of the mind" that could be integrated with psychoanalytic knowledge . . . if the former renounced the concept of the unconscious. In my book, *La memoria, la inventora*, (México: Siglo Veintiuno Editores, pp. 103–122. I consider his research and his life.

My method and point of departure challenges the reductive hypothesis: the study of the personal reasons for memory—always variable for every subject—is inaccessible to the techniques of magnetic resonance, positron emission and the measurement of electrical activity and potential changes in the neuronal synapses linked to events and tests that rely on devices for the detection of lies. Conversely, it is permeable to the dialectical experience of the encounter between those who believe they "have" memory and other speaking persons trained to understand how a recollection—without taking into consideration the "authenticity" of the experience evoked in it—is a conveyer of the truth for the subject. The inexactitudes of memory are not lies that must be detected but rather carrier pigeons of the real motives active in the emotionally functioning mind; they can be studied; they are accessible to dialectical and not to instrumental reason.

The Freudian hypothesis can be summarized in a few lines: both remembering and oblivion of episodes in one's own life are motivated, they respond to a principle of causality and of multiple decisions. Remembering and forgetting are not mechanical gains or losses, nor could they be completely one or the other. However, as I have already suggested, *Freudian memory is a three-sided coin.* In addition to memory and forgetting, there is also repression, that is, the function of the unconscious deciding what, how, and how much shall be remembered and forgotten. Freudian memory is unfaithful to historical truth, to the chronicling of "real" events. It acts not as a supposed "objective journalist"—which, as we know, does not exist—but rather it distorts memories and mixes them with fantasies, with familiar novels and individual myths. Memories are collages that mix traces of lived experiences with the desires and driving aspirations of the person who *evokes* them and they also depend on the person or the context in which the evocation is produced; this is increasingly the case as the memories pertain to earlier periods of the subject's life. In other words, the context in which the memory is recounted is just as decisive for understanding it as the text itself of what is remembered.

Memory is not independent of its audience. Childhood memory resembles a dreamlike construction (that requires interpretation) more than a photographic reproduction of a past event that is naively contemplated and accepted as a *fait accompli*. We know that photographs are not entirely innocent either, that there is a driving desire behind the decision to snap the shutter, behind the framing, the lighting, the selection of what will be visible and what will remain hidden. Photography is also a discursive act, a message in search of an audience. A letter (*lettre*). And even more so, the narration of a memory.

In the Freudian framework, a memory is not accepted at face value. The question of process is always considered: how it was constructed and came to assume its current form. What is of interest is *the work of memory*, the process of its distortion, more than its current form. All memory is suspect.

The human being—this is an elementary principle—begins existence in a defenseless state from which it can only escape through the help of others and, in particular, through the intervention of cultural institutions, most importantly language and family. The two which are essentially one: it is in the bosom of the family that the subject acquires the "mother tongue." Memory and forgetting are linked to the function of language in the field of the word. If we consider the "history of memory" as an institution (it would be an original operation) we would see that the cerebral mechanisms and structures at work do not function on their own; they are at the service of the "person" immersed in the language who is, precisely, the subject of the unconscious.

The brain intervenes, of course, but subordinating itself—and not always out of loyalty—to the necessities and conveniences of the subject in his/her social relations with others.

Modern scientists who are familiar with neurological structures and specific neurotransmitters distinguish with precision two complementary mechanisms in memory: one of memory production which has to do with the inscription of its impressions, or *encoding*, and another which is the "utilization" of codified memory, that is, recovery of memories through the activation of these impressions, or *retrieval*. Freud referred to them, respectively, as processes of *formation* (*encoding*) and *emergence* (*retrieval*) of memories. This conceptual couple will reappear when we study the childhood memories of writers that will help us test Julio Cortázar's hypothesis and, very particularly, when we study (in Chapter 13) the theoretical consequences of Georges Perec's surprising—and rigorously Freudian—assertion: "I have no childhood memories."

Freud was not concerned with the "authenticity" of the remembered event or the way in which a memory is recorded or retrieved but rather by the way in which it is constructed by the unconscious and the influence it exercises in the ensuing life of the subject. Some have spoken of a "narrative truth" in order to distinguish it from the "historical truth."[40]

The founder of psychoanalysis was convinced, as stated in the epigraph to the first chapter, of the capital and enduring importance of the first memory. If a recollection survives the amnesia of the early years, Freud supposed, it is because there is something contained therein that, directly or indirectly, had exercised and continues to exercise throughout the life of the subject, an orienting function. Researchers of the mind cannot remain indifferent to the manifest and symbolic contents of the first memory.

Freud was very familiar with the writers of his time. In his article of 1899 ("Screen Memories") he referred to "investigation" (in the form of questionnaires) by Binet and Henri (1895) and the Henri brothers (1897) that seems to favor the hypothesis we have provisionally made our own: "Memory begins with terror." Freud cites these studies without highlighting that they do not seem to offer any support for the pleasure principle and the avoidance of displeasure.

---

40 Spence, Donald. *Narrative Truth and Historical Truth*. New York: Norton, 1982. Spence, Donald: "The Rhetorical Voice of Psychoanalysis," *J. Amer. Psychoanal. Assn.* 38: 579–603, 1990. S. Wetzler: "The Historical Truth of Psychoanalytical Reconstructions," *Int. R. of Psychoanal.* 12: 187–197, 1985. Ricoeur, Paul. "Narrative Identity." *Philosophy Today.* 35:1 (1991—Spring), pp. 73–90.

The most frequent content of the first memories of childhood are on the one hand occasions of fear, shame, physical pain, etc., and on the other hand important events such as illnesses, deaths, fires, *births of brothers and sisters*, etc. (my italics).[41]

Sigmund, who had no conscious memory of the birth of the two siblings who followed him (Julius and Anna), expressed surprise upon learning that, contrary to his hypothesis, the first memories of some adults involve everyday and unremarkable impressions that could not have provoked any affect in the child and that nonetheless remained imprinted in great detail in the memory whereas other important events from the same period left not a trace. Why should such trifles be recorded?

The memories of unremarkable emotional content caused Freud to wonder about the reasons for their retention. Investigating with his new psychoanalytic method and using himself as both object and subject of the search, a search with powerful Proustian overtones *avant la lettre*, he arrived at the conclusion that those memories are also of capital importance even though, due to the action of unconscious mechanisms of dissimulation, they appear quite innocent. The formula that emerged was that the *anodyne* content, that is, literally, painless content, of such memories is the result of a complicated process of *conflict* (to gain distance from the displeasure), *repression* (of what is irreconcilable with the or-ganization of the self), and *transactional substitution* (of the carrier representations of pain and anxiety for other seemingly innocuous ones). The structure of memory is comparable to the symptom and its composition runs parallel to that of dreams. Because of the intromission of the unconscious it is difficult to distinguish a recollection from a dream within childhood memory.

Clearly there are important episodes in the first years of life that leave no trace behind (they have not been *encoded*), for example being weaned, or recognizing oneself in the mirror for the first

---

41. Freud, Sigmund [1899]. "Screen Memories," p. 305.

time. No anamnesis successfully retrieves those buried monuments of one's personal odyssey. Other episodes exist that seem to be lost but they can be retrieved in the event of some occasional or accidental meeting with an object or a word that liberates the memory (retrieval cues, like Proust's legendary madeleine and García Márquez's example of the crib).[42] Later, as a grown child, in charge of the logical functions inherent to language, it will be possible for the child to order in memory a chronological sequence of the paths traversed by the self. These later memories that pertain to a period appropriately referred to as "school age" pertain, topically, to the area of the preconscious: they are not conscious memories of the moment, but they can become so without the necessity of breaking through barriers of repression or battle with stubborn resistance. They are there, in a manner of speaking, at the disposition of whoever is speaking and narrating. This is *autobiographical memory*, the mnemic variety that rides the juncture between the semantic and the episodic and is infiltrated by phantasy work that transforms truth into fiction and fiction into an instrument of truth. That transforms desire into history.

Psychologists have long recognized the variability of the period from which we retain our first memory. Some people claim to retain memory from the first year of life; others have memories from as late as eight or ten years old. Many of us, Freud included, are surprised at the trivial nature of these first memories. If the memory seems banal, it is because processes of displacement are at work that lead us to reject its true significance. In this case, there is *repression* to overcome. The memory is like the manifest content of a dream: it is material that must be interpreted in order to gain access to unconscious knowledge that is hidden behind a screen (*pantalla, Deck, écran*) of an anodyne surface. These are screens. This "screening" characteristic is not a property of some memories; indeed, some might even be considered "revealers." Freud maintained that, without exception, "childhood memories" (placed in inverted commas by Freud himself to express his distrust

---

42. See Chapter 6.

of them), are brought about as compromises that express desire at the same time as they dissimulate desire through phantasy work. These "memories" of individuals

> ... come *in general* to acquire the significance of 'screen memories,' and in doing so offer a remarkable analogy with the childhood memories that a nation preserves in its store of legends and myths[43] (my italics).

A feature of these first memories is their visual nature, their physical composition ("comparable only to those represented on a stage") and the protagonist's role played in them by the child. Psychologists today,[44] citing Freud's 1899 article as precedent, assert the necessary distinction between memories in which the child is an object immersed in a scene, and those in which what is remembered is seen from the visual perspective of the subject himself. Cinematic narrative technique provides a way for us to illustrate the difference between scenes filmed with a subjective camera (in which the camera films what the protagonist sees) and scenes filmed from an objective externality, chosen by the cameraperson and independent of the characters being filmed. An appropriate analogy is also found in the context of the short story and novel, where a distinction is made between the narrator who tells, in first person, what he or she can see and know, and the omniscient narrator, who embodies a third person error-free perspective, generally endowed with a bird's eye view of the action that includes being privy to both the external and internal workings of each character. Schacter refers to them, respectively, as *observer memories* (in first person) and *field memories* (in third person). Field memory is, necessarily, as Freud previously indicated, the effect of a falsification.

---

43. Freud, S. [1901], *Psychopathology of Everyday Life*. Translated by Alan Tyson. New York: W.W. Norton & Company, 1960, p. 48.
44. Schacter, Daniel L. *Searching for Memory: the brain, the mind, and the past*. New York: Basic Books, 1996, p. 21.

> In the majority of significant and in other respects unim-
> peachable childhood scenes the subject sees himself in the
> recollection as a child, with the knowledge that this child
> is himself; he sees this child, however, as an observer from
> outside the scene would see him [. . .] Now it is evident that
> such a picture cannot be an exact repetition of the impression
> that was originally received. For the subject was then in the
> middle of the situation and was attending not to himself but
> to the external world.[45]

"Childhood memories" betray their condition as devices insofar
as they are "field memories," that is, episodes viewed in the eyes
of the other who controls the video camera. The original impression of the "acting self" (who lives the experience) has been lost
in translation to language and to the interests of the "recording
self" (who evokes the memory, attempting to be identical to the
former).

Freud did not naively believe that memories offer knowledge of
what truly happened in the past; on the contrary, he thought that
what was most important was precisely the *distortion* (*Entstellung*,
the opposite of exactitude) that the subject imposed on the remembered material so that the memory would serve the purposes
of the pleasure principle and of personal convenience. The objective for the psychoanalysis of memories is to detect the degree
to which a remembrance is obedient to pleasure or enjoyment of
æsthetic beauty, or dread in the face of the uncanny (*unheimlich*)
and, ultimately, inevitable oblivion. This is the utility of the
memory and this is more important than a problematic retrieval
of history using some vehicle to travel backwards, into the past,
venturing into a temporal dimension as imagined by those who
enjoy entertaining ideas of science fiction. Thus, memory becomes
a tool for the research of hidden phantasies and for the exploration
of the unconscious. Strictly speaking, Freud maintained, it is not

---

45. Freud, Sigmund [1899]. Op. cit, p. 321.

possible to differentiate between falsified memories and phantasies. There is nothing unusual in this; we all "recall" stories, works of the imagination: our own and those of others. We swim in a sea of stories, those we invent and those that others invent for us.

Historic truth resides in those memories, but hidden and deformed. Here I might venture an aphorism: "If memory is called upon for something, the result will necessarily be false." Thus I place myself in direct alignment with Freud who ends his exploration of screen memories expressing the suspicion that *all our conscious childhood memories* reveal our existential beginnings not as they were but rather as they appear to us in later periods of our lives. Memories do not emerge from those periods but rather they were formed then for reasons and motives far removed from the goals of "historical accuracy."[46] Freud notes the distinction, reinforced by "memory scientists" today, between the moment of the formation of memories (encoding) and the moment of their retrieval. Childhood is not seen exactly as it was but rather exactly as it is (re)presented to us at a later time: we shape those years, we *construct* them, we novelize them.

Personal memory constructs myths. Freud was among the first to liken community histories to individual memory. He did not hesitate to compare the individual's personal narrative via these "memories" with the historiography of peoples who fabricate a contrived history of what has been forgotten, "a story of prehistory," which fits perfectly with the opinions and desires of the present.

> . . . many things had been dropped from the nation's memory, while others were distorted, and some remains of the past were given a wrong interpretation in order to fit in with contemporary ideas. Moreover people's motive for writing history was not objective curiosity but a desire to influence their contemporaries, to encourage and inspire them, or to hold a mirror up before them.[47]

---

46. Freud, Sigmund [1899]. Op. cit. p. 322.
47. Freud, Sigmund [1910]. Op. cit. pp. 83–84.

Thus, by way of memories, the conscious memory of one man becomes the harlequin's disguise to be tendentiously elaborated later on. Nonetheless, the examination of such costume materials is fundamental for reconstructing the irretrievable historical truth. These memory traces, which the subject himself poorly understands, "cloak priceless pieces of evidence about the most important features in his mental development."[48] It is upon this base that Freud conducts his detective-like investigation to fill the gaps of the childhood histories of both Leonardo da Vinci and Goethe.

2. The First Memory Narrated by Goethe and Read by Freud

I will quickly mention, without spending too much time on it, Leonardo's account of his encounter as a baby in the cradle with a vulture that put its tail in his mouth—a vulture which was most likely a kite. Much has been written in this regard and I can add little to it. Freud's commentary (1910), touching upon the story's improbability, is still a great source of aesthetic and intellectual pleasure to read, a narrative that follows the rules of the not-to-be disdained crime genre.

Seven years after his study on Leonardo, during World War I, Freud undertook the analysis of the only recorded episode from the early childhood period of his literary idol, Johann Wolfgang von Goethe. The article is entitled "A Childhood Recollection from '*Dichtung und Wahrheit*' (1917)" and includes references to the life of the writer; to that first memory of the child poet who destroyed the family's new crockery by throwing it out the window for the amusement and at the encouragement of his young neighbors; to a patient that Freud was treating and who had also destroyed and thrown family possessions out a window; to two patients treated by a colleague who was a precursor in the analysis of children; as well as other references.

---

48. *Ibid.*, p. 84.

At this time I am not concerned with reconstructing Goethe's memory but rather interpreting Freud's method of studying it and his conclusions. As we shall see, his study offers more for the psychoanalysis of Freud himself than of Goethe. This brief text, written in 1917, ends with Freud's interpretation of the recollection written in first person, that is, inserting himself in the place of the narrator as if he were actually Goethe. In this way, by substitution of one person for another, he directs at himself the interpretation that is aimed at the other, that is, at the author of *Faust*:

> I was a child of fortune: destiny had preserved me for life, although I came into the world for dead. Even more, destiny removed my brother, so that I did not have to share my mother's love with him.[49]

We will never know if this interpretation is valid for Goethe—who never wrote such a statement—but undoubtedly it is valid for Freud, the older brother of a child, Julius Freud, born in 1858, deceased and promptly forgotten at the age of six months, days before Sigmund celebrated his second birthday. In his conscious memory Freud retained no recollection of this brother or his death, nor does he recall the birth of a sister, Anna, when he was two-and-a-half years old, for whom he never bore much affection.

We don't know if Goethe really hated or hoped for the death of his little brother, as Freud so interprets from "what we believe we have obtained through observations of other children"[50] (about himself, undoubtedly). Certainly, to affirm this we would have to be spiritualists and invoke the spirit of the great poet himself in order to confirm or rectify this hypothesis. However, we can believe Freud when, already in his forties, he confesses: "I can only indicate [. . .] that I greeted my one-year-younger brother

---

49. Freud, Sigmund [1917]. "A Childhood Recollection from '*Dichtung und Wahrheit*' (1917)" in *Character and Culture: Psychoanalysis applied to anthropology, mythology, folklore, literature, and culture in general*. Editor, Philip Rieff. New York: Collier Books, 1963, pp. 200–201.

50. Freud, S. [1917]. Op cit. p. 200.

[Julius] (who died after a few months) with adverse wishes and genuine childhood jealousy; and that his death left the germ of [self]reproaches in me."[51] One effect of this guilt—according to Freud's own interpretation—was his fall from a high stool shortly thereafter, an accident that severely cut his cheek and compelled him as an adult to cover it with a beard for the rest of his life. Freud does not remember the incident but the skin on his face bears traces of the event and perpetuates the memory of the desired fratricide. The memory is a scar, like a circumcision.

It is worthwhile to remark that Freud should compare himself to Goethe and that, at the same time, he should try to erase the very possibility of having felt such lethal jealousy towards his little brother as he reveals and communicates to Fliess in the letter written twenty years before his analysis of Goethe's childhood recollection. In his study of the life of Goethe, Freud observes that when the young Johann Wolfgang was 15 months old, his sister Cornelia was born on December 7, 1750. His comment is surprising:

This slight difference in age almost excludes the possibility of her having been an object of jealousy [. . .] Nor is the scene we are endeavoring to interpret reconcilable with Goethe's tender age at the time of, or shortly after, Cornelia's birth.[52]

When Julius was born, Freud was 16 months old. Julius died just days before Sigmund's second birthday. On the basis of which arguments could Freud exclude Goethe's jealousy towards Cornelia without negating at the same time his own towards Julius, which he had recognized twenty years earlier in his letter to Fliess?

It seems that, without realizing its significance, Freud transcribes the notes prepared for him by a friend regarding his "discovery" in *Dichtung und Warheit*: "*Goethe, too, as a little boy saw*

---

51. Freud, S. [1897].*The Complete Letters of Sigmund Freud to Wilhelm Fliess: 1887–1904.* "October 3, 1897." Translated by Jeffrey Moussaieff Masson. Cambridge & London: The Belknap Press of Harvard University Press, 1985, p. 268.
52. Freud, Sigmund. [1917]. Op cit., 195.

a younger brother die without regret" (Freud's italics).[53] The rest of the text appears in normal typeface. The emphasis on the word, *too*, explains the reason for Freud's interest and his interpretation in this regard. To be like Goethe—to be able to identify with the poet—signifies for him an absolution, an annulment of any implication in the wished-for crime. If Goethe—idealized and venerated by all of society—could have wished for and celebrated such a death, why not Freud *too*?

The *Glückskind* (the lucky child) bears the burden of a guilt-laced desire since that death enabled him almost exclusive enjoyment of his mother's love—absolutely exclusive if it hadn't been for the birth of Anna, the new intruder. We can say that his mother's adoration of her "*goldene Sigi*" (her golden boy) is the key, according to Freud himself, to his entire life. It is not a coincidence then that he again imposes on Goethe—his model, the marvelous artist with whom he identifies—using the first person singular (again!), an interpretation that corresponds to himself. We read in Freud's words, not to be confused with those of Goethe:

> . . . he who has been the undisputed darling of his mother retains throughout life that victorious feeling, that confidence in ultimate success, which not seldom brings actual success with it. And a saying such as "My strength has its roots in my relation to my mother" might well have been put at the head of Goethe's autobiography.[54]

Notice the subtle use of the impersonal "he who" at the beginning of the quotation. Who does this refer to? If Freud had written: "I was fortunate because I did not have to share my mother's love with him," one would immediately understand that the statement was not Goethe's; the same might be observed of his statement that the other, Goethe, *might* have had the right to begin his autobiography with the words, "*my* strength." We have before us

---

53. Freud, Sigmund. [1917]. Op. cit., p. 196.
54. Freud, Sigmund [1917]. Op. cit., 201.

a good example of "potential autobiography" or, in other words, identity usurpation.

Whose autobiography is Freud referring to? Goethe's *Dichtung und Wahrheit*? No. He is writing about *his own* autobiography as "poetry and truth." Goethe wrote his autobiography without pausing to discuss the love of his mother. It is not unusual to find that analysts formulate interpretations that are more veiled confessions than accurate propositions relative to their patients. For this reason caution is recommendable regarding the quantity and phrasing of interpretations, maintaining some healthy skepticism when considering the object of the affirmations, remembering what we learned as children when we have to respond to the charge that "You are what you say about others." And we should recognize that Freud was aware of this when he invented the term "projection" to refer to this lack of self-knowledge which surfaces in reflections on supposed knowledge concerning others. Be that as it may, it is certain that Freud knew and always admitted that—Goethe or no Goethe—the reciprocal love between him and his mother was the source of all his achievements.

At the age of seventy Freud was invited to write "An Autobiographical Study" for a collection consisting of the autobiographies of outstanding members of the medical profession. The book contains little more than "semantic memory"—personal data, the evolution of ideas, references to the psychoanalytic movement. But if one wants to know who Freud really was, it is necessary to refer to his bona fide autobiography, which gives substance to *The Interpretation of Dreams, The Psychopathology of Everyday Life*, the article from 1899 on screen memories and revelations about the subject of the enunciation such as—and this is a beautiful example—those that emerge from his analysis of the childhood recollection (Kindszeiterinnerung) in *Dichtung und Wahrheit,* a text in which Freud never writes in the first person "I" to refer to himself. The true story of Freud's life may be found between the lines: it is not contained in the factual details of his life but rather in the formulation and distortion of his memories, in the associations that constitute the "latent content" of his dreams. Like all men, Freud hides behind memory and allows his truths to filter through the cracks. Memory veils; the word reveals.

3. A Childhood Recollection from Sigmund Freud

Following this necessary reference to Freud's orientation regarding early childhood memories, we can now turn to what few people remember about the most distant memory of Freud himself. Psychologists themselves, all of whom have read at least half a dozen biographies of Freud, beginning with the canonical and canonizing Ernest Jones, when asked about the first memory that our founder—elevated to the level of Father—wrote about, it is possible that they will hesitate and finally pronounce that it is the "screen memory" published in 1899 in which the color yellow of the dandelions and the marvelous flavor of the bread given to the children by the peasant-woman are so outstanding. This being the case, the memory is a screen but not of Cortazarian dread, though certain of Freud's associations point to a feeling of dread. We should remember the insight of previous analysts who discovered Freud himself falsifying information about the protagonist of this paradigmatic memory, described as "a man of university education, aged thirty-eight [. . . whose . . .] profession lies in a very different field" and in addition "is not at all or only very slightly neurotic."[55]

Freud says that he retains many memories of Freiberg, the town in Moravia where he was born in 1856 and from where he had to move in 1859, thus all memories that date from his second and third years. We may now say that this famous episode recounted in 1899, with the yellow flowers, is a triple-fold screen: it is a *Deckerinnerung* because its content is deformed and only accessible after a laborious and at times unlikely interpretation. It is a screen because Freud disguises his identity as "completely" as he

---

55. Freud, Sigmund [1899]. Op. cit., p. 309.

uses that same adverb to deny that the subject's profession is that of a psychoanalyst. Finally, it is a screen because it occupies the place of an early memory to which, curiously, there have been few references among the writings of vast hosts of Freudologists that exist and have existed in the world—among whom I include myself.

At the end of the fourth chapter in *The Psychopathology of Daily Life*, Freud no longer conceals his identity as he did in the case of the screen memory *princeps*, but rather offers a recollection that supports Julio Cortázar's hypothesis. His early memory, retrieved after celebrating his forty-third birthday, though it may have surfaced previously in his conscious, is calculated to be from "before the end of my third year" given its location and the people involved, in addition to himself: Freiberg, his mother, and his half-brother Philipp who emigrated to England at that time. Freud himself emphasizes that his younger sister "was born at that time."[56] The text is brief but should be placed in context—something that Freud does only partially, very partially, in both senses of the word.

I saw myself standing in front of a cupboard ['*Kasten*'] demanding something and screaming, while my half-brother, my senior by twenty years, held it open. Then suddenly my mother, looking beautiful and slim ['*Schlank*'], walked into the room, as if she had come in from the street.[57]

Before proceeding we should take a moment to become oriented in this narrative and review the context: Amalié, the mother of Sigismund (which was Freud's name at that time), was the third wife of his father, Jakob Freud. Jakob was already advanced in age when he married the young Amalié and he had children the same age as his new wife. One of these children was Philipp, who appears in this memory. The family situation was confusing for the child. He supposed that old Jakob was married to Resi

---

56. Freud, Sigmund [1901] *The Psychopathology of Everyday Life*, pp. 49–51.
57. *Ibid.*, 49–50.

Wittek, the nurse, who was also an elderly person; he would have considered them to be his grandparents, a confusion that was reinforced because his cousins of his same age, who also lived in the neighborhood and were children of his other half-brother, were the grandchildren of Jakob and, logically, called him "grandfather." He also assumed that Philipp and his mother—both in their twenties—were married and, consequently, were his parents. As a result, he was perplexed by the complex family structure since old Jakob shared his bed with Amalié.

These elements alone are enough for us to follow the thread of associations that lead Freud to his interpretation, his "unexpected view" of the enigma of his crying in front of an open cupboard.

> I had missed my mother, and had come to suspect that she was shut up in this wardrobe or cupboard ['*Schrank oder Kasten*']; and it was for that reason that I was demanding that my brother should open the cupboard. When he did what I asked and I had made certain that my mother was not in the cupboard, I began to scream. This is the moment that my memory has held fast; and it was followed at once by the appearance of my mother, which allayed my anxiety or longing.

What accounts for this strange idea that Amalié Freud could be shut up inside the cupboard and why look for her within? Why suppose that Philipp could allay his anxiety? Freud, insatiably curious, interrogates his mother, who is nearing the age of seventy (in 1899) and finds out something heretofore unknown to him: that Resi, at the time of his hated brother's birth, had carried out certain thefts in the house for which Philipp had taken her to court and had her put in prison. Upon learning of this, Freud "understands" the sequence of events: when he noticed the absence of the nurse, the little Sigismund asked Philipp where she was, suspecting that he had something to do with her disappearance. Philipp "answered in the elusive and punning fashion that was characteristic of him: "She's 'boxed up' ['*Sie ist eingekastelt*']."

Philipp uses a vulgar expression in German roughly equivalent to "being in the can" (in jail).

Sigismund understood the answer (*eingekastelt*) in a literal way and stopped asking questions but, sometime later, when he noticed the absence of his mother he suspected that the "naughty" (*schlimme*) brother had done the same with her as he had done with Resi, he had "boxed" *her up also*. Driven by this phantasy occasioned by a verbal misunderstanding, by a polysemous signifier, the desperate boy began to scream and demanded that Philipp open the box, cupboard, or wardrobe that was in the room. It is the box in his first memory. The anxiety subsided when his mother reappeared, "looking beautiful and slim,"[58] free and refreshed. The sexual and thanatotic connotations in the memory are obvious. Philipp seems to be in control of the mother and to be able to imprison or liberate her at will. The boxes, following Julius's death, suggest funereal ceremonies. The mother, abducted or deceased, appears in his anxiety-ridden phantasy as forever lost to him.

Freud explicitly clarifies the sexual connotations. In his imagination it is his half-brother who impregnated his mother. The box or wardrobe is the equivalent of the maternal womb and he seems to suspect that there are more children enclosed within. Philipp has taken his father's place as Sigismund's rival. Freud thought that it was Philipp that had put (*hineinpraktiziert*) the recently born baby girl in his mother's womb.

The memory springs from dread. However, it has been displaced. Freud has forgotten everything about the birth of his younger sister but remembers this traumatic memory and, at the same time, it is screened by a memory (*Deckerinnerung*), which permits reliving the anxiety that ends happily with the reappearance of the mother whose slimness is a relief to the child: she has no more babies inside her womb. It also displays his anger and anxiety towards his naughty brother who enjoys the body of his mother and shuts her up in a wardrobe. He insists on knowing

---

58. "Slim" . . . *die Schlankheit der rückehrenden Mutter* (*Gesammelte Werke.*, vol. 4, p. 60, note added in 1924).

what is inside that wardrobe filled with secrets. Here we should recall our first epigraph as well as the claim that our most distant memory holds the key to the secret wardrobes of mental life (*welche die Schlüssel zu den Geheimfächern seines Seelenlebens in sich birgt*). Is this memory the box in which lie hidden Freud's mother and his rival brother who has taken the place of his father? Is our memory—the memory of each and every one of us—a wardrobe brimming with ghosts?

At a certain point in these texts, Freud indicates the succession of associations that implies a causality connecting them all together.[59] Then, when he writes for the first time in a letter to Fliess from October 15, 1897 about the story of his mother in the box, he immediately goes on to say to his friend:

> A single idea of general value dawned on me. I have found, in my own case too, [the phenomenon of] being in love with my mother and jealous of my father, and I now consider it a universal event in early childhood [. . .] Everyone in the audience was once a budding Oedipus in phantasy and each recoils in horror from the dream fulfillment here transplanted into reality, with the full quantity of repression which separates his infantile state from his present one.[60]

Freud reveals the roots of dread in the face of memory. Anxiety appears when that which should remain hidden emerges into the light. Such is the essence of the uncanny, the *unheimlich*.

The end of the recollection, for Freud as well as for Julio Cortázar, is a happy one; neither the rooster nor the box is frightening. But the anxiety has left its mark on the terribly jealous man who became the little two-and-a-half-year-old boy, crying for his absent mother. It was necessary for her to return, to personify that pacifying other, to reassure him that his fears were unfounded and

59. Freud, Sigmund [1917] Op. cit., p. 198.
60. Freud, Sigmund [1897]. *The Complete Letters of Sigmund Freud to Wilhelm Fliess: 1887–1904*. Trans. & Ed., Jeffrey Moussaieff Masson. Cambridge, MA & London: Belknap Press of Harvard University Press, 1985, p. 272.

that the box could be opened and closed because there was no one inside, alive or dead. To open and close, one, two, here and there, *fort* and *da*, one, two, the lid of a box or the door to a wardrobe, one, two . . . it's child's play.

JEAN PIAGET'S FALSE DREAD

1. A Child Is Kidnapped in a Park in Paris

Almost no one is ignorant of Jean Piaget (1896–1980), the Swiss psychologist who rigorously studied the intellectual development of children and induced from his research certain ideas that he tried to apply to the theory of knowledge, creating a "genetic epistemology." Although these days his name and his work tend to have faded into oblivion, few would neglect to recognize him as one of the pillars of the contemporary "cognitive sciences." I, however, do not come to him for his research or the results they produced but rather because on two occasions—in 1945 and 1969— he related the first of his "childhood memories," a memory that reveals traces of the dread I have detected over the course of my examination of various other authors.

The two versions are almost identical in their wording but were formulated in very different circumstances and moments. One was written as a footnote to an important essay,[61] the other emerged while Piaget was being interviewed for television in

---

61. Piaget, Jean [1945], *Play, Dreams and Imitation in Childhood.* Translated by C. Gattegno and F.M. Hodgson. New York: The Norton Library, 1962.

1969,[62] twenty-five years after publication of the aforementioned essay, *La formation du symbole chez l'enfant*, which has the suggestive subtitle: *imitation, jeu et rêve image et representation* (the English translation was published as: *Play, Dreams and Imitation in Childhood*[63]), with arbitrary syntax, indicative of the magnitude of the author's ambitions at the moment that he endeavored to relate this memory.

Before turning to the text of the childhood recollection, it is useful to consider the context of the televised interview: Piaget was asked about his relationship with psychoanalysis and his clear reluctance to accept Freudian hypotheses; he answered that this was because the childhood recollections that analysis regarded as being so transcendent were not authentic: "they are largely reconstituted" (in Bringuier, cit., p. 120)—which is a rigorously Freudian hypothesis—and that "for the orthodox Freudian, the past determines the adult's present behavior" (*ibid.*, p. 122).

Disregarding certain minimal differences between the two versions of the same early memory, I will provide a third condensed version. Here is the memory:

One of my first memories would date, if it were true, from my second year. *I can still see, most clearly,* the following scene, in which I believed until I was about fifteen. I was sitting in my pram, which my nurse was pushing in the Champs Elysées, when a man tried to kidnap me. I was held in by the strap fastened round me while my nurse bravely tried to stand between me and the thief. She received various scratches, *and I can still see vaguely those on her face.* Then a crowd gathered, a policeman with a short cloak and a white baton came up, and the man took to his heels. *I can*

---

62. Bringuier, Jean-Claude. *Conversations with Jean Piaget*. Translated by Basia Miller Gulati. Chicago and London: The University of Chicago Press, 1980, pp. 120–124.
63. Piaget, Jean [1945], *Play, Dreams and Imitation in Childhood*. Translated by C. Gattegno and F.M. Hodgson. New York: The Norton Library, 1962.

still see the whole scene, and can even place it near the tube station.[64]

The memory is clear—the terror experienced—the story is perfect and concise. True? Alas, Piaget interjects in one version after the other the following comments, demolishing the preceding narrative:

When I was about fifteen, my parents received a letter from by former nurse saying that she had been converted to the Salvation Army. She wanted to confess her past faults, and in particular to return the watch she had been given as a reward on this occasion. She had made up the whole story, faking the scratches. I therefore must have heard, as a child, the account of this story, which my parents believed, and projected it into the past in the form of a visual memory, which was a memory of a memory, but false.

All false, pure fabrication! Piaget concludes: "Many real memories are doubtless of the same order." We are left perplexed by this categorical and rash conclusion. Comparing the two versions of the recollection (separated by twenty-five years) we find that, in front of the television cameras and improvising in 1969, Piaget interjects between the two versions—the convincing account of the memory that he "still sees" and the revelation of the nurse's deception—a sentence that is lacking in the written version: "As a child I had the glorious memory of having been the object of an attempted kidnapping" (Bringuier, cit., p. 121). This statement constitutes a "small" conflict which forms, I believe, the key to the story. It is here, at the divergence of the two versions, where we find *the truth* of the memory and this truth reveals *the desire of the other* which makes the memory "glorious": the desire of the kidnapper to gain power of the baby, the desire of the nurse to defend him, the desire of the police to battle evil in defense of the

64. Piaget, Jean, *ibid.*, footnote 1, pp. 187–88.

child, the desire of the parents who reward the nurse with a watch, the desire (as we shall see) of the mother to shield her baby from the story by whispering about it . . . and even the desire to use this "false" memory as an argument in favor of his psychology of intelligence over psychoanalysis, attributing to Freud hypotheses that he did not hold. It is a desire that is manifest in both of these versions—one written, the other spoken—slightly divergent from one another and to which we are the fortunate audience.

Addressing the cameras, Piaget adds an explanation that is a new, less vivid, memory. More than a memory, it is an explanatory construction; whereas before, evoking what "happened" on the Champs Elysées, he had expressed a sense of security and a return to the experience, here what dominates are clauses that express relativity:

> I *must* have heard it when I was, oh, I don't know, seven or eight. My mother must have told someone that an attempt had been made to kidnap me. I heard the story and *probably* even heard her whispering—you don't tell a child that he was practically kidnapped, for fear of upsetting him—but at any rate, I overheard the story, and, starting from that, I reconstituted the image—*such a beautiful image that even today it seems a memory of something I experienced* (Bringuier, cit., p. 121, my italics).

The "memory" is not authentic, it is the result of a deliberate falsification. How could anyone disagree? Nothing of the sort happened *in reality*. The question that hangs in the air after reading Piaget's recollection is: How and why did this "false" memory reach such a level of conviction in the child? According to Piaget, the "memory" was not formed when he was less than two years old but rather when he was already seven or eight years old. It was at that time that it was "codified" and it remained unaltered until he was seventy years old despite his knowing very well that the recorded event never took place. His memory was content to retroactively retain a constructed event with fraudulent intentions, granting it all the trappings of objectivity. Piaget cites his false memory on both occasions as an argument against Freudian psychoanalysis and this is as striking as his attachment to the nurse's deceitful story. Nonetheless, Piaget, the child psychologist, was far from ingenuous. He was a scrupulous reader of Freud (and all of the important published psychologists of his time) and he could not ignore Freud's contention, expressed in one of his most widely read texts—the text previously cited, from 1901—that all child-hood memories are screen memories, worked by phantasy and distorted at the service and convenience of the pleasure principle.

Moreover, in 1922 Piaget was himself in psychoanalysis for eight months with Sabina Spielrein, one of the most important figures in the history of the discipline. Spielrein was a former patient of Jung's (with whom she had a stormy relationship that has become legendary)[65] and, subsequently, she was a friend of Freud's and a member of the Vienna Psychological Society where she made various important contributions. Her most transcendental contri-bution was a pioneering proposal in the field of psychoanalysis: Spielrein before anyone else, promoted the recognition of a de-structive drive, the direct precursor of the death drive that Freud brought to light years later, in 1921. In the aforementioned televised interview, after relating the story of his "first" memory, Piaget recalls his analysis with Spielrein (without naming her directly) in Geneva, and he states that he considers himself authorized to speak of psychoanalysis precisely because he had this experience: "I've been analyzed—if not, I wouldn't be talking about analysis!" (Bringuier, op. cit., p. 123). He confesses that, yes, indeed, he had resisted, but his resistance was theoretical:

> . . . not at all in the application of the analysis [. . .] I was perfectly willing to be a guinea pig. As I said, I found it very

---

65. Carotenuto, Aldo [1980]. *A Secret Symmetry. Sabina Spielrein between Freud and Jung.* Translated by Arno Pomerans and John Shapley. New York: Pantheon Books, 1982.

interesting, but the doctrine was something else again. In the interesting facts that psychoanalysis showed, I didn't see the need for the interpretation she tried to impose on them. She's the one who stopped. [. . .] She felt it wasn't worth wasting an hour a day on a man who wouldn't accept the theory.

—You would have liked to go on, then?

—Oh, yes, I was very interested. For instance, I'm not the least bit visual. I couldn't tell you what color the wall-hangings in this study are without looking at them. Well, it was simply remarkable how many visual images came back with childhood memories [. . .] I was visual during the analytic hours in a way that really surprised me. I visualized scenes from the past, partly reconstituted, as I told you, but with a whole context, including shape and color—a precision I would have been incapable of at any other time (Bringuier, op. cit., p. 123–124).

This unassailable testimony clarifies some of Piaget's reasons for resisting an experience that may have affected him too intensely. His intellectualizing passion, the wellspring for the great discoveries that brought him his well-deserved fame, conflicted with the wishes of his analyst (the perpetual desire of the other!), apparently excessively interested in steering towards the "cause"—as we shall see—this *Wunderkind*, this prodigal child that she saw in Piaget and that he continued to be until his death at the age of eighty-four.

Thus, as Piaget so clearly remembers his life as a baby, he forgets the Freud he read, memorized and erased, the Freud who wrote:

One is thus forced by various considerations to suspect that in the so-called earliest childhood memories we possess not the genuine memory-trace but a later revision of it, a revision which may have been subjected to the influences of a variety of later psychical forces.[66]

66. Freud, Sigmund [1901]. Op. cit., pp. 47–48.

How can Piaget distance himself from psychoanalysis by using a skepticism motivated by the artificiality of his first memory as an argument when this same skepticism regarding early memories is a distinctive feature of Freudian psychoanalysis? We shall pursue an answer to this question. Piaget comments:

> I'm fairly skeptical of childhood memories. I know that the way a child reconstitutes his own memories, or an adult reconstitutes his childhood memories, can be useful psychoanalytically. But ultimately, I don't think they are pure memories; I don't believe in pure memories; they always presuppose a greater or lesser degree of inference (Bringuier, op. cit., 121–122).

2. Memory Is a Work of the Imagination

If anything fairly characterizes the Freudian position it is its *coincidence* with Piaget's prudent incredulity. Neither Freud nor the Freudians ever believed that they would find a mystical "pure memory." What Piaget calls "one part inference" (which could also be called "interference") is the fundamental and constant addition of phantasy work in the construction of memory. In fact, it has long been known—it is not a Freudian discovery—that it is difficult to differentiate between memory and phantasy. For Hobbes (1588–1679) ". . . Imagination and Memory, are but one thing, which for divers considerations hath divers names."[67] The word "imagination" (which the Greeks called "phantasy") emphasizes the empirical content of the experience and sets aside the fact that such an experience slowly dissipates. The word "memory" focuses on the conservation of the recollection and relegates to a secondary level the sensual or sensorial (*sensuous*) aspect of the experience. For the English philosopher, memory is the perception that one has

---

67. Hobbes, Thomas [1651], *Leviathan* (2.3 and 2.4). Edited by Richard Tuck. Great Britain: Cambridge University Press, 1991, p. 16–19.

previously perceived; it enables one to have knowledge of the world. "Much memory, or memory of many things, is called Experience." But what "we generally call Understanding" is something else: it is the application of the imagination through language, through words. Depending on how one views it, a recollection is either memory or phantasy, that is, it is the conjugation of the two.

It is in this simple yet venerable tradition that Freudian doctrine assimilates memory and phantasy, by combining them, and this is perhaps what Piaget could not, or would not accept with his acerbic intellectualism. Piaget's first memory does not demonstrate so much that the nurse had lied (he did not learn that until later and her confession did not serve to erase the "memory") but rather that the boy needed to believe in the "glorious" reality of the scene that fulfilled his phantasies of being the marvelous object that assured the jouissance of the Other.

In the autobiographical memories of Goethe, at the beginning of Chapter 1, after a long reference to the astrological conjunction of his birth, we find that the poet affirms that:

When we desire to recall what happened to us in the earliest period of youth, it often happens that we confound what we have heard from others with that which we really possess from our own direct experience. Without, therefore, instituting a very close investigation into the point, *which, after all, could lead to nothing*, I am conscious that we lived in an old house . . . (my italics).[68]

Freud begins his article, "A Childhood Recollection from *'Dichtung und Wahrheit'* (1917)," by recalling this observation by the poet that refers to the induced character of childhood memories, but he interrupts it before quoting what Goethe demonstrates: that it serves no purpose to search for "objective" data referring to the source of the memories or to try to determine whether they proceed from a first-hand experience or from a story heard from

68. Goethe, Johann Wolfgang von [1811]. Op. cit., p. 4.

others. What is important is the memory per se. Whether Piaget might have been the victim of an attempted kidnapping, or that the supposed attempt might have been the concoction of his nurse, changes nothing from the point of view of the memory, for the "glory" that accompanies it and which is not a consequence but rather the cause of his retaining the memory and the absolute conviction that the subject has of the nature of the (falsely) lived experience. If Piaget's narrative proves anything, it is that illusion takes precedence over reality. Freud realized this truth after a few years. We might even suggest that psychoanalysis was born when Freud came to understand *the primacy of phantasy over the memory* of a historic event.

Having been the object of an attempted kidnapping is the *manifest* content of Piaget's phantasy, in which he believes to the letter despite his knowledge that it never happened. To have escaped the kidnapping is the *latent* content of Piaget's phantasy. So, was it before or after he was two years old? The Genevese, compatriot of Rousseau's, has said that intellectually he resisted the theory of analysis, yet he submitted to being analyzed by Sabina Spielrein, who he believed (falsely) had in turn been analyzed by Freud. The "information" was false, but of what importance is that? What is important is what he believed. His analyst, Sabina Spielrein, was his work colleague in Edouard Claparède's psychology laboratory; his job at the institute—for which he had been contracted—was to explain psychoanalytical hypotheses.[69] Furthermore, Piaget believed that she did not willingly reveal her personal views but rather that "she'd been sent to Geneva by the Société Internationale de Psychanalyse to disseminate the doctrine" and it was at that time that he had been "perfectly willing to be a guinea pig." Piaget states that he resisted the "need for the interpretation she tried to impose" (Bringuier, cit., p. 123).

Which is the phantasmic scene of Piaget lying on the couch undergoing psychoanalysis? Let us review the scene in 1922. Is it

---

69. Roudinesco, E. and M. Plon, *Dictionnaire de la psychanalyse*, Paris, Fayard, 1997. Article: Spielrein, Sabina.

not transparent? An attempted kidnapping! The specter of the Champs Elysées is still active. Piaget in 1969 remembers how a certain woman, sent by Freud, wanted to trap him in 1922, and he resisted—despite the vivid revival of his past achieved during the sessions, so powerful as could only be experienced by evoking the attempted "kidnapping" that never took place. He resisted to the point that "she stopped the analysis." Perhaps Sabina Spielrein did not wish to take the place of the nurse in the phantasy of her young patient. Let him live his phantasy of being the marvelous object (*agalma*) lacking the Other, who tempts him into participating in a scene of criminal abduction that he should resist! Let him organize his life as a resistance—from the supposedly ignored intellectual trenches—against psychoanalysis! No one is more stubborn and persistent than a phantasy organized around the scene involving a previous and immense *jouissance* . . . and Piaget knew how to extract prodigious results from his. His memory began with a vivid and intense terror . . . albeit unreal. Yes, to be sure, nothing is more stubborn or persistent . . . than the first childhood memory.

5

BORGES YEARNS FOR BLINDNESS

1. The Multiplied Self in the Mirrors of the Wardrobe

One could grow weary or impatient reading the many commentaries written on the seemingly compulsive presence of mirrors, tigers and labyrinths in the Borgesian world. It is almost stereotypical to add anything more to what has already been written on such images in the work by the author of *The Aleph*. Unless . . . unless there is something he still might teach us. Which is invariably the case.

The *leitmotif* of this study is that of a memory—the memory—that commences in terror (Cortázar). On this point we should not overlook Jorge Luis Borges's response to María Esther Vázquez during an interview in 1973 when she asked about those obsessive, insistent references, particularly those having to do with mirrors. The immediate evocation of the celebrated writer was a childhood recollection; I do not know if it is the first in his memory, but I know of no other before (or after), having reviewed all that he wrote and mentioned in the many interviews he gave. In any case, we have already seen that the idea of a "first memory" is an indemonstrable and mythical presumption, rife with fantasies, desires and adventitious information, if not an out and out falsification.

And we cannot put much stock on the reliability of memory, not even in the case of Borges:

> In the house we had a large Hamburg-style wardrobe of three sections. Those mahogany wardrobes which were common in the Creole households of the period. I would lie down in front of it and see myself in the mirror in triplicate and I felt afraid that those images did not correspond exactly to me and I thought how terrible it would be to see myself differently in each one of them . . . When I was a child I didn't dare tell my parents not to leave me in a totally dark room for fear of that anxiety. Before going to sleep I would open my eyes repeatedly to see if the images in the three mirrors remained faithful to my image of myself or if they had begun to change quickly and in an alarming way. To this was added the idea of the plurality of the self, that the self was changeable, that we are ourselves and we are others; I have applied this idea many times.[70]

When there are various mirrors, their respective angles will necessarily be slightly different ("différantes" Derrida would say, as well as "differing," since no two can be seen at the same time, a lapse of "differation" separates the two gazes). The reflections are simultaneous; the gazes cannot be synchronic. Such a difference is valid not only for the body that is viewed but also the retina that views the various mirrors. Thus, no one of them, by virtue of its very multiplicity, can redouble or confirm "exactly" the "me" (*moi*) that observes it. The diverse images disorient the uncertain observer that is the child, unsure even of his own appearance: no one is more "real" (true) than any other, no one is equal to another. All authentic, all false. Each could act with capricious autonomy, which is the classic theme of the *Doppelgänger* and so many sinister tales in which shadows separate from the body

---

70. Borges, Jorge Luis. *Veinticinco Agosto, 1983 y otros cuentos*. Madrid: Siruela, 1983, pp. 80–81 (my translation).

and act on their own. The image of one's own body and face is a needle that functions like the compass of the subject, vacillating. It is left demagnetized (de-northified).

Borges the child's gaze branches into three gazes. In place of the trivium or of the trioply, with the material of the three images almost simultaneously and minimally differentiated, he has to construct a unifying composition, a synthesis of the various "points of view," so as not to become disoriented. Only in this way can he avoid the heartrending experience of feeling himself as one but seeing himself as three, of inhabiting three virtual spaces at once, with barely perceptible variations among them. If it is difficult to conceive of oneself as being one and oneself at the same time when one sees oneself replicated by the virtual specular image, how can one become one and oneself when four representations correspond to the real body: the imaginary, and the three duplications that appear in the various doors of the enormous Hamburg-style wardrobe?

The child's anxiety, it seems to me, recalls Cortázar's childhood recollection in which he describes his situation and states most emphatically: "they made me sleep alone." It is from the parents that the child would have liked to ask for protection.

"Georgie," like Pirandello's character Vitangelo Moscarda (*Uno, nessuno e centomila / One, No one and One Hundred Thousand*), is one, and he sees many without any one being more trustworthy than any other. The variability of the perspectives ranges, at the same time, from "one" to "one hundred thousand" to "no one." The strangeness of mirrors resides in the compulsive mania they have of following us, imitating us, and repeating our every movement. The only way to hold their image is to remain motionless, without so much as blinking an eye or breathing, as if dead. If mirrors are multiple and watch us, there is no way to stand before one of them and neglect the unpredictable curiosity and voracity of the others. And there is no other human being there on the scene at that moment. There is no one capable of guaranteeing life with certainty. There is no one who, with the soft emulsion of words, can offer the assurance that in spite of the threatening spectacle of the proliferation of images, the self will not self-destruct or separate among the images, and that the body will remain one and unique. There should be someone more disposed to intervene and eliminate in one fell swoop the proliferation of so many "selves" capable of deciding how to act each on its own. There is the need for a control that will unify and coordinate into one sole image the anarchic dissidence ("trisidence" in this case) of the doubles.

The child would escape from the interstices of the mirrors if he could drive them off by denying them the food that feeds them, which is the light. The little one, alone, is powerless to eliminate the accomplice of the glass, so active and insidious, sibylline and invasive, pouring into the room. But the Other, perhaps he or she could expel the light. Borges addresses—he would like to address—them, his parents, to deliver a strange paradoxical, irrational entreaty. It would take much courage to ask for something so outrageous, a surgical treatment for his anxiety. His petition is so absurd that it is impossible for him to even formulate it. He would like to ask his parents to put him in a completely dark room. But he does not dare. His words are smothered before they can be pronounced. His anxiety, his impotence, cannot be negotiated in a discourse that seems inadmissible. They remain unformulated, stifled. "I didn't dare tell them that I wanted them to leave me in a totally dark room."[71] Who—which child—would dare *to ask for blindness*? Where is the child who prefers to put out the light rather than protect himself by furnishing the world with vision— even before the advent of the invention of Morel, what is today called television?

To be sure, the child is not Joyce, with his phobia of storms and his fear of the dark. His blindness—that of the Irishman—was also sought after; he did everything possible to obtain it with the invaluable collaboration of the ophthalmologists who subjected him to a series of suspicious operations. Surely the child is not Gabriel García Márquez either, who recalled:

---

71. *Ibid.*

I never could overcome my fear of being alone, above all in the dark, but it seems to me that it had a concrete origin, which is that at night my grandmother's fantasies and premonition materialized. At the age of seventy I still glimpsed in dreams the ardor of the jasmines in the hallway and the phantom in the gloomy bedrooms, and always with the same feeling that ruined my childhood: terror of the night.[72]

The triple gaze of the mirror-machine undoes the person—splits the person like the prism does to light. This triple gaze, which can be infinitely multiplied, causes the unstable representation of the body to tremble (". . . that which I believed to be my image.") It is common and almost universal for children to be afraid of the dark, to need light to reassure them of their own presence in the world, to use their eyes as crutches so that the self does not suffer collapse. This is not the case for Borges, as he himself assures us. He would have liked for "them," the Other, to have given him the "unanimous night" and, in its place, books, so as to avoid meeting up with his own reflection. The mirror did not confirm for him that he was Borges but rather that he was "one, no one and one hundred thousand," depending on the perspective of the observer. With their argent eyes, the crystals de-conceived him.

The mirror is—and it should be—proof of one's existence and of the body's permanence in space, asserting itself as "me" (*moi*), counting itself as "one." But three mirrors! With their proliferation they cannot help but destroy the image, pulverizing it. Humpty Dumpty, me, broken and all the king's men and all the king's horses cannot put the pieces together again. And if every mirror were to capriciously twist its particular vision of what can be seen in it? Who can harmonize them, submit them to rules, restrict their reproductive arbitrariness and obscene profusion of images?

---

72. García Márquez, Gabriel, *Living to Tell the Tale*. Translated by Edith Grossman. New York: Alfred A. Knopf, 2003, p.82.

The permanence of the self-image—the work of memory—is a precarious guarantee of the world in which we live, but without that guarantee we could not live. Borges also addressed this theme in his story, "Funes the Memorious": the incessant variability of the appearances impedes the formation of any single concept: Funes, in his vertiginous world, could not "comprehend that the generic symbol *dog* embraces so many unlike individuals of diverse size and form; it bothered him that a dog at three fourteen (seen from the side) should have the same name as the dog at three fifteen (seen from the front). *His own face in the mirror, his own hands, surprised him every time he saw them*" (my italics).[73] How curious! In order to have knowledge it is necessary to forget the tiny differences that flutter among the memories of perception. Only then is memory possible.

Jorge Luis Borges develops a ritual that might me called obsessive-compulsive. He tries to alleviate his anxiety by repeating, in an almost defiant way, the experience that terrifies him. He repeatedly opens and closes his eyes, blinking. Terrified, in the middle of the night he plays his own game of *fort—da*, just like Freud's little grandchild. Peek-a-boo. He explores the reliability of the gaze that observes him through the wardrobe's mirrors, the gaze of the Other. "Do they remain faithful images?" or do they break the pact and conspire to modify them(selves) in a swift and alarming way? Does he really want the truth? No, he does not demand the truth, but rather the ratification of the image that he has forged of himself ("the one in which I believed"). And, if this were not possible, then bring on the darkness! Are these not the keys to the life and work of Borges?

In time, Borges offered a poetic version of this recollection ("they say that fourteen verses are a sonnet"):

---

73. Borges, Jorge Luis. "Funes the Memorious." Translated by James E. Irby in *Labyrinths*. Edited by Donald A. Yates & James E. Irby. New York: New Directions, 1964, p. 65.

As a child I feared the mirror might reveal
Another face, or make me see a blind
Impersonal mask whose blankness must conceal
Something horrible, no doubt. I also feared
The silent time inside the looking glass
Might meander from the ordinary stream
Of mundane human hours, and harbor deep
Within its vague, imaginary space
New-found beings, colors, unknown shapes.
(I spoke of this to no one; children are shy.)
Now I fear the mirror may disclose
The true, unvarnished visage of my soul,
Bruised by shadows, black and blue with guilt—
The face God sees, that men perhaps see too.[74]

2. Books and Blindness Battle Against Mirrors

Fascinated horror before the mirror, doubt over identity, doubts over who is the author of these lines or who is the dreamer of this dream in the circular ruins, doubts by Chuang Tse over a butterfly that dreams of being Chuang Tse rather than being he who dreams of it, memory of the horror of being seen and the impossibility of escaping the gaze of others, demanding the gift of blindness and of books, the sensation of not knowing where one is in the middle of a world that is a labyrinth, the rejection of that substitute for the mirror that is copulation, capable of producing other eyes that would see themselves in other mirrors, escape from mirrors in the hideaways of libraries, infertility of the body and fecundity in writing which is the "mirror and model" for writers of the future, remote refuge for unnameable and un-concealable

---

74. Borges, Jorge Luis. "The Mirror." Translated by Hoyt Rogers. In *Selected Poems*. Edited by Alexander Coleman. New York: Viking, 1999, p. 405.

sins (from God or even from other men), roughly alluded to by the Freudian notion of the super-ego. Are these not the coordinates of Borges's universe, prefigured in the horror of the multiple mirrors of the Hamburg wardrobes Borges obsessively conjures up "before falling asleep?"

To find a self-fulfilling prophesy for the writer, there amongst the mirrors in a room in Buenos Aires, would be risky. Who could offer aid for such an interpretation? No one . . . no one except for Borges himself. Here is what he says to Antonio Carrizo:

Carrizo: Borges, mirrors . . . you don't like them at all.

Borges: I don't like them at all or I like them too much. Well, of course I have freed myself of them. Because blindness is a drastic way to do away with mirrors.[75]

It is unfortunate—unfortunate for him—that the longed for emancipation should be dubious. It is not enough just to stop seeing them in order to successfully escape their visual field and perpetual ambush. The mirror is an inert object but, at the same time, it is also a specter impregnated with our human form to which it cannot give birth. Mirror, into which we look; looking glass, that looks back at us. Borges can speak to—and even berate—that "mysterious brother" who finds him even in the dark night when there are no eyes to see what the mirror continues to see:

You have always watched. In the tenderness
 Of the uncertain water or the crystal that endures
You search for me and it is useless to be blind.
The fact of not seeing you or knowing you
Adds to your horror . . .[76]

---

75. *Borges el memorioso. Conversaciones de J .L. Borges con Antonio Carrizo*, México: FCE, 1983, p. 92 (my translation).
76. Borges, J.L., "Al espejo" (To the Mirror). In *Obras completas*. Buenos Aires: Emecé, 1989. Volume II, p. 109 (my translation).

To these verses we will return, led by the hands of lucid women writers.

It would no longer avail the aged child—now the blind, wise old man—to control his night watchman by opening and closing his eyes. The many eyes of the tireless crystals still invade and perforate the soul of the blind man who cannot ignore them although, for him, they have gone from clear silver to blurry gray. The child wished for blindness. The adult feels that the battle is lost, that one more horror has been added. And he knows where the terror comes from: not from the visual field but rather from "the true, unvarnished visage of my soul, bruised by shadows, black and blue with guilt."

If it is a metaphor to say that mirrors are prisons, then it is no less metaphorical—a metaphor impregnated by illusion—to propose that one "can free oneself of them" through blindness which is the price of that freedom. It is worth mentioning that the blank sheet of paper into which the writer casts himself is also an annulment of the mirror, a way of escaping it. The mirror is equally abominable to the opaque surface of the printed page, filled with senseless scribbles, filled with that de-imagined reality of alphabetic signs that lack, as such, meaning, that say nothing, but that conjure up a reader for whom they are populated and furnished with signifiers. The book also annuls the destabilizing play of images. To read is, among other things, to invert the crystalline, reflective, and persecutory surface of the mirror, redirecting it and fixing it to the wall. "To submerge oneself in the text," as we tend to say, is to practice a kind of "drastic" abolition of virtual space that can drive one crazy with its "split" message. To read is a way of escaping from the gaze of the other and from mirrors, immersing oneself in a funnel of paper in which the subject can be segregated, can become secret and is no longer seen. Blind men and readers, blind readers, without egos; who can know what they see? Who can see them if they cannot see? Signs that issue the order: "Follow us."

Borges does not dare to ask for darkness in order to escape from the mirrors. Is it a premonition? Is the oracle inscribed in his first memory or is it his unconscious desire, never formulated, but realized in the blindness that, like Tiresias, makes him see again? He knows that blindness is his destiny. He said that "this slow twilight" began in 1899, when he was born.[77] It does not help to know that it was an inherited affliction, one that his father and his grandmother had suffered. For him, Nietzschean like few others, it was a question of *ja sagen*, of saying yes to destiny. He learned to accept blindness as a gift because it corresponded to his most fervent desire.

> . . . if we accept that in the good of heaven there can also be darkness, then who lives more with themselves? Who can explore themselves more? Who can know more of themselves? According to the Socratic phrase [*gnoti te auton*], who can know himself more than the blind man?[78]

Borges compares himself, for his "own modest blindness," to Milton who became totally blind in 1652 thinking "that he lost his sight voluntarily [. . .] and then he remembered his first desire, that of being a poet."[79] Like others, Milton knew that "his destiny was literary [. . .] I too, if I may mention myself, have always known that my destiny was, above all, a literary destiny." Like Joyce, almost blind when he wrote *Finnegans Wake*, Borges passes his life "polishing the sentences in his memory."[80] To disconnect himself from the visual world and take refuge in the auditory world of words, creating a new reality, is his objective. He continues to write subsequent to his blindness but writes his way out of a foretold blindness, transforming the humiliation, the misfortune and dismay—proudly making "from the miserable circumstances of our lives things that are eternal, or that aspire to be so."[81] Nothing less!

---

77. Borges, J.L., *Obras completas*, cit., vol. 2, p. 144.
78. Borges, J.L., [1977], "Blindness," in *Seven Nights*. Translated by Eliot Weinberger. New York: New Directions, 1980, p. 120.
79. *Ibid.*, p. 116.
80. *Ibid.*, p. 119.
81. *Ibid.*, p. 121.

The comparison of Borges to Oedipus could be considered an application of obscurantist and dogmatic psychoanalysis, an object deserving of derision. I will not venture to suggest this. There is no need to insert into his discourse preconceived ideas that he did not need, especially when I am aware of how he maintained distance from Freudian readings. However, this should not prevent us from listening to him when he says, during the same conference on blindness:

> Democritus of Abdera tore his eyes out in a garden so that the spectacle of reality would not distract him; Origen castrated himself.
>
> I have enumerated enough examples. Some are so illustrious that I am ashamed to have spoken of my own personal case—except for the fact that people always hope for confessions and I have no reason to deny them mine.[82]

I will not question the dubious veracity of both references. Democritus, the Laughing Philosopher, could hardly have explored the natural world as he did until the end of his life without the use of his sight. One legend says that he put out his eyes with hot glass to avoid the distraction of what was visible "in a garden" (Borges adds), but this legend has been completely discarded by scholars. There is also much controversy over whether Origen castrated himself, whether it was to avoid scandal since his students were both men and women (!?), or in order to follow the teachings of Matthew (19:12 King James Version), "there be eunuchs, which have made themselves eunuchs for the kingdom of heaven's sake." In the version of the Bible translated into Spanish and annotated by Amat, a note says: "It is not legal to mutilate the body, as Origen did, but rather to calm the passions and live a heavenly life of the flesh."[83]

---

82. *Ibid.*, p. 119.
83. *La Sagrada Biblia* (*The Holy Bible*). Translated into Spanish by Félix Torres Amat. Mexico: Libreros Mexicanos Unidos, 1958, p. 1161 (my translation).

Borges admits the voluntary quality of his blindness and he has no reason to deny the "confessions" that liken him to the legends of self-mutilation attributed to Democritus and Origen . . . one who put out his own eyes and the other who castrated himself.

I still suspect that the dread in his first childhood memory oriented his life towards blindness as well as towards his synoptic visions of the entire universe as depicted in *The Aleph*. Escaping from the prison of his body, trapped by mirrors, resulted in his production, as maker (*El hacedor*), of infinite virtual universes, *orbis tertius*, of new fantasy worlds; there, for humans to inhabit them, gaining distance from their dread of mirrors.

GABO GARCÍA'S DIRTY OVERALLS

1. Where Was the Childhood Memory Kept?

Gabriel García Márquez is a parthenogenetic writer: he conceived and gave birth to himself following a unique process that took him from Aracataca, in the Colombian jungle, to the Nobel Prize for Literature. How was he able to accomplish this unusual voyage from a land filled with legends through which run rivers of blood that empty into a sea of wonder—a sea of marginality in relation to an official culture that disdains this world and writes it off as *barbaric*, as a world of outlandish miscegenation, of protohistoric landscapes and alluvial accidents—to the writing of marvels with universal relevance and the provocation in readers all over the world of an unlimited, spellbound enjoyment of a rhetoric of hyperbole and paradox? This is, perhaps, the greatest mystery that one would like to see clarified and that would drive one to enter into what appears to be the first part of his autobiography.[84] Incidentally, without looking for it (. . . is this true?—I doubt it), over the course of my reflections on the narrative construction of the subject as "I" and the supposed oracular value of first memories, I have found in the text of the Colombian writer another "first childhood memory" concisely narrated and evocative of daily and

---

84. García Márquez, Gabriel. *Living to Tell the Tale*. Op. cit.

Cortazarian dread. It is no less coincidental that this first memory should be clad, I believe, in the lights (and shades) of a personal reference. Let us listen to García Márquez:

> There, out of the blue, my mother gave me the most unexpected surprise with a triumphant emphasis:
> "Here's where you were born!"
> I had not known that before, or I had forgotten it, but in the next room we found the crib where I slept until I was four years old and that my grandmother kept forever. I had forgotten it, but as soon as I saw it I remembered myself in the overalls with little blue flowers that I was wearing for the first time, screaming for somebody to come and take off my diapers that were filled with shit. I could barely stand as I clutched at the bars of the crib that was as small and fragile as Moses' basket. This has been a frequent cause of discussion and joking among relatives and friends, for whom my anguish that day seems too rational for one so young. Above all when I have insisted that the reason for my suffering was not disgust at my own filth but fear that I would soil my new overalls. That is, it was not a question of hygienic prejudice but esthetic concern, and because of the manner in which it persists in my memory, I believe it was my first experience as a writer.[85]

This narrative is typical: it submerges us in a searing and traumatic episode, in a seemingly banal setting. The evocation is abundant with elements that characterize the "screen memory" (Freud, 1899). The episode may seem banal, but that is not the case for its oracular function, indeed the writer himself attributes to it a certain stamp of destiny, an indelible mark that conveys him, in a surprising way, toward the craft of writing.

The memory was buried, the recollection eroded by oblivion and it might have never surfaced had the writer not turned out to be the modern Aesop that he is, and had that memory not exercised

---

85. García Márquez, Gabriel. *Living to Tell the Tale.* Op. cit., p. 34–35.

its irrepressible and unforeseeable effects from within the brimming void we call the unconscious. Is the memory inside him or does it lie dormant, crouching, in that crib, always waiting for him, though it might never have been seen again by the sensitive poet, who even as a child standing behind bars, is remembered as capable of turning into himself (*sich erinnern*) and of expressing himself outwardly, of making a "deposition" of his memory (*eräussern*, if I might be so bold as to invent a strange word in German, a language that is always open to lexical innovation)? The crib, revisited in the company of his mother, is a repository of saved memory lying at the ready for just such an accidental encounter: "I had forgotten it, but as soon as I saw it I remembered myself . . ." At this point, the sentence may be left in suspension. What García Márquez had forgotten—he tells us—was not the crib; it was himself. The memory obeys a strange peristalsis: when memories return, the subject is overcome by incontinence. The excrement of the past recovers its organoleptic qualities.

The memory of García Márquez's inopportune excrements is not an encounter with something lost in the past, but the possibility of producing himself through the expression and externalization (*Eräusserung*), through the de-recording, as I am tempted to say, of memory. *Erinnerung* is the German word for "memory." What is notable in this word is the root, *In/Inner*, which refers to the interior. *Aus*, in contrast, is that which is outside, exterior; thus, *Eräusserung*. The German language is very fortunate to be able to clearly distinguish memory, *Gedächtnis*—the effect and learning of past perceptions and actions—from *Erinnerung*, the memory of an episode laden with affective connotations and pertinent to speaking beings. *Gedächtnis* is something you have; *Erinnerung* is something you tell.

Hegel explored this relationship between the "interior" (*Erinnerung*) of memory and the objectified, externalized, savable aspect of memory (*Gedächtnis*). In his *Encyclopaedia* [1830],[86] the

---

86. Hegel, Georg Wilhelm Friedrich [1830]. *Philosophy of Nature:Encyclopaædia of the Philosophical Sciences*. Translated by A.V. Miller. Cambridge (Ma): Oxford University Press. 1971.

philosopher does not resort to my innovation, *Eräusserung*; he uses the expression, *Entäusserung*, a word that was popular in Marxist theory and that is normally translated as "alienation." If this word is imported into English somewhat differently, as externalization (*Eräusserung*), it may coincide with Hegel in his line of thought, especially when the philosopher says that internalization and externalization are not so directly opposed as they are complementary: the subject broadens his or her internal life and thoughts insofar as experience of the past is expressed in discourse and writing. To write an autobiography, to live to tell the tale,[87] is not a way to materialize something previously existing as a memory, but rather to construct a new subjectivity through the spoken or written word. This is none other than the foundation for the technique and practice of psychoanalysis: that someone, through the very act of telling, may produce him/herself as an other that is different in place of him/herself, to be different from the way he/she was. Life—shall I venture to say this?—is born of the story. Through *performance,* the act of narration in a certain scene of the narrative, in a certain moment of life, creates the life being narrated. By addressing another person, who becomes a listener or a reader, life is not merely evoked, it is produced. We are the stories we tell. Characters in search of an author; stories in search of receptive ears. Vainly heroic narratives that conjugate and segregate "I."

The retrieval of what has been forgotten, which should not be confused with the (analytic) reconstruction of what has been repressed, is triggered by the mother's voice saying: "Here's where you were born!" and "this was your crib." The mute object, awash in the limbo of an ignored memory, was an entity deprived of significance, stupid in its condition of combustible wood, on the verge of going up in smoke. The mere perception and location of the small artifact in the family narrative (like Proust's madeleine, the retrieval cue of the neuro-physiologists), ratified by the mother's words, is sufficient to project the radiographic image of

---

87. Cit., unnumbered page. Epigraph: "Life is not what one lived, but what one remembers and how one remembers it in order to recount it."

the "bones of the memory," the ever illusory first memory. The hyper-clear (*überdeutig*) elements appear with the almost hallucinatory clarity of memory emphasized by Freud and endorsed by our writers: "the overalls with little blue flowers" recently worn for the first time. Others—relatives and friends—will argue and go on arguing with the memory-endowed writer about the reasons he gives for the feelings he does not hesitate to refer to as "anxiety" and "anguish." "Reasons," "causes," "motives?" One can search. "Rationalizations," users of psychoanalytic jargon would say. A question that is impossible to settle, skeptics will say, since we cannot overlook multiple determinations for the mind and we risk falling into caricature when trying to impose "reasons" or "explanations" either from inside or outside of the subject. Memory is like the stuff of dreams, of the nightmare of waking up in a desolate world. It resists interpretation.

The writer of these lines can recognize in his own history a similar first memory. There are, in him, certain imprecise impressions of an earlier time, shadows of a memory. But the precise moment from which the memory is torn seems to be "the same" as that of García Márquez's. At three years old he was also left alone, in this case in a red-tiled courtyard, beside a gray washing machine, during a brilliant blue afternoon, and he found himself with soiled diapers, crying inconsolably because no one came to clean up the mess he had made without wanting to, but unable to avoid doing so. Where is the trauma in these two trivial and similar memories? It lies in the unanswered cry, in the lack of response from the Other. It is worth emphasizing García Márquez's illuminating words: "for somebody to come and take off my diapers." In an evocation of the same type, Cortázar says: "They had left me alone . . . and then the rooster crowed."

It is not only the writing vocation that recognizes its source here. Perhaps all redeeming ideals share this humble origin. Why not, as well, the need for a God that protects the helpless, confidence in a system of just social relations, the search for magical or scientific answers to avoid destitution? And why not love with its promises, friendship, mutual fidelity that is demonstrated in the consistent response to cries for help, the interchange of goods and services, physical fitness techniques, drugs, a total human effort to alleviate "cultural adversity," which may be read as the attempt to pass from a world in soiled diapers to a forever lost world of new overalls with everlasting blue flowers?

That "memory should begin with terror," as Julio Cortázar claimed, signifies the beginning of the project of "living to tell the tale," including "telling the tale to live." One narrates, one searches for meaning, one calls for the solidarity of the Other. Someone must arrive and keep at bay that atrocious nucleus of the being, to chase off the Thing (*Ding*), the ominous and un-representable Thing, the closest and most distant, not intimate but rather *extimate*, the Thing that releases the first and most horrifying scream to arise from helplessness. The Thing that emerges from the guts and is the object of the greatest rejection by the intolerance of the Other. The indicator of that intolerable neighborhood of the Thing is the scream, the inconsolable wail beneath a naked sky aimed at people who seem to drift away creating with their distance the setting for traumatism. The abandoned subject awash in his own excrement—himself become excrement owing to the sad predicament of his desolation—is born from terror and tries to improve his circumstances by imposing ideals of cleanliness, comfort, beauty and love. García Márquez's first memory, as false and screening as any other, could serve as a paradigm of how the subject of exchanges is constituted, "quid pro quo, tit for tat."

No one comes to aid the helpless Narcissus, with his dirtied and foul-smelling self, with feces clinging to his skin and penetrating to his soul. There must be the Other but the Other does not arrive. The world's harmony has been upset. The situation is hopeless. The pristine beauty of the little flowers on the blue overalls has wilted. Can it be revived with pretty words? Perhaps yes; but with a different fragrance.

The love one may have for oneself takes root in—becomes attached to—certain objects: in this case, the crib that the ancestor—his maternal grandmother—in her role as the great Other, keeps "forever," and the overalls with the little flowers which, no matter what happened to his body ("hygienic prejudice"), had to be kept clean ("aesthetic concern"). The injury consists in not being able to resolve on his own the embarrassing situation of having soiled himself, in having to depend on the other who may capriciously, with no explanation, simply disappear . . . or remain trapped within the wardrobe whose key is in the hands of the evil Other.

The self is adrift, at the mercy of the currents—invisible yet turbulent—in "Moses' basket," which is as fragile as himself. To live is to be aware of the great initial trauma: the self cast away, afloat on the Nile, appealing with tears in the eyes to the supposed omnipotence of the Other, the daughter of Pharaoh, anyone capable of saving the despairing baby. Later he will pass from behind the bars of his crib-prison to the vast but frightening world of years of solitude, of waiting for that letter that never arrives because there is no one to write it, the times of cholera, of abduction and of foretold death, carrying at all times the messianic hope of saving and freeing himself through clear writing.

This is his misfortune, the writer's crib of desire. This is, indeed, "living to tell the tale."

2. The Retrieval of Memories

It is worth returning to an earlier question: Where were the sensations that were aroused in Proust upon tasting the madeleine? How is it possible that Piaget, in his sessions with his analyst, saw again the exact place where, as he rode in his baby carriage, the attempted abduction took place—an event that never occurred? Why is it possible for Nabokov to "see again" his nursery in the paternal mansion and feel that nothing will ever change?[88] How

---

88. Nabokov, Vladimir. *Speak, Memory: An Autobiography Revisited*. New York: Alfred A. Knopf, Inc., 1999, p. 56. See below, Chapter 9.

is it possible that Martha Robles's memory[89] was aroused by reading another writer's account of a memory? Why is it enough for García Márquez to see his crib for him to recall his "forgotten" first memory?

These memory retrievals were not sought after; each one was an accident, an unexpected occurrence, which gave rise to an explosion of reality. I refer to "reality" as that which is not symbolized, as corporeal experience that is expelled both from the word and the image. In this example, the childhood experience that lies buried and waiting is like a burr that can be carried off on the wind or clinging to a piece of clothing, dropped somewhere else to germinate and become a narration, charged with blood and life. I will refer to this concise resurrection of memory as epiphany,[90] when the "I" that one presently is disappears and is replaced by what the "I" was at the remembered moment. It is a phenomenon with a hallucinatory appearance that transpires like a dream when it encounters a "trace of daylight," enabling the old and forgotten event to return to life. Without a return to García Márquez's origins—the visit to his grandparents' home—aided by the words of his mother, how long would the crib's ostracism from his memory have lasted? Would it have returned in time to be included in the autobiography of the conjurer of the sad whores?

The latent recollection (from *latens*, occult, hidden) is a phantom in search of a body, a body of words, of images, of integration into a narrative, of dates and points of reference, of ideas about the place of the self in relation to its temporal and genealogical coordinates of space, people, and meaning. It is a phantom thirsting for history, begging for a place in the story of life, a nook where it can nestle down in memory.

The memory specialists (mnemologists, I affectionately call

---

89. See sections 7.3 and 7.4.
90. I will return to the notion of "epiphany," as it occurs in Joyce, when I discuss Virginia Woolf's remembered first impressions of life (see Chapter 7.1). We can distinguish between *epiphany*—a revived sensual and corporeal experience—from *episode*, which is recalled and transmitted as a narration.

them) often vehemently debate two opposing hypotheses. The first, favored by the majority—at least, a majority of the "romantics"— proposes that all lived events are recorded in memory but access to them has been lost. We may recall that Paul Valéry shared this view (see page 24 fn 27): what is lost is not the memory but rather the path leading to it. The second hypothesis states that, in fact, irreversible forgetting and loss of information takes place and this loss is proportional to the passage of time. Clearly, the first of these affirmations is the more attractive and it can never be proven false (it is not "falsifiable," according to Popper's epistemology). Faced with the impossibility of remembering something, it can always be sustained that the failure is transitory and due (for the moment) to a lack of the appropriate clue or retrieval cue. There are memories that sleep in obscurity awaiting the torch that will illuminate them. Psyche and Eros.

There are legendary cases of hypermnesia, such as the fabulous Simonides, inventor of the science of mnemonics, immortalized by Cicero; Borges's Nietzschean Funes; the prodigious Sherasevski, a supposed patient of Luria, the Soviet psychologist[91] and Georges Perec—we will deal with the onslaught of his memory in Chapter 12. These "cases," fictitious or real, show us that forgetting is a necessary and adapted function that enables the memory to function better, with less interference by obsolete or unnecessary information. What good would it be for us to remember what we had for breakfast exactly a year ago? Why would we keep our worn-out childhood shirts (or overalls) in the closet?

Memory fades with time but, occasionally, it grows stronger, it revives with new stimuli, it receives vitamin and hormonal complements in the form of photographs, conversations, accidental encounters with aphonic objects that nonetheless become eloquent, like the blessed crib in which the child García Márquez slept.

---

91. Funes and Sherasevski have been further examined in Chapters 2.1 and 5.2 of *La memoria, la inventora* (Braunstein, Néstor. Mexico, Siglo XXI, 2008). In English this second part of the trilogy on memory will be published as *Memory: the Inventor.*

It is a fact that there is memory that is present but not utilized. As I think about, and read for, the chapter I am currently writing, I run across the expression "dormant memory" and, suddenly, certain verses I once learned in high school enter my head though I have not thought of them for several decades: *Recuerde el alma dormida, / avive el seso e despierte, / contemplando / cómo se pasa la vida / cómo se viene la muerte* (*Remember the dormant soul, / revive the brain and awake, / contemplating / how life passes / how death comes*). Except that, given that my topic is "memory," the recollection has come to me with a deformed first verse owing to an unconscious intention: *Despierte la memoria dormida* (*Awaken the dormant memory*), which is more consonant with the expression, *dormant memory*, the retrieval cue operant in this case. These "Coplas de Jorge Manrique por la muerte de su padre" [1476] ("Coplas of Jorge Manrique for the death of his father") were recorded in a more or less mysterious way but, not only did they have to be awakened by key in order to provide access to their bedroom, but the very key gave form to the recollection and induced the "error"—an error, without a doubt, which could be corrected through the comparison I performed later with the text of the verses I searched for and found in an anthology of classical Spanish poetry. With the book in hand, I could "correct" my "recollection" and "wake the dormant memory . . ." in agreement with my desire and in disagreement with literality.

How does the record of a sleeping past persist in memory? Where is it kept? Here begins the realm of metaphors. About the "place" there *seems* to be no doubt.[92] More than five hundred years ago, Manrique himself said that it was in "the brain"—and, certainly, he is not responsible for inventing the cerebral location. From the "garbage heap," which is how Funes refers to his memory, to the "vast palaces" of St. Augustine; from the impressions located somewhere in the brain to the immense neuronal networks without any specific *topos*; from the warehouses with their shelves to the digitalized holograms—somewhat listless, somewhat lascivi-

---

92. More than doubtful, known to be false, is the view that memory has one or various brain "centers."

ous—depending on the inscrutable will of the laser; everything has been said and more metaphors are in waiting. It was not in vain that Mnemosyne, the tireless matron of metaphors capable of evoking her, gave birth to the muses.

One very logical idea for philosophical and scientific speculation has been the search for the *memory atom*, that is, the elemental particle that, in combination with others, would constitute the molecules, tissues and, finally, the vast organism of the brain. It is not an easy matter to name this atom: is it a bit, acronym for "binary digit," which, when added to another seven to form eight, becomes a byte?[93] Is it a neuron with hundreds or thousands of dendrites and synapses? Is it a signifier, is it a phoneme? Is it a letter contained in the twenty-some Western alphabets, sufficient for stocking the shelves of the library of Alexandria? Clearly, the metaphor chosen to represent memory determines the nature of the "atoms," which, as the name would indicate, are not vulnerable to fission (but rather to fiction). The signifier that has come to have the most success in this atomic race is the "engram," which refers to the idea of an "element" inscribed in the "brain," which was so dear to Jorge Manrique. It is now time for some definitions: "Engrams are the transient or enduring changes in our brains that result from encoding an experience.[94]

In a notable chapter, Schacter reports that the word "engram" was coined by Richard Semon (Berlin, 1859—Munich, 1918) but was not widely used until it was dusted off by "the great neuroscientist Karl Lashley" in 1950 (who "forgot" to cite his predecessor). Like Freud, Semon was a disciple of the evolutionary biologist, Ernst Haeckel. In a work that was promptly forgotten, titled *Mneme* (1904), he had spoken of "hereditary memory"—which we prefer

---

93. "The byte is a unit of digital information in computing and telecommunications. It is an ordered collection of bits, in which each bit denotes the binary value of 1 or 0. Historically, a byte was the number of bits used to encode a character of text in a computer and it was for this reason that the basic addressable element in many computer architectures. The term octet is widely used as a precise synonym of the 8-bit byte where ambiguity is undesirable." (Copied from Wikipedia.en .)

94. Schacter, D.L. *Searching for Memory*, cit., p. 58.

to call "Darwinian memory"—as distinguished from "everyday" or psychological memory. Semon proposed distinguishing three stages of everyday memory: *engraphy*, for encoding information into memory, the *engram*—whose definition I cited above—which is the "memory trace," and *ecphory*, which "is the process of activating or retrieving a memory."[95] Semon died in relative obscurity (he committed suicide in 1918 following the death of his wife). His ideas on the "engram" gained recognition posthumously when Lashley took them up and especially when the neurosurgeon Wilder Penfield's research gained enormous notoriety in the 1950s. Penfield electrically stimulated certain areas of the temporal lobe in fully conscious patients and elicited surprising memories of seemingly long-forgotten events. The results he produced led to the rapid confirmation of the supposition that memories are not forgotten or lost, but rather they are *latent* and awaiting appropriate stimulation (in this case electrical but also sensorial or psychic . . . why not?) to reactivate them so they will reappear in the conscious. Unfortunately, Schacter notes, the enthusiasm of those who thought they had found the location of memory—the vault containing the engrams—was not long-lived. Only 40 of the 520 patients who received temporal lobe stimulations experienced what could be called memories and even they could not decide if they had experienced memories of actual past incidents, hallucinations or phantasies.

My decision to limit this essay to a specific aspect of memory—first memories as well as certain select features ("paper scraps")—compels me (for now!) to leave until later a review of the exciting field of memory research by contemporary neuroscientists and computer model specialists. Advances in the field of psychophysiology are noteworthy, although it is my opinion—moreover, my conviction—that they will never penetrate the secrets of memory if they do not take into account subjective aspects and the relation of the subject to the audience of memory, in particular those others—witnesses and listeners—that such methodologies

---

95. Cit., pp. 56–60.

exclude. Questions such as what is remembered, why, what is the meaning of memory in the life of a subject—which is a mass of relations with others in a social world—will be difficult to answer through research of the temporal lobe.

I propose an analogy to the relations between the apparatus for film projection and the film that is projected. Knowledge—all possible knowledge—of the mechanisms of film projection that enables film viewing on the screen to improve or worsen will hardly be decisive in order to understand a given film. However, we have to concede that we would see nothing at all of the film without the apparatus that materializes it in the form of fleeting shadows on a screen. This is how I conceive the relation between the brain and memory. The script of the film we view with pleasure or dread does not depend on the apparatus used for its projection. The story is based in language.

The retrieval cues—cribs and madeleines—depend on the situation of the subject who remembers in relation to the other who must "authenticate" the memory. One remembers for someone, for some other. In the case of writers, and in our case also—the case of neurophysiologists—certainly we are faced with the relationship between the memory and a vital objective, a phantasy, an effect of the imagination of each person, concerning what it is that one wishes to obtain. We all excavate the caverns of memory and make discoveries therein. We are all interested in showing the energetic value of the black gold that we extract and we free ourselves of rhetorical exercises to prove the validity of our evocations in support of our hypotheses. The knowledge we achieve is partial; no knowledge excludes other knowledge although, possibly, some may not be available for a simple formulation. The moment for synthesis does not seem to be at hand and the opposition between the memory sciences that form part of the natural and symbolic sciences, including psychoanalysis and literary criticism along with linguistics, history and anthropology, is not harmful; it is rich and fertile because it stimulates a double quest. The divergence of paths broadens the territory to be explored.

Indeed, speaking of territories: was Gabriel García Márquez's crib in his grandmother's house in Aracataca, or in the pharyngal nucleus of the writer, or on page forty of his autobiography, or transported to the pages I am currently writing and, subsequently, to the readers who will read them tomorrow, or . . . where in the world is it? A reward has been offered for its capture, dead or alive.

VIRGINIA WOOLF: SHAME IN FRONT OF THE MIRROR

1. Who Believes in Virginia Woolf?

Virginia Woolf (1882–1941) is one of few writers to venture into the writing of autobiography and the narration of personal recollections with so much precaution and with so much knowledge of the risks involved. Her meditations are lessons that no one who is interested in the subject should ignore. "A sketch of the past"[96] puts into practice this caution based on the following sad affirmation: the subject who writes, at a given age, generally after having published a more or less large body of work, believing her/himself to be writing about her/himself, writes about an other, to whom certain things have occurred . . . but the subject is now very different from the person to whom these things happened. The person being written about is no longer there. The previous beings that one formerly was are now phantoms that, lost in the fog of the past, are hardly recognizable; *identity*—who can deny it?—*is discontinuous*. Memory aspires to correct by filling in gaps and painting over. The practice of narration, as Claude Simon said both truthfully and beautifully, is "an intellectual effort devoted to caulking up the time sequences that have escaped

96. Woolf, Virginia. "A Sketch of the Past," in *Moments of Being*. (*MB*). New York: Harvest / Harcourt Brace & Co., 1985, pp. 64–159.

our perception."[97] Only the author's name remains unscathed. However, in the case of Virginia Woolf, not even this can be said. The wife of Leonard Woolf is not even the daughter-in-name that she was—by genes or the battle she fought against him—of Sir Leslie Stephen. Many book covers with her husband's last name written in large letters following "Virginia" bear witness to the intermittence of her name; particularly, her feminine name.

Virginia Woolf knew very well that the speaker and the writer, the *subject of the enunciation*, mistakes and misleads the reader believing and simulating that s/he is the same as the *subject of the statement*. When we speak, using the term "I," we are not of whom we speak. "I" is a screen; it is itself a screen memory. The clarity of our affirmations—together with the succinctness of our memories and our self-image—functions as an illusion that hides, even to ourselves, the self we are. Whoever says "I" usurps the place of the subject and dons a mask with which he or she identifies. We all can and should say: *"I" is unknown to me; it is a capricious invention of my memory.* And this is the mistake in identification that mirrors give rise to. More often than not, whoever proclaims himself as "I" is an imposter, which is what Borges addresses in "Borges and I." For this reason, understanding the relationship between the author and his or her image in the mirror can be very revealing in every autobiography. We have already had a glimpse of this with Borges reflected in triplicate by the mirrors of the Hamburg-style wardrobe. We will see it explicitly as we examine the different types of autobiography, distinguishing them according to the type of relationship established between the writer and his or her own face (*prosopon*) in Chapter 14.

The distance between the two subjects (the subject of the enunciation and of the statement) is inescapable. In 1939, how could Virginia Woolf, the acclaimed writer, consider herself the same person as the little Jinny who had lived certain peripeteias in 1885, the date of her first memory?

---

97. Simon, Claude. *The Wind.* Translated by Richard Howard. New York: George Braziller, 1986, p. 153.

Virginia Stephen came from a family abundant with literary personalities. The hurdle she faced in order to give expression to her experiences in an autobiography had already been a stumbling block for her father, Sir Leslie Stephen, who had written, a year before the birth of his illustrious daughter:

> The autobiographer has *ex officio* two qualifications of supreme importance in all literary work. He is writing about a topic in which he is keenly interested, and about a topic upon which he is the highest living authority. It may be reckoned, too, as a special felicity that an autobiography, alone of all books, may be more valuable in proportion to the amount of misrepresentation which it contains. We do not wonder when a man gives a false character to his neighbor, but it is always curious to see how a man contrives to present a false testimonial to himself.[98]

Virginia Woolf adds her own reasons for agreeing with him when she finds that the majority of autobiographical writings are failures. Why? Because "[t]hey leave out the person to whom things happened" (Woolf 1985, 65). Do we dare claim—following her suggestion—that all autobiographies, without exception, are mystifications and frauds? Yes, because there are no examples to the contrary. Distortion (*Entstellung*) is structural and essential; it is not accidental and it cannot be avoided. The best autobiographies are the ones that recognize this shortcoming, that accept without ambivalence this inevitable corruption, subtly passing from the "autobiographical genre" to the novel (Joyce, Proust, Perec, Amat, and also Woolf). Thus, despite all claims of objectivity, the result is always, in the end, a novel. Obscurity proceeds from both memory and the unconscious: the duo cast their shadows equally—that of forgetting and repression—over the writer. By

---

98. Stephen, Leslie. [1881]. *Hours in a Library*, "Autobiography." New York and London: G.P. Putnam's Sons, 1904. (Republished: Grosse Pointe, Michigan: Scholarly Press, 1968), p. 185.

projecting more light into the mirror one is overcome by the glare, not by transparency.

The first recollections narrated by Woolf do not coincide with the Cortazarian formula. Far from being memories of absence and terror, they are pleasant experiences of presence and exaltation. In the first recollection, she is lying in her mother's lap as they travel by train. She supposes, because of the late afternoon light, that they were returning from St. Ives; but "it is more convenient artistically to suppose that we were going to St. Ives." (A splendid example of autobiographical objectivity!) In this setting she sees her mother's flowery dress (anemones?) on which the vibrant colors stand out (blue, red and purple) on a black background. The perception of her mother's dress opens the way towards the first true moment of memory, the most important of all.

Woolf imagines that her life could be compared to a bowl that is emptied and refilled over and over. The bowl sits on a base that is the always renewable presence of one memorable instant, *a single moment*, the most voluptuous conceivable. Her memory is:

> . . . of lying half asleep, half awake, in bed in the nursery at St. Ives. It is of hearing the waves breaking, one, two, one, two, and sending a splash of water over the beach; and then breaking, one, two, one, two, behind a yellow blind. It is of hearing the blind draw its little acorn across the floor as the wind blew the blind out. It is of lying and hearing this splash and seeing this light, and feeling, it is almost impossible that I should be here; of feeling the purest ecstasy I can conceive.
>
> I could spend hours trying to write that as it should be written, in order to give the feeling which is even at this moment very strong in me. But I should fail . . . (*MB*, pp. 64–65).

The next recollection is from quite a bit later but also takes place in St. Ives, at the country house, which is Virginia's equivalent to Proust's legendary Combray. Everything there is sensuality, "as if everything were ripe" (*MB*, 66): humming, the light of the sun, many pleasant aromas all at the same time descending towards the beach, the apple trees on a level with her head, the murmur of bees, the colors of the garden. These two moments, she says with wonder, are:

> . . . more real than the present moment . . . I can reach a state where I seem to be watching things happen as if I were there. That is, I suppose, *that my memory supplies what I had forgotten*, so that it seems as if it were happening independently, *though I am really making it happen* . . . I often wonder—that things we have felt with great intensity have an existence independent of our minds; are in fact still in existence? (*MB*, p. 67, italics added to highlight the element of artifice in memory and its analogy to sleep work.)

In another paragraph, she narrates her ecstasy upon seeing a flower and understanding that it is part of an immense whole. We, the readers, grasp that these objects which give rise to states of ecstasy and rapture are in themselves trivial but the experience they refer to is that of dissolution of the limits and of existence itself, on the whole comparable to Joycean *epiphanies*, those sudden eruptions of reality that are like revelations for the young artist. In the work Joyce sent to the printing press, the epiphanies only appear in the first pages of *Ulysses* in order for him to make fun of them. These moments of revelation, so famous and commented upon, were only described and defined as "epiphanies" in a posthumous text [published in 1944],[99] *Stephen Hero* [1906], published without the approval of the author. The term, epiphany, was discarded from the publication of the work for which *Stephen Hero* was an early draft: *A Portrait of the Artist as a Young Man* [1914]. Woolf, unfamiliar with the literary meditations of Joyce, describes her own states of mystical rapture: irruptions of jouissance for which words cannot do justice; intimate, ineffable, transcendent experiences

---

99. Joyce, James. *Stephen Hero*. New York: New Directions Publishing Co., 1963.

about which any commentary would not only seem inadequate but inopportune. They are corporeal sensations and thrills that no document could possibly validate. These experiences are not stories. They simply are. Perhaps for this reason, because of their inexplicableness and their artistic value, Joyce omitted them. On one hand, they were objects for theoretical reflection pertaining to a literary figure capable of designating them; on the other hand, he indeed included them in certain texts: *Ulysses*, while poking fun at them, is a vast anthology of the young Jimmy's epiphanies.

How many similarities there are between Jimmy and Jinny (Virginia's nickname)! They were both born and deceased in the same years (1882–1941)—she entered the world fifteen days after he did and she committed suicide two months after Joyce's "almost suicide," as he permitted himself to succumb to a poorly treated perforated ulcer. Between them they renovated English literature; nonetheless, they remained worlds apart and nothing could bring them together. They were opposites in almost every way: he was a man, she was a woman; he was heterosexual, she was bisexual; he was Irish, she was English; he was a plebeian, she was an aristocrat; his father was a drunk, a failure and much loved by his son, her father was respected by society, but ridiculed and hated by his daughter; he was indifferent to the death of his mother, she suffered the death of her mother as an intolerable fated blow; he chose to escape his environment and live in exile, she lived her entire life where she was born and raised on the outskirts of London; he lived captive to financial debt and unable to gain recognition for his literature, she was the owner of a successful printing press; he was the author of a shameless style of writing, she was the author of literature that was respectful of convention; he was satisfied with his masculine status, she was violently opposed to the relegated situation of women in society. They never met, but when Joyce's patron, Ms. Weaver, brought the manuscript of *Ulysses* to Virginia for publication by her press, Hogarth Press, she kept it at home for some time, read it superficially, and rejected it. Virginia Stephen-Woolf scorned Joyce's scatological vulgarity;

he disdained the author of *The Waves* out of total ignorance and a seemingly divine conceit.

Despite the staunch opposition, we may consider Virginia Woolf's first impressions as *"epiphanies"*—which are somewhat more transcendental and less accessible to reason than *memories*. "I am hardly aware of myself, but only of the sensation. I am only the container of the feeling of ecstasy, of the feeling of rapture" (*MB*, p. 67). Following the narrative of her first and very precocious epiphanies, her memoir, aptly titled *Moments of Being*, does indeed turn to the narration of a recollection. In leading up to the narrative of this first memory, she mentions that "instead of analysing" the trance-like sensations, what we would call "epiphanies," she will show us what she means when she affirms that memories are more complicated and less intense than epiphanies:

[. . .] here is an instance of what I mean—my feeling about the looking-glass in the hall. There was a small looking-glass in the hall at Talland House [. . .] By standing on tiptoe I could see my face in the glass. When I was six or seven perhaps, I got into the habit of looking at my face in the glass. But I only did this if I was sure that I was alone [. . .] A strong feeling of guilt seemed naturally attached to it. But why was this so? One obvious reason occurs to me—Vanessa and I were both what was called tomboys [. . .] Perhaps therefore to have been found looking in the glass would have been against our tomboy code [. . .] the looking-glass shame has lasted all my life [. . .] I cannot now powder my nose in public. Everything to do with dress—to be fitted, to come into a room wearing a new dress—still frightens me; at least makes me shy, self-conscious, uncomfortable [. . .] What then gave me this feeling of shame [. . .]? [. . .] Yet this did not prevent me from feeling ecstasies and raptures spontaneously and intensely and without any shame or the least sense of guilt, so long as they were disconnected with my own body [. . .] I must have been ashamed or afraid of my own body [. . .] Though I have done my best to explain why I was ashamed of looking at my own face I have only been able to discover some possible reasons; there may be others; I do not suppose that I have got at the truth [. . .] Let me add a dream; for it may refer to the incident of the looking-glass. I dreamt that I was looking in a glass when a horrible face—the face of an animal—suddenly showed over my shoulder [. . .] I have always remembered the other face in the glass, whether it was a dream or a fact, and that it frightened me (*MB*, pp. 67–69).

So writes Virginia Woolf. At the risk of seeming persistent, I will insist that—drawing a distinction (as Virginia Woolf does) between "moments of trance" and memories—this is the first memory, strictly speaking, that she evokes. And it is up to us to continue her analysis. The author's account of the face in the mirror sets off alarm bells for Lacanian psychologists, accustomed to considering the moment of encounter with one's specular image as a jubilant moment, initiator of an endless love-affair between the subject and her own image, like Narcissus. For this little girl, the encounter with the mirror is colored by shame. And, as the pen goes on to tell the tale, terror follows immediately with the apparition of the monster in the dream that succeeds the memory in her autobiographical narrative. The combination of shame and terror in this first memory approaches—albeit in an atypical way— Julio Cortázar's formula. In the next section of this chapter I will consider in detail the aspect of mirrors in the memory of writers.

The memory of the small Virginia leads us to a conclusion that we will have to carefully support even though we now state it rather laconically and with a degree of dogmatism: *the gaze, of everyone, is always gendered.* Perhaps many of us (or all of us?) already know this; few of us state it. To see a face—and this, I believe, has been the case since time immemorial—is to assign that face, and to the person wearing it, a place among the two sexes, unless we find, to our surprise and discomfort, some kind of ambiguity. This process is not voluntary; it is automatic. It is not personal; it is universal.

If this aspect of the human gaze, which is so elemental, has been neglected, it has been even less emphasized that *the gaze of mirrors also, in their metallic and obscene innocence, is gendered.*

This is true when seeing oneself or seeing an other: Virginia Stephen is a girl; what others see is the figure of a girl, they offer her a feminine world as "her own space" (*"A Room of One's* [*her*] *Own"*). The girl seen in the mirror (like Nabokov with his moths and butterflies, as we will see) sticks pins into the girl-chrysalis with the destiny of a woman, a destiny that is comparable to the mother's. Is this how she would prefer to see herself or does she prefer her "tomboyish" code, which she shares with her sister (Vanessa Bell), playing cricket, skipping among the rocks and climbing trees, not to mention her lack of tidiness? Has she inherited, as she hopes, a paradoxical *ancestral terror of femininity* and beauty just as she sees and admires them in the beautiful composure of her mother? We are not the ones who grant her this inheritance. She is the one who has proposed it, literally (*MB*, p. 82).

Nonetheless, there she is, watching the little girl who peers back from the other side of the mirror, frightened by the possibility of being seen. There she is, straining to reach the height at which she can see her own face ("standing on tiptoe") and finding, perhaps, an inaccessible image and, therefore, placed at an astronomical distance. The mother, in this particular case, is the object of an ideal and idealized love.

Without falling into the complacent innocence of applied psychoanalysis we can hear Virginia drifting away from the marvelous feminine image of her mother and becoming a rival to her father in her condition as a writer, a woman of the world and a witty person. At the same time as she considers him to be a conventional man, she recognizes, near the end of her life, that she envied him "yet he is not a writer for whom I have a natural taste" (*MB*, p. 115). Sir Leslie Stephen was a divine as well as puerile presence for his family. In one recollection, the little girl Virginia was twisting her hair the same way he did. When her mother scolded her, she answered, "Father does it," and the mother responded in a way that must have been a challenge for Virginia: "Ah but you can't do everything father does" (*MB*, p. 111). No? Why not? From her torrid romances with friends (in particular with Victoria Sackville-West) emerges her enigmatic character, *Orlando*, who traverses without difficulty the centuries of history, national borders and sexual identities, capable of passing overnight from the masculine to the feminine condition, demonstrating the instability, dissolution and the constant re-composition of what many call "I."

According to their etymology, the words speculum (mirror)—*espejo* in Spanish, *Spiegel* in German—and specter (aspect and species, spy and spectacle) pertain to the same conceptual family. The image in the mirror is a specter that prophesizes. This reflection coagulates and consecrates the image that is there, in advance, the image that lives in real space, ordering it to identify with an effigy of a woman that is imposed as being her true and constant figure, that she will have to incarnate, by design of the Other, for now and forever. The question then arises—and neither Virginia Woolf nor we can answer it in a hasty manner—"is it the same to look in the mirror and see the image of a boy as it is to see a girl and then discover that it is 'yourself'?" I believe that both she and we, as well as Martha Robles, who we will discuss later in this chapter, and Nuria Amat, who we will consider in the next chapter, would tend to answer in the negative. Because the mirror gazes at us; it is *a looking-glass*. And its gaze is classified into two species: masculine and feminine; it is "sexuated."

What relation does the male or female image have with the desire of the other or the gendered image that the child already has of the maternal or paternal or fraternal other? I insist on irrefutable evidence: the specular image is always, and cannot be otherwise, an image that is fundamentally linked to the "gender identity" of its "owner." Mirror (*espejo*) and specter, and spectacle: whoever observes us also classifies and catalogues us according to what we show. The mirror reflects the gaze . . . the gaze of the Other.

If the face glimpsed in the mirror is, by chance, that of a man or that of a woman, the image demands of us—and we demand of it—signs of agreement with our desire or with our anxieties and uncertainties in relation to our sexual identity. We ask it to relieve us of doubts. The mirror receives a question (like the one asked by the mother in Snow White) and it must answer. It cannot refuse to answer the question of gender. The transvestite best illustrates the frequent eagerness to invert the gendered image, transforming it into its opposite by putting on new clothing. However, clinical psychoanalysis reveals unusual situations, including the much more frequent case of exaggerating features that are normally associated with one's sex as a way of combatting anxiety over being perceived as pertaining to the other sex. I am referring to the show, the representation, the masquerade, the exhibition of one's gender. Men who are adept at body-building and women who excel at applying make-up and exhibiting their physical attributes illustrate the intersection of sex in "The Garden of Forking Paths." We have already alluded to the feminine "masquerade"; there, the exaggeration of female features tends to obscure and to "compensate" for assuming certain characteristics that traditionally define masculinity. When Virginia Woolf's character, Orlando, changes from a man into a woman, the character discovers (it)self staring for a long time into the mirror. The author comments:

> She was becoming a little more modest, as women are, of her brains, and a little more vain, as women are, of her person. Certain susceptibilities were asserting themselves, and others were diminishing.[100]

Bear with me at this point to make three digressions—one playful, one clinical and one literary—before returning to Woolf.

Here I offer a joke—something that always serves the psychoanalyst well. A man asks: "Why do you women always try to conquer with beauty instead of using intelligence?" And the woman answers: "Because it's easier to find foolish men than to

---

100. Woolf, Virginia. *Orlando: A Biography.* New York: Harcourt, Brace and Company, 1929, p. 187.

find blind men." As we can see, it is a question of image. They say that it is not easy for women "who know Latin" and show off their intelligence—they don't get married nor do they end well.[101] Those with feminine wiles have discovered that it is more convenient to hide this attribute as there is an abundance of men who are not willing to pardon this quality, which they consider the domain of men.

We can also review a clinical case, for which the psychoanalyst should not be reproached either. A young biology researcher has to speak in several conferences in the United States and finds it very difficult to pronounce words that begin with "W"; for which reason she tries to avoid such words. The problem does not occur with the words "what" or "which," but it does happen "with words such as . . . such as . . . *woman*." In her presentation at a conference on physiology she has to be careful to avoid using this word. She does not hide her feminine features but this phobic symptom appears in the area of language. Through analytic work it is soon apparent that she harbors a great deal of anger over the professional limitations that she has to suffer as a woman, she resents the prerogatives that—she supposes—men enjoy, and, strangely, that the letter "W" in English corresponds to the letter "M" of "mujer" in Spanish, which is the same letter but inverted "like in a mirror," and that this "M" is the initial letter of her mother's name, the person who has created most of the hurdles in her life and with whom she still struggles, even though she is a scientist with considerable prestige. As if that were not enough, people who know her are unanimously surprised by her physical resemblance to her mother, that is, with the hated image from which she has always wanted to distinguish herself. The mirror, for her, is not a good companion. Rather, the mirror is an insolent messenger that always brings the worst tidings.

The relationship between the image of the woman in the mirror and the image of the mother, as an ideal, or as a vague, indifferent figure, or as a hateful model, is recorded with searing letters

---

101. In Spanish: "Mujer que sabe latín, ni se casa ni tiene buen fin."

and remains like a shadow that accompanies all women in their encounters with the mirror. We can illustrate this with a previously mentioned literary reference. The protagonist of the excellent novel, *Wittgenstein's Mistress*,[102] by David Markson conducts a humorous and profound monologue:

> Once, in the Borghese Gallery, in Rome, I signed a mirror.
> I did that in one of the women's rooms, with a lipstick.
> What I was signing was an image of myself, naturally.
> Should anybody else have looked, where my signature would have been was under the other person's image, however.
> Doubtless I would not have signed it, had there been anybody else to look.
> Though in fact the name I put down was Giotto.
> There is only one mirror in this house, incidentally.
> What the mirror reflects is also an image of myself, of course.
> Though in fact what it has also reflected now and again is an image of my mother.
> What will happen is that I will glance into the mirror and for an instant I will see my mother looking back at me.
> Naturally I will see myself during that same instant, as well.
> In other words all that I am really seeing is my mother's image in my own.
> I am assuming that such an illusion is quite ordinary, and comes with age.
> Which is to say that it is not even an illusion, heredity being heredity.

There is no symmetry. Markson could not have put these words into the mouth of a masculine character. Nor could he have done it by substituting the word "father" for "mother." It seems that the behaviors of men and women are different in front of the mirror. The stereotypes, which are not entirely gratuitous, cast suspicion

---

102. David Markson [1988], op. cit., p. 67.

on the virility of a man who adores his reflected image and tend to consider complacency and the constant use of mirrors to be a feminine trait. With the exception of Borges's metaphysical anxiety in front of multiple mirrors, the autobiographies of men make no reference to the specular reflection, whereas the reference is practically inevitable in the narratives of women who recount their lives.

The first encounter with the mirror, that artifact in which we recognize that the observer on the other side "is me," is indelibly recorded in the memory—the true, involuntary, Proustian, Freudian memory. The image is redemptive, it confers unity. In addition, depending on the bias of the gaze of the other, it may be shattering, caustic and destructive. We may say that the first gaze into the mirror restores the being from corporeal fragmentation. It constitutes an "ideal self," a model of perfection to which it will always wish to return. Later—necessarily later—knowledge of sexual (genital) differences will be gained, and of gender, induced by culture through the family. Both anatomically and socio-culturally (which endorses the division between masculine and feminine), the subject must admit that this ideal self is unattainable because whoever is a man cannot be a woman, and vice versa. What is import about sex are not the genital attributes that one has or must have, but rather that whatever one does indeed have, there still remains a discrepancy in oneself—perceived as a negative—which appears as a positive in the sex of the other.

Completeness does not exist; there is and always will be something lacking. The mirror, reflecting a gendered body, informs us of this restriction. The ideal must concede to the pressure of stereotypes and to indications of this sexual deficiency-difference pertaining to both men and women, both on the level of the image and the plane of reality. From this moment forward, the subject will endeavor to recover the "ideal self," "sated, full of itself,"[103] but

---

103. José Gorostiza [1939] *Muerte sin fin*. En *Poesía completa*, México: FCE, 1996, p. iii. *Death without end*. Austin (Tx): Harry Ransom Humanities Center. Translated by Laura Villaseñor. 1971.

it will have to do so by submitting to regulations that compel it towards the search for lost integrity in the minefield of love, hoping to find in the other the substitute for its discrepancy. To approach the ideal self it must yield to "moral" exigencies imposed by the Other: a certain "ideal of the self" will have been formulated, a set of commands without definite form, more or less filled with contradictions. Virginia Woolf poetically lived and confessed these difficult-to-reconcile exigencies. Life and work—both in love and in books—appear to conspire around the enigmatic gendered mirrors, the silver-plated siblings of that first mirror—the one she peered into in Talland House.

The same crystal that first excited the illusion of self-satisfied integrity now endeavors to negate it. Heterosexuality, homosexuality and transvestitism will be three of the responses—all of them insufficient—to the recognition of incompleteness that derives from the difference between the sexes. Difference-deficiency, as we proposed above. Order and regulation of incompatibility: the subject is invited to the carnival representation of an "identity" that it can accept or reject depending on the models it is offered by its surroundings: male or female.

2. The Specular Function of the Mother

Let us prepare ourselves for the adventure of a theoretical exploration of the virtual continent of mirrors, that continent where (I believe) we live. For now it is a question of recovering Jinny Stephen's first mirror, the girl who would become Virginia Woolf, a woman who spoke of the little girl, admitting that she knew her very little and poorly—that she had forgotten her.

The "simple incident of the mirror," which happened to her "personally" and aroused in her feelings of guilt and shame, seems inexplicable to her when it returns to her memory and demands to be written half a century later. She knows there is a secret. I would now like to rummage through it. Her reserve about appearing as a woman was still active fifty years later; it was the feature that defined her relationship with others: the manifest shame every time she showed her feminine image. No one was supposed to see—not even her—the deep satisfaction that came over her as she contemplated herself. For, without a doubt, she must have enjoyed studying herself, alone and hidden. What did she see? The maternal figure? The figure she always admired? Or the rejected figure of the tomboyish little girl that the others—those who applied normalizing pressure on her—wanted to correct? Let us venture to enter into the mirror and verify what Jinny Stephen found there. I would suggest that she did not see either one of the aforementioned images. She was not seeing: she was *reading*. She was reading the contrast between the two; the mirror showed her ideal self, unburdened of external pressures that tried to compel her to define herself as man or woman. The jouissance, the ineffable shiver that had to remain latent, the heart of her desire, was in the dissociation from herself and the game of hiding her jouissance from the smothering gaze of the other. Her own image—that of the tomboyish little girl—was sought after, she strived for it (on tiptoe) as the source of jouissance. The displeasure and dread arose from the possibility of being caught enjoying her challenge to sexual difference. Her phantasy, clearly bisexual, assumes body and life, to the amazement of her readers, in *Orlando*.

In the culminating moment of this "biography," the narration turns to the fabulous transformation of the thirty-year-old man who went to sleep one night in Constantinople, was awoken by the peal of trumpets, arose and stood "in complete nakedness before us" and "we have no choice left but confess—he was a woman" (cit., p. 137). As soon as she tells what has happened, in these words, Virginia Woolf, embarrassed, departs from her own story, fearful of being caught looking at herself in the mirror and discovering her feminine self: "But let other pens treat of sex and sexuality; we quit such odious subjects as soon as we can" (cit., p. 139).

To confirm our construction of Virginia Woolf's phantasy, we need to return to the most painful event of her life, the death of her inexpressibly beautiful mother when she was thirteen years old, a death that sunk her into a deep depression from which she could only emerge through writing—driven by the irrepressible call to poetic creation . . . thirty years later!—the novel, *To the Lighthouse*.[104] Once she had finished writing this autobiographical novel, in which she reserved for herself the place of a boy (James), she was able to stop being obsessed by her mother, to stop seeing her and hearing her voice. She comments, "I suppose that I did for myself what psycho-analysts do for their patients" (*MB*, p. 81). What does she mean? I will state it clearly: to remember (and to write the memory) in order to forget. Many pages later she says that, just as she had "rubbed out a good deal of the force of my mother's memory by writing about her in *To the Lighthouse*" (*MB*, p. 108), she had also rubbed out the force of her father's memory. With the writing of this novel she could put to an end her constant, obsessive struggle with Sir Leslie Stephen following his death. Until she wrote the novel, Virginia's Woolf's lips were constantly moving in bitter discussions in which she angrily told herself what she had never dared to say to him. Writing *To the Lighthouse* was the ritual ceremony necessary for burying her parents. However, even afterwards, they, or their specters—like Tito Monterroso's dinosaurs—continued to haunt her. It was not enough for her to awaken, nor was it enough for her to read Freud for the first time in 1939, a fact that she mentions in her diary immediately after describing her bellicose relationship with her father, the writer, her rival.

At this point, let us remember that James and Alix Strachey, Freud's official translators into English, were intimate friends with the Woolfs and members of the Bloomsbury group which she founded. For this reason it seems very strange—or, conversely, completely understandable—that she did not want to undergo analysis nor, until shortly before she committed suicide, find out what psychoanalysts were capable of telling her. Moreover, Virginia

---

104. Woolf, Virginia [1927]. *To the Lighthouse*. London: Wordsworth Classics. 1994.

and Leonard Woolf were the founders of Hogarth Press, which was practically the official publisher of the English psychoanalytical movement. Still today the Standard Edition of the Complete Works of Sigmund Freud is published by Hogarth. Virginia's brother, Adrian Stephen, was a psychoanalyst and married another psychoanalyst. Virginia's husband, Leonard Woolf (*rara avis*, a penniless Jew in the elitist Bloomsbury group), declared himself a Freudian throughout his life. Nonetheless, when Virginia fell prey to her melancholic and hallucinatory episodes, they did not accept any treatments other than rest and abundant feeding (the Weir-Mitchell treatment). The proclaimed relationship between the Woolfs and psychoanalysis was strictly intellectual. It might better be referred to as a manifestation of snobbery, a way of being up-to-date, while they tenaciously maintained their mask of Victorian conformity in real life. What most irritated them about Freud and his disciples was the insistent focus on sexuality. I could continue to write about the ambiguous relationship Virginia Woolf maintained with Freud and psychoanalysis but this is not the objective of this study. I am concerned with memory and dread. And, to be sure, mirrors.

As Virginia Woolf made clear, we must also recognize the same: she could only alleviate her grief and rid herself of her two ghosts—that of her beautiful mother who died when she was just becoming a woman, and that of her father who was her role model and rival—by submerging them in the same river where she delivered her own body at the beginning of Autumn 1941.

In Lacanian theory, the mirror stage,[105] experienced by the child before attaining the ability to speak, usually between the ages of six to eighteen months, is formational of the *I*. The *infans* (without speech), who previously experienced his body as an

---

105. Lacan, Jacques [1936–1949] "Le stade du miroir . . ." *Écrits*, Paris: Seuil, 1966, pp. 93–100 [ed. W.W. Norton & Co. pp. 75–81]. This is the most widely disseminated aspect of Lacan's teachings. Its repetition may seem superfluous but I think it is necessary for clarifying the essential features of the memories of the three writers under consideration here: Virginia Woolf, Martha Robles and Nuria Amat.

anguishing and chaotic collection of dispersed sensations, finds in the image staring back at him from the other side of the glass an integrated, ideal and complete figure, a messenger of unity that heretofore was lacking for him. He falls in love with the other who is himself, he smiles, jubilantly looking at himself, he is unhinged, identifying with an image that is not himself but rather his double and who he has just called "I." He becomes conscious of his existence through a universal game that consists in entering and leaving the visual field of the mirror: "Now you see me—now you don't." *Fort—Da*, one, two, one, two—just like the waves in Virginia Woolf's first epiphany (*MB*, p. 64). The adults fit into this infantile reflection and they also appear duplicated by the mirror, confirming for the child that, yes, it is him/her, this is how s/he is seen and has a name by which s/he can recognize him/herself, be recognized by others and to which s/he can answer, "Present!" when spoken to.

It is said that the specular image is redemptive, it holds us together, it occupies a center around which the world is organized. Indeed, this is so much the case that "insanity" consists in not being able to recognize oneself as being the reflected image in the mirror, being oblivious to and rejecting the abysmal differ-ence manifest between the virtual space of the mirror and the body that exists in real space. In the mirror we identify ourselves as "one" at the same time as we see ourselves duplicated and we appear as "two," if not three or more, as in the case of Borges. "Alienation" (*Entäusserung* in Hegel) consists, paradoxically, in *not* being alienated and deceived by the belief that one is the image seen on the other side of the mirror and that the name one is assigned designates who one is: "John Doe; that is who I am, that is who I see (they see), in the mirror, in the photograph." Psychoanalysis has studied the roots of this fascination with one's own image, back to its mythological foundations and thus, following Freud, has appropriately denominated it "narcissism," which evokes and forewarns of the mortal condition of falling in love with oneself.

This captivity in the cell of one's own image is the foundation for subsequent love relationships—we fall in love with those who know how to recognize us—and it is rooted, as previously indicated, in epic experiences of conquest uniquely taking place between the ages of six and eighteen months. But its effect does not end there, it persists throughout one's life. We know (we *believe* we know) who we are and we uncritically accept the idea that we remain one and the same person from birth to death. It is—as we have just seen—one of the essential functions of memory to trick ourselves into making ourselves the bases upon which is constructed this credulous belief in personal continuity. The mirror stage is not transitory; it is a permanent structure: it is the root of being as a fictional entity, haunted by the belief in being where one is not: in mirrors and in the gaze of others. "I am what they see. They see what I am." It is in those around us, in the moments when we feel our identities to be so frequently threatened, where we seek confirmation of our being, recognition that will allow us to affirm (or to suppose) that "we are." However, perhaps—why not?—there may be an abundance of reasons for us to feel ashamed of what we are, of what we reflect, of our unnamed flaws. We might consider it a sin to be discovered indulging in that image, to be revealed enjoying the visual autoeroticism of Narcissus copulating with himself. Is this what happened to Virginia Woolf? It would be very simple and very false for us to restrict ourselves to that. We would miss out on the complex value of her experience and her memory. We must seek beyond that and, if possible, see what relation is woven into the experiences of shame and dread of Virginia Woolf with the hypothesis proposed by Cortázar after relating the effects of the disconcerting rooster's crow (if that was indeed the cause of his awakening).

We know (and we cannot forget) that in the encounter with the mirror not all is a bed of roses. Inevitably, the image that gazes back at us when we stare at our own face is that of an inaccessible interloper; we understand that we can never bridge the gap separating us and grasp the vain promise of unity. That, as soon as we have recognized ourselves, we have also had to admit the terrible dissociation, the permanent disconnection with that idealized other, with the ideal self. *The glass, that of all mirrors, is fragile*: it gives us our reflection, and at the same time it notifies us that it is impossible for us to cross over and reduce the miniscule yet infinite distance—the profound abyss—that separates us from ourselves. To this jubilant recognition there is a dramatic and distressing backdrop. This companion, as perpetual as a shadow, watching us from the other side is, at the same time, the reporter of our uncompromising solitude and the informant conveying that, just as it watches us, we are always an object captured by the gaze of the Other, of any other who may recognize us. We will never be able to see ourselves from the vantage point of the other. We will never be able to control—even by multiplying the hours spent in front of the mirror—the image the other perceives of us.

Are the others—that Other who keeps us forever centered in the viewfinder of the photographic camera—extraneous? Could we do without them? No. They have a duty to guarantee the imaginary identity, that of the fictional being that emerges from the melding of the real child with the child that appears in the beyond, in the virtual space of the mirror. *"You are who you see. You are because you see yourself."* They must confirm the child's identification with his/her own image and ratify his/her insertion into the network of family and social relationships, into the history of a community. The experience of the mirror reveals the dissociation between the side that is here (*real*—R) and the side that is over there (*imaginary*—I) of oneself, and it requires the presence of a third party (*symbolic*—S) who sanctions and conjugates, in language, the advent of the self into existence. R-I-S, interlaced, not dissociable. There is no "I" before specular recognition. It is because of this necessary presence of others—those who speak, those who give names—that even blind children, unable to see themselves reflected in optical apparatuses, emerge into existence and "see themselves" as "I"s; they, like all of us, need someone who sees them and names them in order to be able to identify themselves through the gaze and the word of the other. For this reason, all mirrors are enigmatic; in the mirror the question of destiny is posed. Virginia Woolf's case is not different in the moment that she stands on childish tiptoes, straining to see her image. So long as—what terror!—no one catches her at this shameful game.

Specular recognition is, as mentioned above, a function of memory. The person who appears there is the same as (one remembers) the person who was there before. There is a circular return of the figures that generate the illusion of continuity in time. Nonetheless, time imposes its erosive changes on images. In *Remembrance of Things Past*, Proust affirms, "When we observe the face of a woman who was beautiful it is not enough for us to read her present features; we need to translate them." One also reads the future in the mirror: it is an instrument for predicting what is to come. *Catoptromancy* is one of the few resources we have for predicting what will become of us. Popular masculine knowledge has come up with proverbial expressions in this respect, not without some degree of misogyny: "If you want to know how your wife will look in the future, don't look at her, look at her mother." Thus, the mirror occupies three dimensions of time and bridges three verbal tenses. It is a perception of the present, a history lesson, and a reliable prophecy, a view of the future.

Perhaps it goes without saying, as it is manifest, that the gaze of this other can bring with it love, hatred, or indifference. If the child defines his/her identity by sharing what the other "sees" in him/her when told: "That image in the mirror is you," the identification with the image brings with it the evaluation made by the adult of the child's being. In principle, one is what the other sees in you, one sees oneself through the eyes of the other. The mirror is thus weighted down (or relieved) by the bundle of love, or the hostility of others, that it contains. To be a desired child is not the same as being the object of others' hatred or fear. It is not the same to be accepted as one is as to be pressured into being different, beyond what one could possibly ever be. It does not matter how one is in reality (who knows what one "really" is) but rather the compatibility or the difference that there could be between oneself and that which constitutes the ideal of the other. The narcissistic valuation (love of oneself) of the child depends on uncontrollable eventualities: if the other regrets that the child is a girl and wishes that the image that appears in the mirror were a boy, or vice versa, if the other wanted a blond rather than a brunette, etc. *The mirror does not reflect, it compares*; it forms a comparison with the image desired by the Other. It measures and generally finds something wanting. For this reason it causes depression. We believe we are looking into it when it is looking at us. Thus, the ambiguity in the English language is marvelous with its synonym for the word "mirror" (*miroir*, in French): "looking-glass." The ingenuous reader is comfortable and used to hearing the *glass* in which one *looks at* oneself. But the reader who has learned to question the signifier, hears something more: the *looking-glass* is the crystal that looks at us. Lewis Carroll's Alice could not have passed through the mirror. She passes through the looking-glass in the two senses—active and passive—of the visual drive. She penetrates into the realm from which she is seen. The mirror, Borges discovers, watches us. It induces paranoia.

The author of *Les Fleurs du Mal*[106] is wrong when he expresses his belief that he can intervene in the image of the other and inject it with his prejudices. When Baudelaire sees a horrible man looking at himself in the mirror, he reproaches and rebukes him for stopping to stare at an abominable image. To which the other responds that, according to the sacrosanct principles of the '89 revolution, he has the right to stare at himself and the question of the pleasure or displeasure he derives from it concerns no one but his own conscience. But Baudelaire insists that he is mistaken. He recognizes the other's legal position but believes that his protest is founded in "good sense." His error is in believing that he can put himself in the place of the gaze of the "horrible man" who—why

---

106. Baudelaire, Charles [1860], *Œuvres complètes*. Paris: Gallimard, La Pléiade, 1975, p. 344.

not?—could well be observing himself through the eyes of some other, a loved one, for example his mother, for whom, proverbially, there are (almost) no ugly sons. There are, however, so many young and beautiful women who suffer from aesthetic hypochondria, thus helping to feed the plastic surgeons!

The possibility of loving oneself and, consequently, transferring that love to others, resides in the basic fact, beyond the control of each subject, of being loved, approved of and absolved, by the un-appealable judgment of that foundational and fundamental Other who is the mother. The indifference or disdain of the mother, just like her love, may be the source from which the subject acquires form and consistency, the space in which the subject may be able to find delight, enjoyment or become embittered with the image of him/herself.

Lacan's innovative perspective in promoting the mirror stage [1949] has had an important influence on the studies of subjectivity since that time. This was recognized by a researcher who made a decisive addition to the Lacanian postulate: D.W. Winnicott.[107] For this original contributor to the field of child psychoanalysis, "In individual emotional development *the precursor of the mir-ror is the mother's face*" (111, italics in original). When the baby looks at the face of the mother, "ordinarily, what the baby sees is himself or herself" (Winnicott, cit., p. 112). When the mother looks at her baby, the baby sees the image that she sees in him or her. If the mother cannot respond to the emotional expectations of her children, "[t]hey look and they do not see themselves." Consequently, their creative capacity atrophies and "they look around for other ways of getting something of themselves back from the environment."

The mother's face, according to Winnicott, has an oracular function. If babies do not find a confirmation of their existence in the expressions of their mothers, they feel lost:

---

107. Winnicott, D.W. [1967]. *Playing & Reality*, "Mirror-role of Mother and Family in Child Development." London and New York: Tavistock/Routledge, 1989, pp. 111–118.

Some babies, tantalized by this type of relative maternal failure, study the variable maternal visage in an attempt to predict the mother's mood, just exactly as we all study the weather. The baby quickly learns to make a forecast: 'Just now it is safe to forget the mother's mood and to be spontaneous, but any minute the mother's face will become fixed or her mood will dominate, and my own personal needs must then be withdrawn otherwise my central self may suffer insult.'

[. . .] A baby so treated will grow up puzzled about mirrors and what the mirror has to offer. If the mother's face is unresponsive, then a mirror is a thing to be looked at but not to be looked into (Winnicott, cit., p. 113).

It is unfortunate that Winnicott did not distinguish between the specific reactions of female and male babies to the mother's face, first, and the mirror, later. He seems to have ignored a perspective that would have been fruitful and, perhaps, it is therefore up to us, his readers, to complement his article focusing on the maternal gaze as a driving force behind the emotional development of children. Although Winnicott does not distinguish between cases of male and female babies, the importance of the mother's gaze is illustrated by four cases that he presents and in all four the women are adults. One of them, evidently a psychoanalyst, is someone that had read Lacan's work on the mirror stage "but she was not able to make the link that I feel I am able to make between the mirror and the mother's face" (Winnicott, cit., p. 117). The approach we are pursuing, that of studying autobiographical paper scraps [*petits papiers*] may not only open the way towards crucial discoveries regarding the importance of mirrors in sexuation (Lacan's term) but also regarding the precursor of the mirror, as indispensable as it is unpredictable, as temperamental as the weather: the gaze of the mother.

Winnicott's contribution to Lacan's discovery (who, in turn, based his work on Henri Wallon's), is central to our study of the memories of the three women writers concerning us. They provide three paradigmatic cases of the special relationship women have with the mirror and literature, a relationship that is different from that maintained by men with the "looking-glass."

3. Martha Robles and Mirror Phobia: I Would Prefer Not to

See Myself

My comments and conclusions on Julio Cortázar's first memory (see Chapter 2)[108] came to the attention of a good friend, the distinguished Mexican writer, Martha Robles.[109] For her they acted like a trigger that fired off an old memory, possibly her first, a memory that confirms and, in my opinion, enriches Cortázar's proposal on the relation between anxiety ("memory begins with terror") and the ability to create oneself as an "autobiographical I." Goaded by the testimony of the author of *Hopscotch*, Martha Robles remembered and conceived a splendid text that throws new light on certain classical aspects of psychoanalytic theory. More specifically, Lacanian concepts that we reviewed when considering Virginia Woolf and her visions of childhood that I relate to the ideas of R.D. Winnicott on the mirror stage, that is, on the relation that each of us has with our own image vis-à-vis the first mirror which is, in turn, the mother's gaze. Let us take advantage of like to acknowledge and express gratitude for the generous license granted us by the author to cite her narration at length, whenever we can resist the temptation of paraphrasing it.

What does it tell us? First, it recognizes an effect I will call "redemptive" for her, based on her reading of Cortázar's first memory. Let me explain: when Robles was small, "*infans*," before

---

108. Braunstein, N.A. "Ficcionario," in *Excelsior*, México, May 2, 9, 16, 23 and 30, 2001.
109. Martha Robles is celebrated as a novelist, essayist and journalist. She is the author of many books. Among her novels, *La condena* (México, FCE, 1996) and *La ley del padre* (México, FCE, 1998) are worth mentioning.

she could speak, she had an inner, incommunicable, overwhelming experience that left a lasting impression on her. The event was not an intense sensation like an epiphany, impossible of being transformed into a narrative but more accurately, an *episode*. It was more like an earthquake in the infantile ground that supposedly escaped from the conscious because it was impossible to calm it by integrating it with the complicated structure that we call *language*. The memory of that "moment of being" was there, of course, before her reading of "Cortázar's rooster," only inaccessible to her. If not, how would she have been able to retrieve the memory? It was there (where?), buried in her memory, "repressed," far from forgotten, ready to leap into the light of consciousness when it met her madeleine, the appropriate retrieval cue, just like the crib in García Marquez's case. Martha Robles received my first and still protean reflections through several newspaper articles ("paper scraps") on Cortázar's childhood recollection. Robles identified with the metaphor of the terrifying first memory as the core of memory from which a person begins to exist and she saw that she could retrieve, confront and give the form of a literary narrative to her first encounter with the ominous. Thus chained to poetic imagination, the event could emancipate itself from the chains of oblivion (from repression, to be exact) and enter into the files of her official memory. The way to the world of writing had opened up and that is where it now resides. It had drifted unredeemed; thus it was "redeemed." From the "medicinal" effects of having discovered Cortázar's episode with the morning rooster, Martha Robles sensed—I would even say, declared—a fertile assimilation: the precocious memory retrieved vis-à-vis the oracle. I say this without forgetting, even for an instant, that oracles are always retroactive (*nachträglich, après-coup, a posteriori*). *They will have become oracles once they are fulfilled,* either literally or figuratively.

The oracle is a dark and mysterious pronouncement that contains the cipher of a destiny. A cipher that also contains—the author herself senses this—the first memory. But there is one notable difference: the oracle is an enigmatic message that points forward with the arrow of time while the evocation of the infantile past reveals destiny moving in reverse; it shows in the past—thanks to memory—the signs that give coherence to life.

Prophecy towards the past or a reverse prediction. Like the prophecy, also ciphered, the memory gains its full significance when it abandons its inner silence [. . .] By understanding yesterday's revelation, glimpses have also been caught of today and the direction of what is to come. Thus, with similar provenances, although from different directions, the elucidation of memory joins with the oracular function.

Martha Robles agrees with the Freudian supposition cited in the epigraph about the decisive character of the first memory in the life of the being in formation, the key capable of opening the secret wardrobes of the soul. She ventures even further: she sustains that the "core of memory" functions as a retroactive oracle, a point from which she can read the cipher of her destiny, establish herself and become one with her own myth. The phantasy of continuity is implanted: I am the plant, I was the seed, I will be the fruit. To remember is to embark on a journey towards the seed and anticipate along the way the flavor of the fruit. It is to give oneself the gift of narrative coherence that, before receiving permission to remember, condemned the memory of the episode to oblivion. However, if Cortázar is correct, if terror lies at the beginning of memory, not just anyone is always ready for a reencounter with the embryo of memory. Thus, as flying is for birds, remembering our origin is for the brave. Martha Robles narrates:

As I read Julio Cortázar's first memory I also remembered. I saw what I knew without knowing it. I was small. So small that the wardrobes with three mirrors that were in my grandparents' house seemed so tall as to never end. Perhaps I went around in a walker, passing the time under the hot sun going from here to there while the adults conversed. I was sucking on a pacifier from a baby's bottle when, in one of the best-lit rooms, I stopped and stared at my own reflection. I felt panic. I don't know if it was for a long or short time, but I was aware of the terror of being and not being the person that was there inside, inside a terrifying mirror. Everything happened in a flash, as if discovering the mirror and my own duplication were one and the same thing. I understood nothing, except that an *I*—or what I assumed to be *I*—was trapped in one of the mirrors of that wardrobe and was looking at me. I screamed. Then I began to cry. I left and came back, but my fear was so great that, since then, I would go around the courtyard in order to avoid passing by "that" which only I knew and which had given me the knowledge of terror.

This is the memory that Martha Robles had and did not have . . . that she "knew without knowing it." As we have said in previous cases, the nuances of her narrative are characterized by expressive intuitions that reveal the verisimilitude of the experience (the *narrative*, not the *truth*, which is unverifiable) and which render it exemplary. The memory is distressing and its consequence is a symptom, more specifically, it is a phobia of mirrors that specialists in esoteric words would probably call "*eisoptrophobia.*" Cortázar's memory was able to trigger Robles's memory, liberating its message of irremediable desperation.

Let us return to the "paper scraps" [*petits papiers*]. In this case, newspaper pieces which usually end up the next day in the waste-basket among the other things that no one wants to keep or reread; like the ones that I have written—for example, the one on the memory of some other, Julio Cortázar—may stir up buried memories; they may fall unexpectedly on a spirit prone to receive its message and suddenly stand before a clearing in the forest of memory. The simple question, "What is your first memory?," posed in propitious conversational conditions, serves as a constructive device for reconstructing memories, if not *from childhood*, then *about childhood*, albeit distant and forever lost. The paper scraps of those brief journalistic notes prompted, first, the writing of an E-mail, then—perhaps incited by me, but also responding to an inner command—that of an eloquent published article that became another "paper scrap" destined for the short life of an article in the literary supplement of a Mexican Sunday newspaper.[110] Although its winding paths are unpredictable and arduous, we graphomaniacs struggle against forgetting and indifference, fishing out bottles cast into the sea by travelers lost into the black hole we call infant amnesia.

I have insinuated that Martha Robles's memory was chained, like Prometheus, to a rock, waiting for the daily visit of the flesh-eating eagle, but it could also have been subject to an encounter with chance or a cause-and-effect meeting with another memory, in this case that of a boy terrorized by the cry of a domestic eagle—called a rooster—that would enable it to assume its place in the world of words. It is worthwhile to compare, to establish similarities and differences.

We tend to consider traumatic whatever is impossible to assimilate, whatever cannot be "swallowed" or metabolized, whatever one cannot integrate or conciliate with the "self," or the memory when it is something hostile to the subject. Referring to the encounter with the mirror for which Martha Robles was not prepared, she says:

> The interpretative limits of that little girl did not encompass familiarity with a mirror. Without the possibility of becoming part of my personal fiction, the experience traced its oracular message in a subversive way: it ciphered my personal history.

The little girl, terrified in front of the mirror, is—like Jinny Stephen in relation to Virginia Woolf, the woman—the ancestor of the writer who came across a memory of Cortázar's and published

---

110. Robles, Martha, "El primer recuerdo. Su doble espejo" ["The First Memory. Its Mirror Double"]. *Arena*, literary supplement of *Excelsior*. Mexico, Sunday, June 3, 2001.

a vivid description of her own memory. Why "the ancestor"? Is she not one and the same person? She points out the difference: "Between the date of the episode and the reading of what enabled me to remember, there is the word that defines me, the language that has made me what I am." Let me lend her a few words (as if she were in need of any), usurping her position as writer:

> No; I am not that little girl. What I am now came afterwards, when, between that sinister episode and the now of today, the heavy mantle of language intervened with its signs that allow me to translate that ancient panic into this succession of sounds that aspire to poetic precision.

Let me risk a hypothesis that will group together this memory with those we will consider from Leiris and Perec.[111] The trauma of the spectacle of one's own distress, of one's helplessness in front of the mirror, is not an episode involving the abovementioned black hole. It is not a lost instant in that inaccessible period that takes place between birth and the age of five, and let us not forget Tolstoy's lesson about the two eternities, one previous to the first cry of the newborn child, the other subsequent to the last breath, framing the brief interlude that is our life. No. "The heavy mantle of words" was constructed in Robles to tame and domesticate the voracity of the image of helplessness. Her defenselessness, like Cortázar's, had to be patched with cotton so as not to remain trapped in that terrible chance encounter with the enemy mirror that pitilessly reflected her own bruised image. *The trauma of mirrors is the trauma of the birth into language*, into the function of the word that rescues the person in the making, removing him from the atmosphere of inert objects that surround him and converting him into an "I." In Robles's case—and in so many others—the trauma is magnified by the indifference of adults.

The retrieval of memory functions as a prophecy that sheds light on the life emerging from the shadows of a remote past

111. Doubts that will be the focus of chapters 11 and 12.

and an unforeseeable future. Now she can say, employing other words—and again I take the liberty of interpolating myself into her text and usurping the use of the first person singular—that:

> I am the consequence of my infantile panic; however much I live and do—my writing—it is a convoluted attempt to go on escaping from the phantom of myself that attacked and terrorized me that dazzling afternoon of heat and shadows.

The adults (the parents?) arrived and provided consolation to the other child, Julio Cortázar. They coddled him, they stayed with him for hours, they spoke to him and explained things to him, they gave him names and words and composed for him the onomatopoeic song of the rooster, trying to help him understand that he should not be afraid, that he had the wool, the silk and the cotton to weave into words in order to cover his nudity against the unknown and to calm the infernal machinery that had been set in motion, as he supposed, that morning in 1917. It was transformed from terror into music. Martha Robles, in contrast, tells us that her experience took place "while the adults were talking," indicating that they did not stop and pay attention to her. The walkers are devices that allow the child to move about freely and independently. At the same time, they are instruments that allow adults to relieve themselves of the constant and restrictive infantile presence. Robles confides in us that she was just one more in a long succession of siblings who did not seem to mean much to anyone, the last of several sisters before the beginning of a series of brothers; one, perhaps, two, had already been born at the time of the mirror episode. So, what importance would the cries and protests, the sound and the fury of a baby girl have had?

Whereas they lavished Cortázar with tranquilizing words, Robles was left alone and frightened, defenseless. Perhaps she sensed that no one would hear her *scream*—that of a Munch in a baby walker. The words came later. They had to be invented, if not stolen, and then woven into clothing to protect the spirit from the discouragement that invaded it when it saw that the defenseless little girl watching it from the other side of the mirror was a double from which it would never again be able to separate itself, a perpetual companion, a pursuer that carried with her the same desperation, the same rage, that it carried: "I was sucking on a pacifier from a baby's bottle when, in one of the best-lit rooms, I stopped and stared at my own reflection. I felt panic." Thus we witness the birth of the *Doppelgänger*, host of so many literary works.

Martha Robles did not only see her own image. In the mirror there were also reflected two items of baby care, two products of human industry—baby walkers and pacifiers—so that the child can get along without the mother's arms or breasts. Lost like Cortázar in the immense universe, in front of mirrors (three, to be exact, like Borges) that continue upwards without hitting the roof, in front of windows that reach to the empty sky without end, in an abyss extending higher and higher, the incipient being is exposed in all her triviality, in her total vulnerability. The walker and the pacifier, desperately held between gritted teeth, reveal her rage at the absence of the others, only interested in what is happening in their own far off and distant world. *Geworfenheit* (Heidegger: "thrownness") of the child cast into the world.

For lack of a loving glance (from the mother, the first mirror, as Winnicott taught us), unable to love what is reflected in the mirror plates of the wardrobe, there only remains the possibility of identifying with that rejected and degraded image, residual or excrement of the Other's desire. Such is the very frequent destiny of men and women who lead lives bearing the burden of having arrived into the world without the favorable winds of the mother's desire that Goethe and Freud encountered, whether because she soon disappeared, as in the cases of Rousseau, Yourcenar and Tolstoy, or having arrived as nuisances or shameful objects for one or another reason relative to the (unconscious) desire of the mother, the ancestor of mirrors. Thus I believe we can interpret Martha Robles's panic in front of her own image:

I stopped and stared at my own reflection. I felt panic. I don't
know if it was for a long or short time, but I was aware of
the terror of being and not being the person that was there
inside, inside a terrifying mirror. [Her own effigy, even in
terror, is captivating] I stopped and stared . . . I left and came
back . . . For how long? Was it for a long or short instant?
[. . .] I don't know.

The language appears to be imprecise: how can an instant be
long without contradicting its very definition which assumes
fugacity? If the ever diaphanous writing of my friend crosses
into hesitancy, employing this oxymoron of a "long instant," it is
because it is incumbent upon us to find the precise truth. It was
an instant, the instant of a gaze, but that instant initiated time,
"time for understanding." There was no "time" *before* that surprise
encounter with the little girl captured inside the rigid frames of
the wardrobe's mirrors. At that moment the long years of latency
began—of memory; the haunting horror became constant from
that moment on following the encounter with her own image. Her
destiny was not to forget. The instant became immune to time, it
was the spring for an eternal return, like the Promethean eagle,
without before or after, until, reading something about Cortázar's
memory, she could end time, understand, and then the decisive
moment arrived, the "moment of concluding."[112] Martha Robles
adds a prologue to the "prolonged instant" of her infancy through
an act of writing—these carefully composed pages she turns over
to us and whose meaning it is up to us to decipher and expose.
Diegesis—the act of telling a story—while maintaining distance
from one's own character, is cathartic.

Her life, following the unfortunate encounter with the specular
image, has a condition, a phobic condition. She will have to live

112. Lacan, Jacques [1945]. "Logical Time and the Assertion of Anticipated
Certainty: A New Sophism." In *Ecrits: the first complete edition in English.*
Translated by Bruce Fink in collaboration with Héloïse Fink and Russell
Grigg. New York: W.W. Norton & Co., 2006, pp. 161–175.

anxiously rejecting, and suffering reactions of intolerance and auto-immunity when confronted with, her own image. Martha Robles would only be able to continue with her existence if she managed to escape from the perpetual and aggressive vigilance of mirrors which could return her to that moment when she found herself hunted by the gaze of the other, by the frames of the looking-glass, by objectifying expressions, whatever they might have been, by "judgments" that imprison in invisible and inescapable cells, by reductive and limiting "interpretations," by invasive affirmations that wished to tell her "this is how you are." Likewise, Virginia Woolf's reaction was phobic, in her case when faced with being seen as a woman or exhibiting feminine attitudes in front of the unexpected gaze of the other: she succumbed, for example, to the inner prohibition against powdering her nose and of trying on clothing. In the final chapter on the autobiographical genre, we will see that writing is, perhaps, the most effective means for escaping from the mirror-spies: creating—and not receiving—one's own face in a risky adventure of being called prosopopeia.

The other is a gaze that pierces into and dissects a person. The other is a mirror, a danger from which one can only protect oneself by taking long detours. Borges, as terrified as Martha Robles, seeks the repetition of his fear in order to domesticate the trauma. He reacts with a compulsion to appear and disappear in the blink of an eye. He longs for blindness in order to escape by drastic and definitive means. Virginia Woolf seeks and finds herself through the looking-glass but she also bumps into her own guilt and shame due to the mysterious jouissance that invades her being. Martha Robles flees. I have come to believe that all three find refuge in writing.

> Until deciphering that remote event (that is, until today) I had not realized that I had never reconciled that first encounter with my reflection. Almost unnecessary, I grew up at a distance from the "aggression" of the mirror. Even today I avoid it . . .

That experience was deprived "of the possibility of joining with my own fiction" and, precisely because of this, "it ciphered my history." What does Robles suggest in a sense that is no longer personal but rather universal? We all construct a fiction of ourselves based upon our sense of "I"; this narration is our "own fiction." And she adds: but, in my case, this fiction is cryptically ciphered around a moment in which "I" do not want to know—and at the same time I cannot help but know—who I am. This is because this "I," reflected in the mirror, frightens me. Perhaps I could say, daring once again to insert words into her text that are not there (as Freud did when he would interject phrases in the first person singular and then attribute them to Goethe), "I live by writing so as to escape from the image of the furious child sucking on her pacifier and who mercilessly attacked me that day from the other side of the mirror. I live and write so that she will not trap me as she did then; in order to persuade myself and so that others understand that I am not her."

Why was she afraid of her image in the mirrors of the great wardrobe that sat in her grandparents' house? Robles proposes several hypotheses and she does this, like Virginia Woolf, in an interrogative manner; she ventures interpretative guesses, she proposes intelligible sketches of the mysterious. That seems appropriate when one recalls that "the mysteries of the Egyptians are mysteries to the Egyptians themselves." (Hegel, quoted or misquoted by Lacan and Zizek). Faced with the fundamental secrets of ourselves we are all Egyptians (and so is Moses, Freud would add).

The writer's *first question*: "Was the discovery of my trapped and duplicated self the cause of such extreme terror?" The little girl could believe that she was one who enjoyed the freedom to move about "from here to there" with her walker, that no one was paying attention to her. Thanks to the disinterest of the adults speaking among themselves, she could sense not only her state of neglect but also the advantage of being able to do whatever she wanted. And here the mirror suddenly reflects her, showing her—maliciously, though without premeditation—that there is another Martha. The triple mirror watches her and fixes her in its rigid frames. The specular *Doppelgänger* reveals her impotence to her. She is squeezed by two corsets, both made of wood: the frame of the mirror and the frame of her walker, that prosthesis that keeps her erect in her clay feet. Those eyes that come from the other side order her to stay in that virtual space, hypnotized; if she manages to break away, she must return: "I left and came back." By placing her body once again in the visual field of the mirror the horror is reborn which causes her to flee again, this time definitively. She does not want to pass in front of herself again "other-ized" by a gaze of glass, inert and uncontrollable. A mute gaze that proffers and prophesizes fates of which one would prefer to remain ignorant. It is impossible to gag a mirror. That is why they are routinely covered with black cloths when there is a death in the house. And, as Borges has already told us: "You have always watched. In the tenderness / Of the uncertain water or the crystal that endures / You search for me and it is useless to be blind. / The fact of not seeing you and knowing you there / Adds to your horror . . ."[113]

Second question: "Did it intimidate me to meet with another little girl who replicated my shock from inside the looking-glass?" It is difficult to endure the anxiety of seeing oneself as an other. The repeated face reveals and amplifies her anxiety, her helplessness, her need to escape. Passing through the looking-glass Martha Robles meets another little girl who is like her but who comes a little after her. The repetition, as we said in the words of Borges, always implies a differing and a difference (Derrida). The terror reaches into virtual space and returns, posing an enigma: am I myself or not? The image requires a paradoxical answer: *I am myself and I am not*. Thus it intimidates and silences.

Third question: "Did it perturb my vision to be and not to be in two irreconcilable spaces?" Broadening the question: "If this

113. Jorge Luis Borges, "Al espejo" (To the Mirror). In *Obras completas*. Buenos Aires: Emecé, 1989. Volume II, p. 109 (my translation).

helpless figure is there, where I see her, where am I? Are we both equally real or equally false or is there one that is more real than the other? Which one should I believe? Am I her in the instant that I look at her and she looks at me or is there a delay, that miniscule amount of time that passes between my looking at her and her looking at me, that makes a difference between us? Am I her or is she a poor imitation that aspires to substitute for me by usurping my place? Does she confirm my being or does she rob it from me or does she take it from me in the moment that she gives it to me, producing me like a fiction in which she becomes the one pulling the levers? Do I find myself in her or do I lose myself or am I alienated from myself?

We can continue to learn from Robles's first memory: the little girl collapses out of terror. Why is she alone without anyone to explain to her that what she sees "is her"? How does she know or sense that "she" indeed "is her" and, upon seeing herself reified and alienated in the mirror, outside herself, why does she lose the vague certainty that she believed she had? Or why does she reject, at such a tender age, her self identified as *little girl* and sense that the acceptance of the gendered image that she sees will sweep her along a path that will impede her differentiating herself from the detested feminine figures that surround her and, very specifically, from her mother? What kind of void has opened beneath her feet from which no walker can possibly hold her back?

Considering the previous possible interpretations I see that it is impossible to settle the question but, on the other hand, there is nothing forcing us to choose between the different solutions. In the same way, when a patient has recounted a dream, he or she proposes different associative avenues without knowing which one to choose and the psychoanalyst points out that all are valid because there are no contradictions between them. The various questions that Robles poses prompt a single laconic answer: "Yes."

First, there is *solitude*. Yes; there must be an other, a third party, so that the child can identify with her image. I know who I am when there is someone else to confirm it. This is a fundamental aspect of the constitution of the "I" that falls to the mirror role of the mother (Winnicott), which was discussed in section 7.2. If there is no one to recognize me, how can I know that I am myself? One needs the support of the Other's words.

Second, *identification*. If I accept that the figure is mine but my reflection inspects me from the outside, I become the object of a gaze and of all the gazes that regard me without my being able to see myself. I cannot liberate myself from the eye of the other, the eye that reads and interprets me. From there to paranoia is no more than a single step: "Why are they looking at me? What do they see in me?" From the other side of the mirror my image hounds me, it harasses and objectifies me.

Third: *sexuation*, directly related to the first two. The form that the other recognizes and with which I identify is that of a woman in the making. How do other people view, and how do I relate myself to the fact of being a woman? Is this how they want to see me and how I want to see myself? Can I escape the fate of women in a phallocentric world? How?

So, the little girl has three reasons for being horrified and fleeing from the mirror. I will say something more about the third as it is the least recognized and I would like to expand on what was said about Virginia Woolf in the preceding two sections. When we meet another human being, the first distinction we make, with a high degree of certainty, is between their being masculine or feminine. How could this not also be the first distinction we make when encountering the puerile anthropoid that repeats our every gesture, our most intimate and unreachable companion, the intruder who lives on the other side of the mirror?

One night, after dinner, Borges and Bioy Casares conversed while, from the remote depths of a corridor, a mirror spied on them. As they concluded they discovered something, which was inevitable in the wee hours of the night: that mirrors have something monstrous about them. Bioy Casares then recalled something he had read by a nameless author from a conjectural country who claimed that "mirrors and copulation are abominable, because they increase the number of men." For Borges it was a memorable sentence, and also for us, and even today we do not know if it was written by an anonymous author or if it was the product of Bioy's modesty, who said that he had read it in an unobtainable encyclopedia, or Borges's modesty, who attributed it to his supposed best friend— a friend who was also a mirror that interpreted Borges without holding back any cruelty, a malicious Boswell. Mirrors, monstrous and abominable, are domesticated by industry. They are hung in predictable places and they are relieved of their ominous qualities. Custom has rendered them harmless. But who does not recall the odd sensation that comes over one when accidentally confronted by one's own specular image, sometimes crouching down in the form of another human being whose features are very similar to one's own?

Not only Borges and Bioy Casares have spoken of the monstrous aspect of mirrors. It would be a futile act of erudition to review all the literary texts—both plentiful and precious—from the myth of Narcissus in Oviedo's account to some contemporary film always to be found in theaters, that represent the sense of alienation at the moment of finding oneself face to face with one's own image, or one that bears a strong resemblance. Cortázar said that memory begins with terror and Lacan speaks of the child's encounter with his or her own image as a moment of jubilation. It would seem that, between them, there is a contradiction, but Martha Robles's recollection might resolve the disagreement. Her first encounter with the mirror could well have been horrific and upsetting, just as she (like Borges) remembers it; the subsequent euphoric exalta- tion in successive encounters with "the other I" would be the result of domestication and dominance over the underlying anxiety of confronting the *Doppelgänger.* Proust, and perhaps Borges, finally grew accustomed to mirrors and could ignore their discomforting presence, their reproductive obsession.

In *Beyond the Pleasure Principle* (14, footnote),[114] Freud tells of

---

114. Freud, Sigmund [1920]. *Beyond the pleasure principle.* Translated by James Strachey. New York: Liveright, 1950, p. 14, footnote. *St. Ed.* Op. cit., vol. XVIII, footnote 6, p. 15.

how his eighteen-month-old grandson learned, while his mother was away at work and his father was at war, to identify his own image in the mirror that reached almost to the floor and then, crouching down, he could make his mirror-image disappear from his field of vision. When the mother returned, he could tell her, in his half-language, that he had gone "out." The grandfather's interpretation proposed that the child, the passive object of the mother's abandonment, succeeded, with this mirror-game, in transforming himself into the active subject who manipulated his own appearance and disappearance, thus gaining dominance over the uncontrollable absence of his mother, that is, his being outside of his mother's field of vision while she was at work. This dominance over presence and absence is confirmed by the precarious use of the word (*fort—da*) and by the use of memory which enabled him to relate, with limited phonemes taken from his mother tongue, his feat in front of the mirror. The feat of appearing and disappearing from view, one, two, one, two, like Freud's mother in the wardrobe, like the waves in Virginia Woolf's epiphany, one, two, one, two, behind a blanket or in front of a mirror, duplicated by word-play, "now you see me, now you don't," is the beginning of one's voyage on the road of life.

We should look into how one overcomes initial anxiety: that of knowing oneself to be the *object* of the gaze before being able to be the *subject* of that gaze. Or how to configure the fate of not being able to overcome that helplessness, confirming over and over that the anxiety forever remains untouched and the soul lives, and will continue to live, condemned to suffer owing to the imminent possibility of remaining caught between the question marks of an ill-fated mirror.

That is what happened to Martha Robles. She lived in a world of sounds and shadows, and perhaps of smells. She was absorbed by the pitter-patter of her own uncertain first steps, by the drip of a faucet, by the voices and words without meaning that filled the air around her, by the language of the street, the songs of canaries and sounds of the kitchen. "That entire infantile world was composed of sounds that multiplied in echoes and strange duplications." What could she sense about herself? The only information came from that doubtful and archaic form of the double that is one's shadow. She enjoyed following it, stepping on it, fascinating herself "with that game of light and dark silhouettes, lacking gestures and features," that is, without faces.

The shadow is a duplication of oneself that lacks a face; it is faceless, in contrast to the image in the mirror which is filled with signs of identity and precise spatial limits. The face ("*la figure*") perceived in the mirror, fixes and shows itself to be, as Martha Robles says, "what it is" (mortal) and "how it is" (gendered) such that in the face we find a synecdoche and a metonymy of the body: "That is what I am; that is how I am." It is in the countenance that one focuses the search for resemblances and genealogical connections of the child. "S/he looks like . . ." It is not rare that based on the child's traits doubts might arise as to the child's "true" paternity, which is the same as harboring doubts about the mother's desire—for the father and towards the child.

> Neat, faithful and in its entire appearance, the figure glimpsed in the wardrobe pertained, undoubtedly, to the universe of repetitions, like the already familiar echo and shadow. But at the same time it was different because my reflection could be seen clearly showing me. The little girl met for the first time with an indication of reality, a concrete being. The discovery terrified me [. . .] It was as if the shadow, suddenly, came to life.

The shadow brings with it a halo of uncertainty; its identity is doubtful; its "two-facedness" is infinite. One sees the shadow, but it is blind. On the other hand, the face seen in the mirror, with eyes that look back from virtual space, unreal, compel the subject to live identified with that gaze and, therefore, to live from that moment forward a virtual, immaterial and stark life. The face is not what we find in nature or in reflective surfaces, it is not the result of a perceptive experience. *The face is a construction*, signed by those who see us and confirming for us that "that" is who we are. There is no face without the intervention of the signifier and the letter. The face (*prosopon*) is a poetic effect (*poiesis*): prosopopeia. We shall return to this, as anticipated, in Chapter 14.

Because of mirrors we exist in a fictitious world, but the unreality we are dragged into becomes our most authentic reality, where our bodies are observed. We are "there" and, in a certain sense, we are no longer "here." Martha Robles glimpsed something of this and was frightened because she could no longer shake free of the framed image, she could not isolate herself "as the solitary figure she had been." Through the looking-glass she entered the prison the rest of the world inhabits, a place of surveillance and control, the "panopticon."

We should recall the structure proposed by the English architect, Jeremy Bentham,[115] for prison buildings in 1785, which ironically coincides with the revolution that enthroned "liberty": a circular space with a central vantage point from which the guards can observe at all times every prisoner in his cells without being observed themselves. God—He who sees all (at least since the times of Bentham and Hegel)—is dead. Yes, he is dead and he has been substituted by this prison architecture that is effectively orchestrated paranoia set in motion. The panopticon is the reality of the contemporary world: nowadays television cameras may be anywhere on the planet, and even in outer space, and every human being can be observed by the great Other, if and when it

---

115. Bentham, Jeremy [1787], *Le panoptique ou L'oeil du pouvoir*. Prologue by Michel Foucault. Paris: La Villette, 1977. In English the facsimile allows us to read: *PANOPTICON OR THE INSPECTION-HOUSE: CONTAINING THE IDEA OF A NEW PRINCIPLE OF CONSTRUCTION APPLICABLE TO ANY SORT OF ESTABLISHMENT, IN WHICH PERSONS OF ANY DESCRIPTION ARE TO BE KEPT UNDER INSPECTION; AND IN PARTICULAR TO PENITENTIARY-HOUSES, PRISONS, HOUSES OF INDUSTRY, WORK-HOUSES, POOR-HOUSES, LAZARETTOS, MANUFACTORIES, HOSPITALS, MAD-HOUSES, AND SCHOOLS: WITH A PLAN OF MANAGEMENT ADAPTED TO THE PRINCIPLE: IN A SERIES OF LETTERS, WRITTEN IN THE YEAR 1787, FROM CRECHEFF IN WHITE RUSSIA. TO A FRIEND IN ENGLAND BY JEREMY BENTHAM.*

is deemed appropriate to do so. What is a camera if not a mirror to which a recording device has been attached to save in memory every scene it captures?

The terrified little girl screamed; later she learned to make detours to avoid meeting "that," the *unheimlich* she had perceived and about which she could tell no one. And no one could explain to her the reason for her fear. It was "something that appears without name or reference," an enemy that is impossible to keep at a distance, as difficult to get rid of as one's own shadow. It was not an imaginary interlocutor with whom so many children converse and find comfort in their fantasies, thus practicing a kind of spontaneous and autoerotic cure for loneliness. On the contrary, it was someone frightening, a pursuer, someone who needed to be silenced. The avoidance of the mirror was repeated in the repression of that memory of terror associated with the first, unfortunate encounter.

Who is so happy that memory causes them no pain? Martha Robles knows what she has repressed and cannot remember. In her own words, uncontaminated by Freudianisms:

> Oblivion is reserve, a pause waiting for the occasion to announce a sudden confrontation with the void or, better yet, with the frightening unknown. What has been experienced, albeit unspoken, does not disappear from the repertoire of being, but rather it remains indefinitely in the shadows, there where the voice may indirectly illuminate that non-word whose power orients the direction of one's own destiny.

What has happened is unspeakable; there is no hope of understanding or discussing it. The small child must do the best she can with her cursed memory, on her own. The corrosive image persists like a relentless mental parasite that pierces with its lances the teguments of the soul. It is not enough to avoid further encounters with the mirror; it is also necessary to escape from the outrage of its memory, to neutralize and exile it from the history of the self. Martha Robles forgets the terror she felt vis-à-vis the little girl in the mirror, terror that "mysteriously hides, even though the inner vocabulary attends to its own laws, responding to the impact in other ways." The little girl establishes a detour, she goes around, avoiding another encounter with that animated portrait of the well-known all too disquieting and familiar baby who upsets her tranquility from the burnished surface of a sheet of glass. She must find a way to save herself from condemnation and discover a lifetime of co-existence—that is, a way to get along with—her mirror-self. She will find the necessary detour along a path that we have already insinuated: that of language, but beyond the word. That has been her destiny. The mirror, in its mechanical stupidity, could not foresee that, by frightening her with what could be *said*, drove her to *write*. Was it to write in order to escape from herself or, at least, to escape from her own image? How could a writer be born from the rejection of her specular image? We may pose the question to the eloquent composition of the writer:

> Thus, as the recording of pleasure assembles and harmonizes, the traumatic reminiscence assaults language, separates it, isolates it. It lashes at its darkness and, confined to the unspoken, the moment of suffering still hurts from a distance, its scar still sears and, deformed, its need for expression expands into the realm of anxiety.

Anxiety is an insatiable beast that devours souls. It must be imprisoned, contact with it must be avoided lest it sink its teeth in. Phobia (of mirrors) and forgetting (of the catastrophic encounter) are the muzzles that hold shut its snout. The muzzled word becomes a symptom . . . and the symptom: letter.

4. Writing as Oracle

Thus it would appear that we have reached the secret of Martha Robles's recollection which has put us on the track of that obscure object that is the writer's desire. We have come to understand in what sense her encounter with the mirror ciphered her history, how it acted as oracle and pointed the way for the writer who today attracts readers by virtue of her literary passion. I do not believe that this formula is applicable to all writers, nor to the majority; perhaps it is only valid for a few. There are no general formulas that define the shape of desire.

Let us return now to a subject that pursues us more than we pursue it in the pages covered thus far and in the pages yet to come. Of all "our" authors we know their mythical "first memory" through the written narrative. Diegesis, the act of narrating with the letter or the word, is certainly an application of memory, a rereading *a posteriori* of certain "mnemic traces." Something of a problematic experience was engraved in the infantile soul and called for a rewriting as a "recollection" mixing "episodic memory" (*Erinnerung*) with "semantic memory" (*Gedächtnis*), according to Hegel's classical terminology, rediscovered by contemporary memory scientists. The doubt that assaults many writers is the following: can the course be inverted such that the childhood experience becomes, not the consequence of the narrative ("Here I began to sing") but rather the cause, that is, the origin of the vocation for the person who "lives to tell the tale?" The possible premonitory value of this "first memory" is that which led Freud to attribute to it a seminal and decisive nature. We could even conspire with Roland Barthes[116] and imagine, as he does, a perverse author who publishes various books in the first decades of his life with the sole objective of earning the right to one day write his

---

116. Barthes, Roland [1980]. *La préparation du roman: de la vie à l'œuvre.* In: *Œuvres complètes.* Vol. V. Paris: Seuil, 2002, pp. 753–54.

autobiography and thus arouse the interest of his readers in the origins of his memory.

In this way, the first memory would set in motion the life of a writer that is lived for the narrative action, often as a substitution for life itself. There are many for whom writing is an addictive instrument that allows for separation from the Other and from the Other's demands, which are more or less impossible to fulfill. This phantasy of emancipation and autonomy is ultimately expressed when a woman or a man is secluded in the intimate, solitary confines of four walls, armed only with pen and paper, or a word processor. The first memory would then be a self-fulfilling prophecy. By bringing these reflections together with the Cortazarian hypothesis, the origin of writing and of the writer would be the horror vis-à-vis a traumatic living experience from which it is impossible to escape. The diegesis (the "literary act," Derrida would say) would enable survival by appealing to the other, to whoever would hear and read the transmutation of terror into poetry, the metamorphosis of the terrified or ashamed face of the little girl in front of the mirror into autobiographical prosopopeia. The arrow of time would flee from the past into the future: from the first wound of terror toward the healing written text.

There is another option when taking the inverse course: the subject, immersed in language networks, ensnared by them, gasping for breath, creates in its phantasy, retroactively, a seminal memory from which flows not only his vocation but also a succession of narratives called fiction or aspiring to historic objectivity, drawing upon, given the case, stored data that will support them. The underlying "prophecy" functions as a precarious construction that ratifies the continuity sought by the self in order to caulk the perforated vessels of memory and draft a fictitious homogeneity, on paper, on the margins of flesh and blood.

In a recent essay, Pierre Bayard, psychoanalyst and literary critic, studied the "cases" of various writers (Rousseau, Verhaeren, Melville, Woolf, Breton, Borges) who wrote about decisive events of their lives before they came true.[117] To explain these "strange coincidences" he distinguishes four hypotheses: the irrational, the rational, the Freudian and the literary.

The first, the *irrational*, sustains a reading that anticipates the future, with a forecasting ability that is inherent to writing or, at least, to some writers. The idea is seductive but it will never overcome the suspicion that it only considers prophecies that have come true and that, to that end, retroactive anticipation is necessary, functioning from the present into the past, thanks to a work that is poetic in itself. André Breton is a case in point. He found precisely the woman he had anticipated in a poem written with the automatist technique belonging to the surrealists. He ends (or begins) by marrying her. For him, there was no doubt: the poem had anticipated their meeting. Can anyone deny it?

The *rational* (or *scientific*) hypothesis proposes that, in certain cases, and there can be no exceptions, there is a succession of more or less fortuitous events that give rise to consequences that, later, retroactively, are read as having been anticipated by the writing of the authors. The peripeteias of the narrator are purged of their symbolic smudges by the rationalist thinker and the recourse of a simple mathematical process of probabilities points to the real events, stripping them of any mystical aura. For example, if Borges ended up blind it is because of a hereditary disease or an accident in which he was hurrying up a dark staircase and bumped his head against the corner of a window that was left open. Another coincidence would be that the accident would have taken place in 1938, the same year in which his blind father died.

The third *Freudian* hypothesis, just as Bayard presented it, highlights the fundamental importance of the past and demonstrates the degree to which texts can find their most authentic inspiration in events that take place later. For that, it is necessary to examine—as an interpretative scheme—the activity of the writer's phantasy, an imaginary, repetitive script in which the subject chooses his or her close family and friends and has them

---

117. Bayard, Pierre, *Demain est écrit*. Paris: Minuit, 2005.

act in situations where they pursue their best interests following certain paths that accommodate their unconscious desire. The literary texts place these phantasies in certain settings before they face them in reality.

> The work obviously depends on life but life depends equally on the work, given that both are different expressions of a common structure that profoundly underlies their development. Such a structure is so much more insistent whenever it situates its sources in very old events in the history of the subject.[118]

Bayard finds that this is a solution that is harmonious with the problem of predestination as it permits escaping, unscathed, from the aporias of both rational and irrational readings. However, he reproaches the Freudian hypothesis for complying with a lineal conception of time and not daring to invert the line by making it run from the future to the past, to recognize a determinism of the future. Personally, I believe that this—what Bayard says is lacking—is precisely the Freudian hypothesis once it has taken into account Lacan's insistence on Freud's conception of the *après-coup*, or the retroactivity of time. In the examples considered in these chapters I have consistently insisted that it is the writer (or analysand) who construes his or her memory according to the needs of the cause that is always present and that points to the realization of the desire in the future guided by the fiction of the writer's phantasy. It is for this reason that "the truth has the structure of fiction," and that memory is written from the future towards the past: the author is the *subject of the annunciation*.

Finally, the *literary* hypothesis situates the book itself at the center of everything, the work as project that guides existence and that both—the text and life—are linked to the certainty of death. Bayard takes Proust as the paradigm and indicates, incorrectly in my judgment, that in Freud the unconscious does not know time

---

118. Bayard, Pierre, cit., 89 (my translation).

whereas the Proustian mind is immersed in time and cannot be conceived in its absence. In Proust, in contrast to Freud, the future, and not only the past, has an influence on our actions. Bayard seems unaware that in Proust the work, that is, the book that drives the author that writes the book, is a phantasmatic construction that organizes his life. García Márquez lives to tell the tale, Proust tells the tale to live, and Neruda confesses that he has lived it. In fact, ignorance of time in the unconscious, proposed by Freud, is precisely the action of the primary processes that indiscriminately bring together, as in a dream, the different moments of the past. Metaphor and metonymy, poetic devices and primary processes that are at its base, do not recognize the chronological sequences and blend the lived events with the writer's phantasies benefiting from a fuel that is timeless desire, the constant and silent driving force, and jouissance, which is the goal and compass. *The future is the animator of the past*; nothing is more part of psychoanalytic thought than this hypothesis. Between the "Freudian hypothesis" and the "literary hypothesis" there is absolute agreement, almost coalescence. "The Horla" is not a premonition of Maupassant's madness, it is one of his first eclosions just as the aura forms part of an epileptic fit instead of announcing its imminence.

It is not necessary to invent new verb tenses to account for the "subject of the annunciation" that is the result of concrete action by phantasies in the configuration of both life and the written work and in the retroactive selection of the memories that give coherence and historic continuity to both. The *future perfect*, "will have been," is the verb tense with which the script of the life of everyone is written. It is a verb tense that is sufficient for demonstrating that—whatever the ups and downs of our existence may be—they retroactively reorganize all the events of the past and will give special relevance to those that serve as materials for the construction of the (auto) (bio) (graphy). What has happened to us *will have been* important as a function of what happens and will happen to us. *The past feeds on the future. It is always today* (the future is an unborn phantasy and the past no longer exists, it has already died) *but the arrow crosses time from tomorrow back toward yesterday.*

Are the life and work of Martha Robles effects of her first and ill-fated encounter with the mirror? No, if we consider it mechanically; yes, if we are wise enough to recognize in her panic and consequent phobia a style that attempts to reveal the mysteries of that instant and a motive for controlling her terror—and escaping from it by means of a smoothness and eloquence in writing that is clear and controlling of the jouissance (terrified and terrifying) vis-à-vis the specular image.

If "memory begins with terror," one can, through writing, circle the ring of fire that prohibits returning to that inferno or one can, like Poe or Kafka, venture upon a voyage without guarantees toward the "heart of darkness" until finding Kurtz, the other self, murmuring as he lies dying, "the horror, the horror!" Marlow could return, but no longer the same as before; he was forever transformed by the voyage upriver (inland) to the center of the black continent. Many have fallen along the way. To go towards terror, to escape from it or to remain wandering on its periphery, such are the alternatives to the voyage. Memory is the vehicle that can convey one, depending on an unconscious decision by the writer, along the centrifugal, centripetal or rotary paths in relation to absence, to the re-presentation of the absent, or to its retrieval in the imaginary. There are three paths of autobiographical memory according to the course programmed for the final chapters of our adventure.

NURIA AMAT: A HOLE IN THE MIRROR

1. Through the Window Across the Way

Nuria Amat is a well-known Catalan novelist who writes in Spanish. To name just the last three of her novels, she is the author of *La intimidad* (*Intimacy*) (Alfaguara, Madrid, 1997), *El país del alma* (*The Country of the Soul*) (Seix Barral, 1999) and *Reina de América* (*Queen Cocaine*) (Seix Barral, 2002 / City Lights, 2005, English version). She has also published a notable book of essays, many autobiographical in nature, *Letra herida* (*Wounded Letter*) (Alfaguara, 1998). In *Babelia*, the cultural supplement of the newspaper *El País*, on 23 June 2001, she published a very concise article, "Vida de escritora," ("Writer's Life") in which she narrates her "first childhood memory which has to do with madness and suicide." Here we have another "paper scrap" [*petit papier*] to add to the present study, and again it is an isolated fragment that was published in a cultural supplement—previously we examined one by Martha Robles, published in Mexico, and now one by Nuria Amat, published in Barcelona.[119] To frame her recollection, she

119. In the same article, Nuria Amat says: "To show (publish) a text is to condemn it to oblivion." She refers to books . . . How much faster does what is published in newspapers disappear from memory! Memorable texts are forgotten as soon as they are printed. But what purpose would memory serve without an audience for this effort to persist? Long live paper scraps! We must give these oddities of non-forgetting a chance.

provides some personal information that cannot but attract our attention, involved as we are in the subject of the "first memory," the "core of memory," which, according to Freudian intuition, probably gives order to the life of many human beings and, according to Cortázar, is anchored in terror—both in a prospective and retrospective sense.

In the article published in *Babelia*, Amat recounts "the terrible experience for a little girl of seeing a woman hanging from the window of the house across the street on the verge of falling into the void." It is debatable whether this could be her first memory, given that in her novel, *Intimacy*, she writes that the woman, spied upon from her "privileged window" (?) that looked out upon the mental hospital across the way, had been seen by her "several times." Imprecision and doubt necessarily characterize—always and without exception—the first memory. Which brings up a question that is not so different from those we posed at the start of this journey through the realms of memory: "When exactly does memory begin, always capricious and enemy to all forms of obedience [. . .] if memories are submerged in the same atmosphere as dreams?"[120]

Whatever the answer, this reminiscence, first or not—it could never be verified—is central to this writer's stories and literary voyage in general. It is the wellspring of her work, the moment of her birth into a second life, that of terrible enigmas demanding explanations. The crazy suicide, seen from the window like the wolves in the dream of Freud's patient, will be an obsessive *ritornello* in her writing because, for her, in a phantasmatic way, it responds to the mystery of the early disappearance of her mother when Nuria was still very little, in her third year of life.

Concerning her mother, the blooming writer retains nothing in her memory, that is, in her "official" memory, the memory banks of her ego. She affirms that, not having retained anything from the body where she was formed, she is "a daughter of words" and,

120. Onetti, Juan C. *Cuando entonces*. Mexico: Diana, 1988, p. 75 (my translation).

like the crazy woman in the white robe in her first memory, "she remains hanging in a silent hell." Presenting herself as an effect of language ("writing to be born"), she denies her corporeal origin or she considers her being as the "verb incarnate," as a creature with a single, belated birth: a traumatic entrance into language submerged in a sinister memory.

Her mother had three children in quick succession. Nuria was the child in the middle, the "mujercita" (the "little lady"). After giving birth to her third child, the mother did not return from the hospital but went directly to a "seaside resort" where she died without anyone knowing precisely why. The inference of suicide is supported by a multitude of indications though no one actually says the words that would clear away the fog of doubt about this death.[121] What the adult—the father—keeps quiet is filled in by the child: Nuria offers us her childhood phantasy: "The future writer seeks to confuse her mother with the crazy woman imprisoned in the attic of the insane asylum across the way." We should pay special attention to her use of the verb *to seek*, since this verb suggests more a sense of desire and jouisssance in the possibility of a confirmatory answer than anxiety over an unresolved question. Thanks to episodic memory, she is able to become an eyewitness to the fact that is the cipher and key to her life: the hushed-up disappearance of her mother who left without saying a word or even a letter to say goodbye.[122] The spectacle of the woman hanging from a window, held by a doctor who finally lets her fall, functions as an "oracle" (aptly designated by Martha Robles), as an indispensable point of reference, an evil magnet and an incitation to save herself by recording in "wounded letters" the irruption of madness and death. The oracle of memory, terrible as it is, calls for the making of amulets that will protect against its influence,

---

121. *Post-partum* depression? Perhaps the doctor would say something to that effect.

122. Similar to the experience of Georges Perec, see Chapter 12. Like the French writer, Amat has only one childhood memory, *the* childhood memory, that of the crazy woman in the window of the insane asylum, allegory for the disappearance of her mother.

for submerging herself for the rest of her life in a world of narratives that capture this unrepresentable absence.

Nuria Amat's traumatic memory has two shutters that converge to close the window of her soul: one, latent, is the enigmatic death of her mother in an uncertain location, kept secret for a long time; the other, manifest, seen through a "photographic eye," is the suicide before her infantile gaze of a "crazy woman" outside her orphan's window. The memory burns (*O rimembranza amara!*): dementia and death and the unbearable pain of life besiege the little lady who has been left without words or with sounds that cross like mute lizards on her tongue.

She lost her mother in the third year of her life. She was left with a newborn brother, a trunk of old clothes in which she would sniff dissipating fragrances, sift through fading photographs and confusing memories of another's life, memories that would reach her through other people who she envied for having actually known her mother, in flesh, blood and sounds. In her article published in *Babelia*[123] she relates:

> Surely I must have said my first words of childhood while my phantom mother was before me to receive my voice and celebrate it, but no one has assured me of such a thing . . . When my mother died, I was still without speech, and I remain without a place from where to speak. My memory was stolen from me. They say my mother was Catalan. [We should note the contradiction between "Surely I must have said" and "I was still without speech"; adverbs are professional informants.]

Amat infers that she was "a mute child" that "did not begin to speak until well into her fourth year." We can venture to reject the contradiction and join the two affirmations: Nuria spoke, like almost all children in the second year of their lives; her first words

---

123. Amat Nuria. *Babelia.* Suplemento cultural de *El País*. Barcelona, July 23rd, 2001.

were celebrated, her genius recognized. Then, suddenly, her mother left to give birth to the aforementioned brother and she never returned from the voyage. The raven of tragedy that fluttered above her home, built across the street from an insane asylum—precisely there—leaves her speechless. The spirit and the voice of Nuria Amat die and are buried in the ever-visited tomb of her mother while her fragile little body insists on surviving. The little girl is erased from the mirror that was her mother and must be born again. She does so slowly, in a birth without mother tongue, a birth that is drawn out into the fourth year of her life and is prolonged further by stuttering, by an anxiety that takes hold of her—and we are compelled to believe her—every time she has to speak.

Her second birth into language is not a repeat of the first. On the one hand, when she decides to speak she does so "in Spanish, in the language not of my mother . . . an inferior language for the family that boasts of being simple and profoundly Catalan." Her inclination for the language of Castilla (and Spain), the language of the invader, the official language of her classmates in the Franco school, sanctions the treason of her mother and the distancing of the incipient writer:

> In my language, the only thing that remains of my mother is the black hole of her disappearance. The imported language excludes me from the family conversations. I rebel against the language of my absent mother (*Babelia*, cit.).

Without knowing it, Nuria Amat made the same decision as James Joyce. He rejected the Gaelic of his Irish ancestors and opted for the language of Shakespeare, degraded by the vulgarity of the daily speech of Victorian England. And Amat would choose to speak and write in the language of Cervantes, the language cheapened by the censure and spiritual baseness of the Franco regime. Irish and Catalans (Shaw and Wilde, Goytisolo and Plá) opted for the language of the invader in order to restore honor and dignity to "the uncreated lineage of their race(s)."

Another point at which the second birth—post-maternal, we could say—differs from the first, is key: Nuria would pass from the spoken word ("Whenever I am about to speak, something unstoppable goes off in my head to remind me of my orphanage color") to the written word. She will take refuge in the opulent Catalan library of her paternal home.

> I had no choice but to exchange the tombstone for the books. The books spoke to me. I believed I could hear my mother through them. They spoke to me of the silence of my abandoned mother [. . .] Novels were like mirrors of memory. In them I saw myself or I didn't see myself, depending on the whims of my mother from the great beyond. Novels spoke to me of the silent death of my mother [. . .] I always had the impression that the library formed part of the cemetery where they kept the kidnapped body of my mother.[124]

Nuria Amat is the daughter of Gutenberg and she inhabits his galaxy. Exiled from the absent body of her mother and the language of her family, with her lips sewn shut for lack of language, like Schoenberg's Moses, she chooses her career: she will be a librarian, a writer and novelist, she will seek silence and end up, necessarily and paradoxically, making her most intimate thoughts public. She will painfully give birth to her books. She will also be a professor of library science in her native city of Barcelona. The library is a world populated by objects—in contrast to those of our common world—that are mute, reliable and comprehensible. Books indifferently permit the silence of their readers, in contrast to humans, who demand answers. They are at rest, impassive, waiting to be summoned by the trumpets of the unpredictable reader, like skeletons in repose while the day of judgment approaches that will raise their tombstones. This shall be a sepulchral yet vital space: a library, "a floating island of compassion and sadness situated at the center of my home."

---

124. Amat, Nuria. *La intimidad*. Madrid: Alfaguara, 1997, p. 169.

Amat emerges from the initial absence of her mother, the ambiguous relationship with her father and the impossibility of speech, all of which limit her to the contemplation of the great spectacle in progress—taking place at her very windowsill: in the mental institution in front of her home with the woman-mother, first, hanging in the void, falling, and then, caught in slow-motion, in an eternal camera. She emerges from there thanks to a special arrangement: her father, half-bibliophile, half-bibliomaniac, allows the little girl to enter his den among the nine thousand volumes he keeps there. The majority of her father's books are in Catalan, the language she abhors. Her father asks her to organize and classify his treasure. The little girl considers herself the "daughter of an abandoned library." At the same time, the man finds in his bibliophilist pride, in his bibliomaniacal compulsion (symbolized by Henri Boulard[125] or doctor Kien in Canetti's novel) in the jouissance of possessing his books, a valuable treasure that is for him—as Amat herself writes—"(almost) my father's wife,"[126] "a cemetery for the living in which my mother could very well have been buried."

The writer whose vocation is barely apparent is bribed (with books, what else?) by her father to work as librarian and the young woman accedes, enjoying it, to his demands.

Only an obedient daughter accepts such assignments from her father. I was the disgraced daughter of a disgraced father, and that condition will lead you to graciously accept jobs and favors that no other daughter would have been disposed to take on in exchange for money or even for a large quantity of books.[127]

125. Braunstein, N.A. "¿Conoce usted a Henri Boulard?" ("Do you know Henri Boulard?") in *Ficcionario de psicoanálisis*. Op. Cit., pp. 7–11.
126. Amat, Nuria. *Letra herida*. Madrid: Alfaguara, 1998, p. 149 (my translation).
127. Amat, Nuria. *La intimidad*. Madrid: Alfaguara, 1997, p. 98.

In any case, it is always preferable to accede to this class of paternal desire than to others that may be more surreptitious and tainted with secrets that are more difficult to confess.

> Many Sunday mornings . . . my father came in pajamas to show me affection or because he needed mine, depending on the moment, and he would get in my bed and he hugged me and caressed me with excessive intensity and duration (. . .) My father would kiss me in a strange way, with the sweetness and affection of couples in love. And as I loved my father above all else and felt, in addition, an immense compassion for his sadness of a widower, I learned to put up with this torture, with considerable skill.[128]

We should not forget that in this paragraph we are not reading a chronicle of true events but rather the novel, *La intimidad* (*Intimacy*). One could easily confuse the ego of the character with the ego of a real person's history. Without confusing them, we nonetheless know that both empty into the same river: the phantasy. The literality of the memory is of little concern to us because we do not believe it. As Freud and Piaget taught us in their moment, memories are constructions. The presence of the father in the little girl's bed, ardent with affection, is either indicative of a real event which could well have taken place, and have been repeatedly elaborated and embellished by the nuclear memory of the daughter, or it is an infantile phantasy that opens the way along a dark path of poetic creation, in which case it is not real; rather, it is hyper-real.

Returning to Amat: the circumstance of the mother-library, the necrophiliac space that unites her with and separates her from her father, turns out to be providential . . . for both persons. The woman grants herself a deferment along her way to becoming a writer and takes the detour through the library. She will care for the books of her traitor father who will end up disinheriting

---

128. *Ibid.*, pp. 12–13.

her from his treasures and leaving them, at the moment of this death, to her brother, who will donate them to the gothic convent of Poblet. In any case, for this young woman who lives among her novels and who receives from the doctors pitiless diagnoses of neurasthenic neurosis, encephalitis and epilepsy . . . for this woman who seems incomprehensible to anyone who believes in the virtues of speech . . . for this fugitive of social contact, nothing could be better than a library where she can while away the hours at her leisure.

2. Period, New Paragraph for the Self-Image

Who can save her? Which talisman can keep the demons of terror away if the loving caress of the other is lacking, in particular, that of the mother, to provide soothing words, lullabies and melodies to allay her feelings of helplessness? What can protect the infantile cocoon from the sinister influence of a memory so devastated by ignorance about the death of her mother and the knowledge of—the knowledge of having seen—what happened to the sick melancholic woman who threw herself into the void on the other side of the street and who created a spectacle that corresponded to the enigma of the absent mother? Peace arrives for Nuria Amat in the form of the printed word, from books that she, like a character in *Fahrenheit 451*, learns by heart, including the "period, new paragraphs." She will be, for a start, a woman of paper, a "book-woman."

"Perhaps my dead mother has become a living library." In *La intimidad* the writer, minimally disguised as the protagonist, narrates her adventures during the early period of her life. She intentionally confuses novel and autobiography (she has every right to her personal *ficcionario/fictionary*) when she speaks of her early life, of the period in which she suckled from the printed page.

She does not see her mother and her mother does not see her. There is no reflection of the child's face to be seen in the redeeming gaze of her mother and Nuria, in *Letra herida*, tries to recover it without fully believing in the truth of the fictions she creates:[129]

> My mother is a chest stuffed full of useless words. I dress myself in her deformed clothing as if these splendid dresses were shrouds of words. This is how I construct my writer's body. I disguise myself as a mother and, thanks to this word clothing, I manage to see her for an instant in the mirror. It's a kind of flash. A period, new paragraph in the mirror. Writing, my writing and, finally, all writing, consists in seeking it.

The little girl does not seek herself, she seeks the Other in mirrors, and they reveal to her the double fiction that she is neither herself nor her dead mother: "In front of the mirror I am so often my mother that it frightens me a little that she can appear from one moment to the next and catch me in the immoral act of usurping her image."[130]

With Amat's narrative, we find ourselves again faced with the shame felt by Virgina Woolf. Moreover, Nuria Amat, with her precise words, helps to illuminate the experience of the British writer. The shame of experiencing *jouissance* in the usurpation of her mother's image before the mirror is manifest. The gaze returned by the looking-glass is pitiless because it comes from beyond the grave, like that of the crazy woman seen from the privileged window. Whoever peers into the mirror, especially if she is the inconsolable daughter of a deceased mother, sees on the other side something that no other gaze could condone: a spectacle of which other eyes are blind, that of a face in search of itself which, if it were to appear in real space, would cause terrible panic. She would have crossed the limit between life and death, between sanity and insanity. The guilt-ridden pastime Amat engages in with her deceased mother's belongings in the attic where they are kept is a capital sin: that of supplanting her mother. It is the same game she engages in with

---

129. Amat, Nuria. *Letra herida*. Op. cit., p. 148.
130. *Ibid.*, p. 111.

her father on Sunday mornings. An "immoral act." Her imposture in front of the mirror, a veritable *quid pro quo*, is obedience to her father's desire and disobedience before the Law that prohibits a little girl from taking her mother's place. According to Amat, her compassion for her widower father underlies the profanation she commits in her imagination. *Zugzwang*, inescapable coercion: whatever she does, it will be bad . . . and she must act. She must represent her mother but she cannot be her mother; she will have to divide herself and live a double life of fiction. The paths that lead to autobiographical writing are mysterious.

We may also recall Martha Robles's terror when she finds herself alone and abandoned in front of the pitiless and indiscreet mirror. The responsible object is the same as that which terrified Borges at night and distressed Proust in his waking hours. Once again, the mirror.

The father has used Nuria to fill the mother's place in order to alleviate a condition of mourning that will not end. The little girl resigns herself to the space she is offered and puts up only weak resistance. The crazy woman has fallen from the window. The mother has disappeared into the void leaving behind the obligation to visit her in the cemetery every Sunday. She is not an angel keeping watch over her orphaned children; rather she becomes a merciless pursuer, particularly because she is impossible to hate. Officially she is "the queen of the heavens and my invulnerable dreams" but, among the library shelves, she lurks like "the most malign and false mother," the only cause of the family's domestic unhappiness, responsible for the family catastrophe and the lugubrious disorder of everyone's emotional state. Nuria refuses to forgive her for having fled the home. The little girl knows the truth without having been told. She can feel deep down that she is "the most awkward extension of her rotting bones." It is not only her image reflected in the mirror, but also her body of a real little girl that is stalked by the mother and submitted to decomposition. Bones are not reflected in the mirror but the eyes that stare into it are like x-rays. The "x" of the rays corresponds to the unknown aspect of her mother's disappearance. The skeleton in the cemetery, coming from the inert glass of the mirror, passes to the other side of the living flesh and is incorporated into the child's face, proclaiming a fated identity. "The memory of her non-existence would remain alive in me until the day I would join her, in the same tomb." By her non-existence the mother has a perpetual presence, an unforgettable nail driven into the little girl's memory.

This is not the moment to develop Freudian theories on identification with the lost object during mourning and melancholy, nor to recall current, debatable theories such as Judith Butler's or that of Queer Theory on the possible consequences on identity for persons who cannot mourn the absence of the loved object when it is of the same sex. Nuria is, after all, still of school age when she becomes the "only woman of the house." She is the recipient of "standardizing" pressures to accept herself as "one" woman with her fate regulated by the common legal prohibition against incest; it is precisely "that" perfect and hated woman that she must incarnate, the cause of all her misadventures. She must substitute for her mother, assuming continuity for her life and denying the mourning process; she is pushed into taking the place of her deceased mother by the father on Sunday mornings and in the two cemeteries: the one in Barcelona, the other in the library. The *père-version* is imposed on her, and it is unappealable.

If not her father, then who could pass the law on to her? In that void—indeed, it is a double-void owing to the absence of her mother and to the dysfunction of the father—stands the mirror. Amat derives jouissance from substituting for her dead mother, incorporating her fragrances, playing at deceiving the mirror with clothes that deform her. Borges is terrified by seeing his image multiplied from one to three, dissolving his sense of the limits of identity; he prefers to flee from the prison of the mirror. Robles was horrified at seeing the specter of her despised mother and also escaped it through writing. Woolf experienced jouissance in playing the double role of mother and conquering lover in front of the mirror, which is why she was frightened by being caught in her guilt-filled and shameful bisexual game: writing enabled her to create a phantasy space where she could hide her guilt without renouncing the game. Amat is afraid of being discovered, not by a living presence but through a hole drilled in the center of the mirror itself and of being punished for relaxing into her imposture. She is stalked and hunted—not much, just "a little"—in those moments of shameful jouissance, by death itself, which could discover her "immoral game."

Writing secures her a space of her own and separates her from the ideal ego, from that deadly and dead mother that calls to her from the heavens and that, at the same time, attracts her to the dungeons of insanity. She writes in order to escape from that hole in the mirror and from the vertigo heights of the insane-asylum window. It is a "period, new paragraph in the mirror"—the power of words is marvelous in the hands of one who brings them, spotless, straight from the cleaners! Amat uses clothing that is not hers, the "clothing of words" that enables her "to see herself" where she is hiding, where she, the mother, witnesses the sinful spectacle of her daughter's transformation imposed by the father. There is no maternal figure she can identify with, one that she would like to resemble. The ego ideal, substitute for the deceased, will have to be achieved, for the greater pleasure of the father, by writing in the way he likes, "like Dickens."

It is fair to say that the literature of Nuria Amat consists of novels that are conspicuously autobiographical in nature. The protagonist of these novels constantly alternates between "it is me" and "it is not me; it is the other." Her work obeys the laws of genre. Paul de Man writes: "The difference between fiction and autobiography is not a polarity, 'it is this or the other,' rather it is . . . unresolvable."[131] Amat tells the truth even as she has the reader believe that she is weaving a fiction. "I want to make believe that the story is not make-believe. It is difficult for me to imagine

---

131. De Man, Paul. "Autobiography as defacement." In: *The Rhetoric of Romanticism*. New York: Columbia University Press, 1984, p. 70.

my writing without that impetus of a constant deception that I maintain with myself." In the end the reader does not know who is writing: whether it is her, or her mother, or the surrealist image of the melancholic woman dangling from the window across the way. The mirror renders them interchangeable. The ego vacillates from one side to the other of the narrow passageway that separates her from the insane asylum, from one side to the other of the mirror that watches her in another's clothing in the attic where the relics of the deceased are kept.

She tells the truth about herself and she does so all the more clearly the more she believes she is hiding it; for this reason she is never entirely sure when she has crossed the limit between what she has lived herself and what she has sketched with ink—ink that is more part of her than her own blood. She invents characters that at times (in *La intimidad*) say "I," yet constantly divide the narrator, that is, they are at once her and the mother who is composed of faint retouches to her infantile, abandoned image, created in the language of others, in the language that her Barcelonan community rejects, in Spanish, on sheets of paper. She said as much in the article published in *Babelia*: "I give names to the silence. I invent memories I don't have. I am a poet without knowing it."

I am aware that I am constructing fiction with the materials provided by the fiction constructed by Amat. To clarify for the unsuspecting reader, I aspire to verisimilitude, not the truth (which I forgot about a long time ago). Nuria Amat sees herself as a character in a novel; thus I write something like a novel of her novel (and of various other randomly chosen writers) in order to test the hypothesis of a memory that begins with terror. I resist "applying" psychoanalysis. I prefer that her fine writing should reveal, by way of words and obeying the signifiers, the structure of her phantasy, that invention that springs from the memory of the woman suspended in air.

The flesh, Nuria Amat seems to be telling us, has the scratchable consistency and combustible property of paper: "My childhood was an abandoned book with its dead letters printed in italics. And my life was a book, and a tomb and some sacred italicized letters." A life of paper, a life in paper, a life through paper, brings out death. Identification with the ever absent mother pertains to the hard shelves of a book-bound necropolis. The spaces of life and death, of sanity and insanity, of commerce and incest, all have imprecise boundaries and the passions for reading and writing will realize the mission of reinforcing these boundaries and of erecting customs offices between the life that is possible and the impossibility of life.

Nuria Amat refers no less than one hundred times to "the abandoned mother." Abandoned by whom? She could tell herself that she is not responsible, the little orphan, but we have to accept her word as truth. The mother left her, yes, but it is no less true that she left her mother lying in a cemetery of entombed letters: "You pass your life doing the opposite of what your father wants just so that, once dead, you do exactly what he wanted." What did her father want?

First, that she organize his book collection and clearly define the spaces between the Catalan (his) and the Spanish (hers). Nuria Amat is today, as we know, professor at the School of Library Science in Barcelona.

Second, he wanted her to write like Dickens. Nuria Amat rebelled. She protested that no one writes like Dickens and she believed that she could only save herself from the treacherous desire of her father if she wrote not *like* but rather *against* Dickens. She goes so far as to explain the death of her father as a murder committed by her:[132]

> My illegible texts, unworthy of a daughter of Dickens, ended up killing him. That is why he changed his will and disinherited me from his books which were mine [. . .] because instead of writing like Dickens, I wrote like the daughter of my father.

---

132. Amat Nuria. *La intimidad.* Op. cit., p. 173.

Her father could not have imagined a more faithful fulfillment of his wishes. Amat escapes from realism and writes an intimate, confidential and autobiographical literature. We do not know what or how much her father knew about the truth of Dickens, but Amat does know:

> My father did not know that the realist novels of Dickens were classified as such for their excess of personal and autobiographical information. Perhaps my father feared, deep down, that I would end up writing like Dickens (*Ibid.*).

What a marvelous game of mirrors! By committing a purely imaginary parricide she becomes the guardian of the royal destiny of her father and, together with her two siblings, deprived of their mother's consolation, they fulfill for their father the redemptive mission of keeping the dead mother alive at the same time that they keep her closed up within the walls of the library. Trying to oppose him, trying to commit parricide, she ends up by fulfilling her own desire which is the desire of the Other: to write autobiographical novels like Dickens and to teach, carrying on the paternal request, the mysteries of the librarian's profession.

VLADIMIR NABOKOV: HOW WOULD THE WORLD BE WITHOUT ME?

1. The Delights of Childhood Memory

Let there be no doubt: it should be easy to find examples that do not confirm (or, that *infirm*, as the epistemologists say nowadays) Julio Cortázar's hypothesis, that is, to find people and writers whose first memories do not have the "terrifying" nature of the rooster at dawn. I confess that I have enthusiastically looked for them. I thought I had found a counter-example in Virginia Woolf, before distinguishing between epiphanies and memories, and I now submit that I have indeed found an author in whom the delight in memory knows no limits and in whom childhood dread appears to be lacking: Vladimir Vladimirovich Nabokov (born in St. Petersburg, Russia in 1899; died in Montreux, Switzerland, 1977).[133] His autobiography is, perhaps, from a strictly literary point of view, the most beautiful ever written: a definitive model for the "genre."

---

133 Nabokov, Vladimir, *Speak, Memory: An Autobiography Revisited.*
   (From here on: *S,M*). New York: Alfred A. Knopf, Inc., 1999.

The beginning of the narrative, chapter one, could well have been given the title, "A perfect childhood in a perfect world."[134] The author takes care to exhibit a detailed map of his parents' three vast estates in Vyra where he passed a large part of his bucolic childhood and photographs of the impressive family mansion of pink granite, Italianate style, in the noble city of St. Petersburg. The year of his birth, 1899, makes it easy to calculate his age of eighteen at the time of the October Revolution, when his world of comfort and privilege fell apart. The first five years of his childhood speak of vacations in Italy and Germany, of a parade of tutors who instructed him in different Western languages, and his learning of how to write in English before Russian, of his family's aristocratic German origins on his paternal grandmother's side, of the wealth of his mother and the nobility of his father, the ideal man, the father of Hamlet risen from the dead, an exceptional human being who lived far above the rest of mortal men.

Let us review first what is manifest in the text, without giving away the surprise that awaits us in the end. Nabokov's supposed first clear memory, the one with which he feels he was born into life, took place on one of his mother's birthdays.[135] At that time, dated with rigorous exactitude, he managed to associate the idea of his four years of age to the twenty-seven years of his mother and the thirty-three years of his father. At the age of eight, he tells us, a severe illness "mysteriously abolished the rather monstrous gift of numbers that had made me a child prodigy" (93). When his mother celebrated her twenty-seventh birthday his sense of time was born; that day he understood that he had been inserted into history . . . history that, for the poor Joyce, was a nightmare from which he

---

134. In fact, the chapter appeared for the first time in *The New Yorker* magazine, April 15, 1950, under the title, "Perfect Past" which was eliminated for the definitive edition ("Foreword," p. 4).

135. In an introduction to the 1999 Knopf edition, Brian Boyd states without reservation that the first chapter "revolves around the first memory that Nabokov believes dates to one of his mother's birthdays" (p. 15).

would have liked to awaken; for the pampered Nabokov, it was a sweet dream that protected him from the history that would later crash down on him in an ominous way. He maintained a profound interest in the age of his parents for many years as the statistics served as a personal reference: "like a nervous passenger asking the time in order to check a new watch" (11). Let us put aside for the moment the information regarding calendar dates, birthdays, the "official" time, and "my first gleam of complete consciousness." All without betraying any hints or signs of death.

Whereas Cortázar formulates a universal proposition that links memory with terror of daybreaks, Nabokov formulates another, diametrically opposed to that of the Argentine writer:

> I may be inordinately fond of my earliest impressions, but then I have reason to be grateful to them [. . .] Nothing is sweeter or stranger than to ponder those first thrills. They belong to the harmonious world of a perfect childhood and, as such, possess a naturally plastic form in one's memory, which can be set down with hardly any effort; it is only starting with the recollections of one's adolescence that Mnemosyne begins to get choosy and crabbed (*S,M*, 13).

There is nothing in Nabokov of the initial horrors of a child born in exile, transported by the winds of history (Brussels, Barcelona, Buenos Aires), surrounded by the strange atmosphere of an apocalyptic war. The young Vladimir senses that "Russian children of my generation" (all equal to him?) lived through a radiant, wonderful period in which they could form impressions of the world in a privileged way, as if destiny were making an effort to reward those children, giving them more than they deserved "in view of the cataclysm that was to remove completely the world they had known" (*S,M*, 14).

This is not an opinion that was shared by another great Russian "writer" who was persecuted by a tragic destiny: Lev Davidovich Bronstein, a plebian Jew, far removed from the imperial capital.

Childhood is looked upon as the happiest time of life. Is that always true? No, only a few have a happy childhood. The idealization of childhood originated in the old literature of the privileged. A secure, affluent, and unclouded childhood, spent in a home of inherited wealth and culture, a childhood of affection and play, brings back to one memories of a sunny meadow at the beginning of the road of life. [. . .] But the majority of the people, if it looks back at all, sees, on the contrary, a childhood of darkness, hunger and dependence. Life strikes the weak—and who is weaker than a child?[136]

Nor is this what we find in another notable poet, also Russian, Jewish, and exiled, Joseph Brodsky. He begins his autobiography recounting two childhood memories that have nothing to do with idyllically staying at home. Rather, they portray his initiation into the art of "estrangement" when he became aware of his identity among strangers, reciting the Marxist catechism or having to define himself as a Jew in the classroom: "The real history of consciousness starts with one's first lie."[137]

Nabokov's past was idyllic and he is tireless in praising the perfection of his memory and of the memories of his mother and father, which he describes as distinctive features. For example his father remembers the exact date—August 17, 1883—when he caught a rare butterfly, a date that his son keeps (why?) in his autobiography. And for all that, he is capable of writing:

The act of vividly recalling a patch of the past is something that I seem to have been performing with the utmost zest all my life, and I have reason to believe that this almost pathological keenness of the retrospective faculty is a hereditary trait (p. 55).

136. Trotsky, Leon. *My Life: An Attempt at an Autobiography*. Mineola, New York: Dover Publications, Inc., 2007, p. 1.
137. Brodsky, Joseph. *Less Than One: Selected Essays*. New York: Farrar, Straus, Giroux, 1988, p. 7.

Nabokov's memory is a sanctuary, a sacred space to fall back on in order to regain strength in the difficult times that life has not spared him. He insists on treating the years of his childhood as objects that have been preserved in a pure state, immune to usury, degradation or falsification. His memory is a jar of formaldehyde. His memories remain there embalmed and incorruptible:

> I see again my schoolroom in Vyra, the blue roses of the wallpaper, the open window. Its reflection fills the val mirror above the leathern couch where my uncle sits, looking with odd satisfaction at a tattered book. A sense of security, of well-being, of summer warmth pervades my memory. That robust reality makes a ghost of the present. The mirror brims with brightness; a bumblebee has entered the room and bumps against the ceiling. Everything is as it should be, nothing will ever change, nobody will ever die (*S,M*, p. 56).

The marvelous memories are classified and filed in order; there is an unrestrained passion revealed in his philatelic collection that is like the album of his memory; almost as dominating as Nabokov's other passion: that of catching, pinning and cataloguing butterflies. This passion, also inherited, began when he was six years old and lasted throughout his life. His enthusiasm for moths and butterflies was overwhelming: "The longing to describe a new species completely replaced that of discovering a new prime number" (*S,M*, p. 93). Such vehement eagerness could not fail to yield rewards: we are informed of certain species that now bear his name: the *Cyclargus* Nabokov (*S,M*, p. 47) and the *Eupithecia nabokovi* (*S,M*, p. 95). With pride he invites his readers to see his collections of lepidopterans at the American Natural History Museum in New York and the Cornell University Museum. The reminiscences are converted into literary material and the butterflies are preserved forever, immobile. *Retrieved*: torn from memory and nature. *Encoded*: once and forever.

Heaven forbid that anyone should want to contaminate the

entomologist and the memory-gifted writer with suggestions of erotic impurities or psychoanalytic secretions; from the beginning of his autobiography Nabokov roars his impatience in this respect:

> Let me say at once that I reject completely the vulgar, shabby, fundamentally medieval world of Freud, with its crankish quest for sexual symbols [. . .] and its bitter little embryos spying, from their natural nooks, upon the love life of their parents (*S,M*, p. 10).

There is too much vehemence in his protest. As if he wanted to take precautions against being reminded of the only dream he describes in detail in his autobiography, a dream for which it is unnecessary that one be a psychoanalyst nor abandon oneself to the calm pleasure of formulating "daring" interpretations in order to understand what it is about. Here, in his inimitable prose, is his account, to be savored for its every word:

> Soon after the wardrobe affair I found a spectacular moth, marooned in a corner of a vestibule window, and my mother dispatched it with ether. In later years, I used many killing agents, but the least contact with the initial stuff would always cause the porch of the past to light up and attract that blundering beauty. Once, as a grown man, I was under ether during appendectomy, and with the vividness of a decalcomania picture I saw my own self in a sailor suit mounting a freshly emerged Emperor moth under the guidance of a Chinese lady who I knew was my mother. It was all there, brilliantly reproduced in my dream, while my own vitals were being exposed: the soaking, ice-cold absorbent cotton pressed to the insect's lemurian head; the subsiding spasms of its body; the satisfying crackle produced by the pin penetrating the hard crust of its thorax; the careful insertion of the point of the pin in the cork-bottomed groove of the spreading board; the

symmetrical adjustment of the thick, strong-veined wings under neatly affixed strips of semitransparent paper (*S,M*, p. 91).

Who or what is this "blundering beauty" attracted by ether,
immobilized, pierced by the pin, providing ineffable jouissance to
the person who "mounts" and "penetrates" its "hard shell"?

Reader of this dream, you can, if you wish, maintain your
Nabokovian candor. There would be nothing to interpret in this
dream if the person who narrates it did not have associations, or
if these associations did not jump out at the reader. The rest of
us—yes, the perverted ones inasmuch as we are spellbound and
bewitched by Nabokov's graceful prose—we would have nothing
more to add. We would simply ask to hear the narrative once more,
and we would ask if the dream had anything to do with the precocious lover of butterflies, with the contention of aggressive impulses,
or with displacement—over an innocent "marooned moth—of a
libido (libido? how "crankish!") that has absolutely no—the last
straw!—sexual content. Perhaps, as readers with limited ingenu-
ity, we might suggest that *Lolita* (1958), the novel that was written
during the same period as *Speak, Memory* (1947–1960), did not just
appear out of the blue.

It might seem that these digressions have led us astray of the
topics of memory and first recollections. It is now time to return
and see how this incursion into the realm of dreams was not in
vain. We have already established the relationship between the
passion for butterflies and the pleasures of memory, a memory
that is as encoded as the butterflies are pinned to the spread-
ing board. "I witness with pleasure the supreme achievement of
memory, which is the masterly use it makes of innate harmonies
when gathering to its fold the suspended and wandering tonalities
of the past" (*S,M*, pp. 131–132).

Nothing has been lost. By the grace of an unmarred memory,
the recollections peacefully hibernate and can be removed from
the storeroom to be defrosted every time they are required for
greedy reminiscence. The marvelous past is retrieved every time

it is summoned by the genie of the lamp. An enviable situation indeed. Let us now return to the pleasant first memory, recognized as such by Nabokov and his exegetes: that of the jouissance Nabokov derived from locating himself in time in relation to the ages of his parents, his passion for evoking his memories in an orderly fashion with points of reference "like someone nervously checking a new watch."

2. Chronophobia

Nabokov is the evangelist of nostalgia. Before the robust reality of the past, the present is a specter and nothing can change, no one has to die. Time has not dissolved: the soap bubbles that fascinated the child have not popped; everything is there, at hand. Indeed, time does not exist:

> I confess I do not believe in time. I like to fold my magic carpet, after use, in such a way as to superimpose one part of the pattern upon another. Let visitors trip. And the highest enjoyment of timelessness—in a landscape selected at random—is when I stand among rare butterflies and their food plants. This is ecstasy, and behind the ecstasy is something else, which is hard to explain. It is like a momentary vacuum into which rushes all that I love (*S,M*, p. 106).

Nabokov uses *memory against time*. The Pascalian fear of the eternal silence of infinite spaces finds in Nabokov an exact counterpart of anxiety over lived time, an inner truth that does not need to take into account the stellar magnitudes. He suffers because he knows—through others, we could say—that life is "only a brief crack of light between two eternities of darkness." This is in the first sentence of *Speak, Memory*, immediately following "The cradle rocks above an abyss." Nabokov cannot resist calculating that death approaches at a speed of forty-five hundred heartbeats an hour (to count, to count everything, "arithmania," according to the classics of psychiatry) and he senses that the eternity that follows death is horrific. The entire beautiful and extensive book is a treatise against time. He speaks of two eternities of darkness and affirms—following Tolstoy, although he does not seem to be aware of it—that there is also a "prenatal abyss." This is all stated in the first eight lines of the autobiography. Immediately, without starting a new paragraph, he launches into a description of the first memory of the book, a memory he prefers to attribute to an "other," someone who is not himself:

> I know, however, of a young chronophobiac who experienced something like panic when looking for the first time at homemade movies that had been taken a few weeks before his birth. He saw a world that was practically unchanged— the same house, the same people—and then realized that he did not exist there at all and that nobody mourned his absence. He caught a glimpse of his mother waving from an upstairs window, and that unfamiliar gesture disturbed him, as if it were some mysterious farewell. But what particularly frightened him was the sight of a brand-new baby carriage standing there on the porch, with the smug, encroaching air of a coffin; even that was empty, as if, in the reverse course of events, his very bones had disintegrated (*S,M*, p. 9).

This is Vladimir Nabokov's first memory—president-for-life of his life and work. *This foundational memory is so precocious it is prenatal.* In his case, in contrast to the other writers who have been our witnesses up to this point, one cannot nor would any-one want to hide the fact that the memory has been fabricated. Subsequently we are distracted by its source: it is an enormously significant phantasy, precisely because it does not try to pass it-self off as a reproduction of a real event. It is a "first memory" of something that never took place, implausible and, for this reason, truly terrifying, a genuine nightmare. It is certainly Nabokov's first, according to the place it occupies as preamble to his auto-biography. But why am I skeptical about his affirmation that the memory is not his own but rather borrowed? Who would the young chronophobiac be if not the writer himself who describes in such detail the home of someone he "knows of"? Who else but Nabokov could be the "young chronophobiac"? Who knows "chronophobiacs" and not mere men and women worn down by age and certainty about death? Who has known anyone deserving of that epithet? I admit that it is a strange condition. Upon carefully reading the autobiography one sees that it is necessary to read a great deal of the text in order to learn that the supreme *jouissance* of the writer is that of *timelessness* and to arrive, 140 pages later, at the confession, already foreshadowed, that Nabokov did not believe in time and could not reconcile himself to the idea of impermanence. Like the young poet who accompanied Freud—almost certainly Rilke—in the short and beautiful text entitled, precisely, *Vergänglichkeit.*[138]

Cortazarian dread present in Nabokov's writing occurs as fear vis-à-vis a precarious existence that could dissolve into nothing, like our childhood paradise lost. In the beginning there was the corpse: the voyage into the past leads him to find the dust of his bones in a baby carriage that has never even been used yet, in a (funereal) wagon that awaits him as his mother waves goodbye. Memory and butterflies have to save him from that original phantom that precedes and governs existence. We have not even turned the first page of the autobiography and we already find Nabokov picketing Nature, who imposes these conditions: "Over and over again, my mind has made colossal efforts to distinguish the faintest glimmers in the impersonal darkness on both sides of my life" (*S,M*, p. 9). He knows that this darkness is provoked by nothing other than the walls of time; he knows that against them he will only bruise his impotent fists. He desperately seeks a way

---

138. Freud, Sigmund [1916]. "On Transience," in *Character and Culture: Psychoanalysis applied to anthropology, mythology, folklore, literature, and culture in general.* Editor, Philip Rieff. New York: Collier Books, 1963, pp. 148–151.

to escape, to flee from time, and he discovers "that the prison of time is spherical and without exits. Short of suicide, I have tried everything" (*S,M*, p. 10).

Now we understand the consoling function of the parade of screen memories that crowd his speaking memory; the entire album helps him keep distance from the frightened young chronophobiac who cannot even admit that he is himself. Nonetheless, in this text of extraordinary beauty, there he is. Nabokov's memory pierces and pins the fluttering memories to cork boards. The strategy that he uses to keep death away is itself mortal. Memory—his memory—lives in order to feed his phantasy. What occurs to the great novelist is both sublime and pathetic, the creator of immortal characters such as Ada, Pnin, Sebastian Knight and his brother, Humbert Humbert and Lolita, and so many others: every time he stirs up one of his own memories and passes it on to one of the characters in his novels he confirms the fleeting nature of memory as it is transferred to paper and the world of fiction. Life fades as it is told. In his mind the memory persists, but it grows languid and cold, it loses its magic and ends up better in print as part of a novel than it is in his memory. The houses where he lived, once they have been described by the artist, collapse without a sound in his memory, like in the old silent movies. Reading this narrative of the man who lives with such joy and the artist, learning of the sense of dispossession that art produces in life, I could not help but recall Poe's story, "The Oval Portrait," the story of the painter who gradually deprives his model of spirit as the painting of her comes to life, until the culminating moment, when the painting is completed, perfect, and the model is also finished, dead.

The ink is still wet on the posthumously published collection of essays by Winfried G. Sebald (1946–2001).[139] The acclaimed German writer, author of the great contemporary novel on memory, *Austerlitz* [2001], begins an essay on Nabokov with a broad reference to the "young chronophobiac" of the first paragraph in *Speak,*

---

139. Sebald, W.G. *Campo Santo*. Translated by Anthea Bell. New York: Random House, 2005, pp. 141–149.

Memory, and points out the effects that the anticipation of death has on the viewer of images taken before his birth: he is transformed into a kind of ghost who, even before having been born, lives among his own family, a specter of the flesh yet to come. Without acknowledging what I have deduced—that the description of the memory corresponds to one of Nabokov's own phantasies—he highlights that the writer's preoccupation with the ephemeral nature of existence underlies his passion for moths and butterflies. Nabokov's entire narrative is infiltrated, according to Sebald, by the impression that our terrestrial actions are being observed by other species "not yet known to any system of taxonomy" and whose emissaries often assume the role of guests in the comedies we participate in as actors. For this reason, Sebald believes, the characters of the Russian novelist, master of the English language, have a surreal consistency and the episodes he narrates have the texture of dreams. They all tread the border separating life from the world beyond, alluding to the world of his childhood which disappeared without leaving a trace in the October Revolution. Sebald is also of the opinion, as I am, that despite the precision of his memories (or, perhaps, precisely because of their exactitude) Nabokov, deep down, questions whether that childhood Arcadia ever really existed. That paradise lost is a retroactive product of exile and of the hardships of work and birth pains. In my view, the original Eden of which his memory of those early years speaks is itself a butterfly that wishes to fly away and therefore he must pierce it with pins and mount it on pedestals of style. It is of the utmost importance for him to preserve it in death, with the illusion of life, fixed to a cork board, splayed among the pages of his books. Sebald remarks:

> Nabokov also knew, better than most of his fellow writers, that the desire to suspend time can prove its worth only in the most precise re-evocation of things long overtaken by oblivion (Op. cit., p. 145).

The clarity of his memories is equal to the careful mounting of long sought-after specimens, laboriously hunted during uncountable arduous hours of recomposing the lines he had written.

Nabokov's objective is clear: to immobilize the wings of fleeting time, fixing them in memory, trapped through the magic of ether, with sharp well-aimed paragraphs. To kill the dead figure of Moses, the legislator, sculpting his perfect image, "consuming the marble so that the statue grows,"[140] and then deliver a hammer blow to the knee, ordering him: *E adesso, parla! Speak, memory!*

I mentioned in passing that the image of the two eternities, one previous and the other following birth, does not belong to Nabokov but to his literary father, Leo Tolstoy. It is appropriate to recall in detail the words of the legendary writer as he describes his first memory, an additional confirmation of Julio Cortázar's hypothesis. In the pages of his autobiography, written at the age of fifty, we read:

It is strange and terrible to think that from my birth to three years of age, during which time I nursed, was weaned, began to crawl, walk, and talk, I cannot find any other impression than these two, no matter how much I may rummage in my brain. When did I begin? When did I begin to live? Why is it pleasurable for me to represent myself then, and why has it been terrible, even as it is terrible to many, to represent myself at the time when I shall again enter into that condition of death, from which there will be no recollections expressible in words? Did I not live then, when I learned to look, hear, understand, talk, when I slept, sucked the breast, and kissed the breast, and laughed, and my mother was happy? I lived and lived blissfully. Was it not then that I acquired everything I now live by, and that I acquired so much, so rapidly, that in all my remaining life I have not acquired one-hundredth part of it? From the time I was five years old until now there is but one step. From birth until five years of age there is an

---

140. Buonarotti, Michelangelo. *Poesie*. Milan: Adelphi, 1996.

enormous distance. From the germ to the new-born child there is an abyss. And from non-existence to the germ there is not merely an abyss, but incomprehensibility.[141]

One anticipates and fears the eternity that follows the period from which it is possible to remember, when the sensation of succession in time will no longer be possible. However, it is impossible to even imagine what so vexed Nabokov: time congealed, empty and infinite time preceding birth, time that separates the embryo from nothingness. It is a supra-individual time: that of silent gestation in a world of speaking beings who, little by little, make way for an obscure desire from which we are descended, burdened as we are with a genetic memory, a collective memory and a history manifested in language, laws, institutions and expectations that we have to make our own, that we will have to appropriate for ourselves through a pronoun that is also imposed on us: "I." Nabokov is an activist picketing against Nature. In the end, his is a rebellion against language, against mortality and against the alienation that is induced by the word: How can there have been a before, and how can there ever be an afterworld without me? Will there be newspapers the day after my death? Will my life have been "a futile passion"?

Tolstoy, as I forewarned, also makes a contribution to the hypothesis of this book, the hypothesis put forward by the Argentine who as chance would have it was born in Brussels. Here is his narrative, which will require no further commentary:

Here are my first recollections (which I am unable to put in order, as I do not know what was first and what later. Of some of them *I do not even know whether they happened in a dream or in reality*). I am tied; I want to straighten out my arms, and I cannot do so, and I cry and weep, and the cry is unpleasant

141. Tolstoy, Count Lev N. Tolstóy. *The Complete Works of Count Tolstóy. Volume XXIII. Miscellaneous Letters and Essays.* "First Recollections (1878)." Translated from the Russian by Leo Wiener. Boston: Dana Estes & Company, 1905, p. 4–5.

to me; but I cannot stop. Somebody is bending over me, I do not know who. All this is in semidarkness. But I remember that there were two of them. My cry affects them: they are agitated by my cry, but they do not untie me, which I want them to do, and I cry louder still. It seems to them that that must be (that is, that I should be tied), whereas I know that it need not be, and I want to prove it to them, and I burst into an irrepressible cry, which disgusts me with myself. I feel the injustice and cruelty, not of men, because they take pity upon me, but of fate, and I feel pity for myself. I do not know and shall never know what it was: whether they swaddled me when I was a suckling babe and I tried to get my arms free, or whether they swaddled me when I was more than a year old, to keep me from scratching off a scab; *it may be that I have brought together a number of impressions, as is the case in a dream, but this much is sure—it was my first and most powerful impression of my life.* And what I remember is not my cry, my sufferings, but the complication, the contradictoriness of my impression. I want freedom—it does not hurt anybody, and I, who need strength, am weak, and they are strong (Tolstoy, op. cit., 3–4, my italics).

My commentary, as I said, will be succinct: Cortázar's affirmation is unambiguously corroborated by this initiation into memory. It would be superfluous to review the life and work of Leo Tolstoy in order to know how, in its relation to literature, political power, his family and conjugal life, the society of his times and the entire history of his long years, the ghost of liberty has played out. This first sensation of impotence and rebellion against the powers of fate was preserved like a scar. His life, plagued by failed but noble undertakings, like death in a dark train station, expresses helplessness in the face of surrounding oppressive forces which—as is stated in the childhood memory—are not even lacking in comprehension. Seeing the contrast between such sublime impotence and such longing for liberty almost provides reason to throw oneself, like Anna Karenina, on the railroad tracks. Or, like Bezukhov, in *War and Peace*, to risk one's own life and end up in chains, imprisoned for trying to kill Napoleon, the tyrant.

Phantasy, dream or memory. Anticipation or retroactive memory. No one can ever know for sure. Nor could anyone doubt the terror and role as fulcrum it plays in joining the two parts of Tolstoy's life and art, just as it is a fulcrum that connects him to his literary descendent, Vladimir Nabokov.

10

ELIAS CANETTI: THE KNIFE ON THE TONGUE[142]

*It is incredible how the written sentence can calm and tame a man.
The sentence is always something different* (ein anderes) *from
the man writing it.*[143]

1. The Tongue Condemned

Biographical information indicates that Elias Canetti [1905–1994]
was an Austrian writer of Sephardic origins. He was, more accurately, a literary transnational, the paradigmatic transhumant
writer who carried within him the saliva of all Central European
languages which he displayed in his writing. He was the author
of a single and celebrated novel written in German—his adopted
language—(*Auto-da-Fé*, 1935), of many essays and an autobiography in three volumes. This autobiography does not begin in the
usual way with an account of who his parents were or the date and

---

142. Elias Canetti was born in Bulgaria in July, 1905, and died in Zurich
in 1994. In 1981 he was awarded the Nobel Prize for Literature. *The
Tongue Set Free: Remembrance of a European Childhood* [1977] (*Die gerettete
Zunge—Geschichte einer Jugend*) is the first volume of his autobiography.
Translated from the German by Joachim Neugroschel. New York:
Continuum, 1983.
143. Canetti, Elias [1976]. *The Conscience of Words*. Translated from the
German by Joachim Neugroschel. New York: The Seabury Press,
1979, p. 40.

circumstances of his birth. He narrates his life without prologues or warnings, but with an account of his first and initiatory memory. The opening lines of *The Tongue Set Free* read as follows:

> My earliest memory is dipped in red. I come out of a door on the arm of a maid, the floor in front of me is red, and to the left a staircase goes down, equally red. Across from us [. . .] a smiling man steps forth, walking towards me in a friendly way. He steps right up close to me, halts, and says: "Show me your tongue." I stick out my tongue, he reaches into his pocket, pulls out a jackknife, opens it, and brings the blade all the way to my tongue. He says: "Now we'll cut off his tongue." I don't dare pull back my tongue, he comes closer and closer, the blade will touch me any second. In the last moment, he pulls back the knife, saying: "Not today, tomorrow." He snaps the knife shut again and puts it back in his pocket.
>
> Every morning, we step out of the door and into the red hallway, the door opens, and the smiling man appears. I know what he's going to say and I wait for the command to show my tongue. I know he's going to cut it off, and I get more and more scared each time. That's how the day starts, and it happens very often.
>
> I kept it to myself and asked my mother about it only much later. She could tell by the ubiquitous red that it was the guesthouse in Carlsbad, where she had spent the summer of 1907 with my father and me. To take care of the two-year-old baby, she had brought along a nanny from Bulgaria, a girl who wasn't even fifteen. Every morning at the crack of dawn, the girl went out holding the child on her arm; she spoke only Bulgarian, but got along fine in the lively town, and was always back punctually with the child. Once, she was seen on the street with an unknown young man, she couldn't say anything about him, a chance acquaintance. A few weeks later, it turned out that the young man lived in the room right across from us, on the other side of the corridor. At night,

the girl sometimes went to his room quickly. My parents felt responsible for her and sent her back to Bulgaria immediately.

Both of them, the maid and the young man, had always left the house very early in the morning, that's how they must have met, that's the way it must have started. The threat with the knife worked, the child quite literally held his tongue for ten years (*The Tongue Set Free*, cit., pp. 3–4. From now on: *TF*).

In Canetti, the Cortazarian terror is presented with brutal frankness, without any cosmetics. The threat of mutilation is direct. The pressure and extortion are backed up by the exhibition of the sharp instrument of amputation and its closeness to the condemned organ. The terror imposed on the child achieves its goals. The ten years of silence prove that it was not a mere threat; the child, effectively, lost his tongue and only regained it when he could tell the story of the knife to his mother, which only happened after woeful misadventures and successive exiles. In the first exile, in England, his father suddenly died at the age of thirty-one, possibly driven to suicide by the infidelity of his wife, or by some other unbearable emotional stress, when Elias was seven years old. This traumatic incident, which we will return to, was a turning point, one that had a profound influence on him throughout his life as a writer.

The first volume of the autobiography is entitled *Die gerettete Zunge*, which means "the tongue saved," or "set free" or, as in the Spanish version, "absolved." The title lends itself to a misunderstanding in different European languages because "tongue" is both an organ in the mouth with which words are articulated and it is the language or dialect that a person speaks. Everyone agrees that Canetti is a writer whose work springs from the intricate linguistic amalgam that characterized the situation in which he grew up. His "mother tongue" was Ladino, the language spoken by Sephardic Jews. The birth of the writer into his definitive language, German, "my second mother tongue"—as he would say later—was caused by the bloody intervention of his own mother.

Literary critics almost always relate the "tongue" in the book's title to Canetti's masterful writing, his gift for languages, his linguistic versatility, and his exceptional command of the German language. However, the episode with the Bulgarian maid makes clear that the threatened tongue—saved, set free, or absolved—is the one that is in the mouth, surrounded by teeth.

The two meanings of the word tongue make it possible to understand the title of the first book of the autobiography in two ways, both legitimate. The title of the second book is less catchy: *The Torch in My Ear* (tr. 1982). That the narrative begins with the threat to the *Zunge*, reinforced by placement of the knife up to the moist appendage, indicates that the organic meaning and the traumatic episode itself precede the whole of the narrative and support the nucleus of the hypothesis of my essay: that human memory is initiated by the sensation of terror and the experience of helplessness. In this case, *six* characteristics are of particular importance for this hypothesis. *First*, the framing of the memory does not form part of the memory itself and it has to be the Other (the mother) who fills in this temporal and spatial information (Carlsbad, summer of 1907). *Second*, the memory is a screen for another scene, a scene of lust that the child could not reveal or else he would lose his tongue. *Third*, in this first memory we find displacement onto a random visual element such as color (yellow for Freud, gray for Cortázar, red for Canetti, and blue for García Márquez). *Fourth*, the clarity and definition of the images is outstanding—and for this reason, we might suspect retroactive falsification—for a child just being initiated into the secrets of language. *Fifth*, the scene clearly exposes the situation of abandonment or defenselessness of the child due to the absence of those others who could have spared him this anxiety. *Sixth*, and last, there are elements that screen the horror and sweeten the memory: the potential executioner is "a smiling man [who] steps forth, walking towards me in a friendly way."

Let us highlight a *seventh* characteristic: what is unprecedented in this narrative by Canetti—in contrast to other narratives of "childhood memories"—is the repetition of the scene: it happened "every morning," it was the usual way to start the day. There is a contrast between the smile of the torturer and the constantly increasing terror of the child who knows that the unappealable sentence will be carried out. It is curious that Canetti does not describe a state of anxious expectation that would be a result of this constant stay of execution: "Not today, tomorrow." Considering the author's work and his entire life, as it is presented in biographies and in light of his way of speaking of his own life and work in his autobiography, one might wonder if Canetti did not wake up every morning, every dawn, hearing the ominous sentence, "Now we'll cut off his tongue," followed by, "Not today, tomorrow." There has always been an affinity between the work of Canetti and that of Franz Kafka, and the Austrian writer took pains to highlight this kinship, especially in his only novel, *Auto-da-Fé*. Is not the story of the child sentenced without a trial to a horrible punishment, constantly renewed, a paradigm of Kafkaesque literature, following in the footsteps of *The Penal Colony*? Would there be jouissance—genuine *jouissance*—in waiting for a threat to be carried out that is not carried out "now" but is always deferred, perpetually surviving, knowing that death will arrive but "not today, not yet"? The confession of early morning jouissance proceeds from the author himself: "Finally, and most obsessively, there is death, which I cannot acknowledge though I never ignore it, which I have to hunt down into its very last hiding-place in order to destroy its attraction and its false charisma" (*TF*, 54). To always have it close at hand, in sight.

From this imaginary agony, from this "I die because I do not die"[144] from this manic persecution by the grim reaper (as if it were not death herself, the fascinating pursuer), Canetti tries to distance himself, like Cortázar and almost all the authors we have considered, by writing compulsively. A man like him ". . . would have to either explode or otherwise burst into bits unless he could

---

144. San Juan de la Cruz [1542–1591] (*Stanzas of the Soul*) albalearning.com/audiolibros/sjcruz_coplas-en.html: "Vivo sin vivir en mí, / y de tal manera espero, / que muero, porque no muero."

calm down in a diary" (*TF*, 40, italics in original). Writing, he confesses, is not voluntary; it is a prophylaxis for madness. Books, exhibiting on their covers his name and his fame, function as cotter pins, those small pins that are inserted at the ends of axles so that the wheels do not fall off. If the cotter pin is lost, if the possibility of controlling the imbalance of the spirit by the magic of careful, perfectionist composition of the word, he will have to be committed. The clear-cut option: write or die (or go mad).

The tongue has been mortgaged against the threat hanging over it. The story, only comprehensible later (*nachträglich*) for the child who, at that moment, cannot understand what is happening between the smiling young man and the Bulgarian maid, will eventually reveal its sexual underpinnings. The presence of the law is conspicuous: because a transgression has been committed one cannot speak or the tongue will be extirpated. This law is even more glaringly apparent when the sentence is executed and the girl is sent back to Bulgaria, not because of something having to do with the child; no, he knew how to keep quiet, but because the parents of Canetti "felt responsible for her."

What did the boy see that he could not tell? What did he hear of the meeting between the two young people? How did he fit himself into the spectacle of the two lovers? As a witness, what enjoyment did he get out of that "original scene"? Nothing in his memory seems anguished except the affirmation, "I know he's going to cut it off, and I get more and more scared each time." It is the banished tongue (the tongue?) of the poet in the making that will have to liberate itself through writing.

However, the central event in his memory, the beating heart of Canetti's life, is not this distressing first memory but rather the inexplicable death of his father, as we saw earlier, when he was seven years old. The relation between this event and the sinister smiling young man with the knife seems evident and I would like to demonstrate that. Only now, the words of curiosity emanate from the child and the person whose tongue is imprisoned behind closed lips or deceitful lips is the mother.

First, it will be helpful to have some background information. The mother "fell ill" a year after the family moved from
Bulgaria to England (1912) and as "the English air didn't agree
with her" she went to an Austrian sanatorium to recover. There
she discovered that she did not want to return to England. She
was excited by her discovery of Strindberg's plays and enjoyed
the company of a doctor who fell in love with her to the point
of proposing marriage and pressuring her not to return to her
family. Although she did not reciprocate this love—at least, according to her—she asked her husband for permission to delay
her return and remain in the sanatorium, until he sent her a
telegram requesting that she come home. In her letters and upon
her return, she informed her husband of her health progress as
well as—out of *noblesse oblige*—her affair with the doctor. When
she returned at last, Canetti's father subjected his wife to a tor-
turous nighttime interrogation from which they both emerged
furious and no longer speaking to one another: ". . . every answer
he received added to his jealousy. He insisted that she had made
herself culpable, he refused to believe her and saw her answers
as lies" (*TF*, 59). The following morning the father was playing
with his children; he said some trivial words. For Canetti, they
were the most memorable words of his life: they were the last he
heard his father pronounce. The master of the house when he
was finished playing, went down to breakfast. He took up the
newspaper, saw the headlines announcing another war in the
Balkans and, moments later, collapsed on the floor with his wife
wailing by his side, in the belief that he was pretending in order
to punish her. She demanded that he talk to her. Hours later, his
mother furiously reproached the little Elias for having fun when
his father lay dead: "Her shouts pushed Father's death into me,
and it has never left me since" (*TF*, p. 56).

Then began a game that Canetti does not dare interpret, but
I do. I should mention that Canetti (like Nabokov and, to a certain degree, Borges) was a determined enemy of psychoanalysis
all through his life, particularly regarding Freudian claims about

the Oedipus complex.[145] As a good disciple of Karl Kraus, Canetti never ceased to sarcastically lance the thinking and work of Freud as well as the pretension of psychoanalysis that it can provide treatment for psychological suffering.

I have mentioned the game played between son and mother, a game that consisted in a police interrogation of the death of the father and husband, a game of eliciting ephemeral confessions that planted doubts to the point of extracting a new confession. These inquisitions were genuine torture (*jouissance*—if they did not "enjoy" them, why would they have repeated them?) for both of them and they reenacted the scene in the bedroom the night before the father died, with the son taking his father's place. It is clear that for twenty-three years they both delighted in the vicious game of half-truths and total lies until, when Elias was already thirty years old and after the publication of *Auto-da-Fé*,—which thrilled the mother—she provided a story that Canetti viewed, finally, as definitive, "the final version, which I still believe today" (*TF*, 58). These words should be appreciated for their true value: he does not consider them a *true* version; they are only an object of belief. He may not be convinced of their truth because they are temporal ("still") and unreliable. Previously he had reported, in words that "sank into me as though Father had spoken them personally [. . .] as though they were a dangerous secret," (58–59) the version that his father had died on that sad morning from the shock of learning that another war had begun and that many people would die. Canetti searches for a consoling explanation but, in what almost amounts to a confession to himself, he recognizes that he does not want to find it: "I *could* not recognize any cause for his death, and so it was better for me if none were found" (*TF*, p. 57, italics in original).

---

145. On Canetti's dissenting views on Freud—the new version of the father— see the second volume of his memoirs: *The Torch in My Ear* (1921–1931). Translated by Joachim Neugroschel. New York: Farrar Straus Giroux, 1982. "It was clear to me that I needed him as an adversary. But the fact that he served as a kind of model for me—this was something that no one could have made me see at that time" (p. 122).

In response to his questions, the mother's initial answers were "he couldn't understand," and, later, others that revealed " 'considerations' because of my youth." The contradictory versions follow one after another; each proving the lie of the previous one:

My mother always smiled when she suddenly said: "I only told you that at the time because you were too young. You couldn't have understood." I feared that smile [*ah, the smile of the forked tongue!*], it was different from her usual smile, which I loved . . . She realized she was smashing me to bits when she told me anything new about my father's death. She was cruel and she liked doing it, thereby getting back at me for the jealousy with which I made her life difficult.

My memory has stored up all the versions of that account, *I can't think of anything I have retained more faithfully.* Perhaps some day I can write them all down completely. They would make a book, an entire book, but now I am following other trails (*TF*, p. 58, the phrase in brackets and the italics are mine).

Canetti kept his tongue quiet for ten years before he told his mother of the childhood episode. His mother was even more persistent and told her last story to her son, not necessarily the true one, twenty-three years after the mysterious death of his father. Throughout those years, the boy, the adolescent, the young writer—all of them—successively pursued the same implacable question begun on that fateful morning in 1912. He repeated the scene of the interrogation by the father who, driven by jealousy, rejected the answers he received from his wife and demanded a confession, knowing that, in any case, he would not be satisfied and his anxieties and detective's sadism would only worsen. Dostoevsky in "The Gentle Creature," Schnitzler, Stefan Zweig and, no doubt, Strindberg, all explored the ins and outs of jealousy and passion. In this case, Canetti, in the place of Hamlet, the son.

Since nothing preoccupied me so much as this death, I lived full of trust at various stages. I finally settled into my mother's last version, making myself at home in it, cleaving to every detail as though it came from a Bible, referring anything that happened in my environment to that version, simply everything that I read or thought. My father's death was at the center of every world I found myself in. When I learned something new a few years later, the earlier world collapsed around me like a stage set . . . (*TF*, pp. 57–58).

Canetti, blind to Freudian hypotheses about Oedipus, so resistant to accepting them, so skeptically Krausian, is, after the death of his father, ferociously possessive with Matilde Arditi, the widowed mother who is disposed to do anything for her son, but who is not really heartbroken.

2. Writing (:) The Mother's Wish

Canetti exhibits a complex that is more that of Hamlet than of Oedipus. He tries to redeem himself for his own sins by attributing them to the wishes of his mother . . . who is very much involved. The only version of his father's death that satisfies and pacifies him is the one his mother tells him in 1935. It is appropriate to recall the context of this final "confession." For his mother, "universal literature, which was dominant, came to constitute the real meaning of life." Nonetheless, Matilde Arditi opposed the will of his father who, just when the boy reached the ill-fated age of seven, began to give him books (in English) and to speak with him at night about what he had read. "I have a solemn memory of these hours" (*TF*, p. 41), the writer comments. His mother's opposition to his reading ("That was the period when I liked my mother least" (*TF*, p. 40)) took place just before she traveled to the sanatorium in Austria for treatment, where the doctor taught her to love Strindberg. I will not enter into a lengthy discussion of the theme of jealousy in Strindberg (*Son of a Servant*) nor of his play, *The Father*. The reader, if he or she wishes, may refer to these works to uncover clues to Matilde Canetti's passion. I will only recall a few words in this respect found in, *The Tongue Set Free*:

> At this point, the jealousy that tortured me all my life com-
> menced, and the force with which it came over me marked
> me forever. It became my true passion, utterly heedless of
> any attempts at convincing me or pointing out a better way
> (p. 120).

Between them, Canetti's parents would speak in German. They had met in Vienna, where they were both avid theatergoers, but they prohibited the small Elias from learning the German language; it was their secret language. When Jacques Canetti died, Elias's mother endeavored, by force and in just a few days, to familiarize him with (which is not the same as to teach him) the language she had previously forbidden him. Her determina-tion was ferocious to say the least: with unreasonable demands, making fun of his smallest mistakes, deriding him for being an "idiot," and the most injurious comment of all, one that was embedded in his memory, would come after he made a mistake, "Your father knew German too, what would your father say!" (68). Canetti, the child, narrates:

> I fell into an awful despair [. . .] Something happened that I
> still don't understand today. I became as attentive as the devil
> [. . .] She didn't notice that I ate little because of my distress.
> She regarded the terror I lived in as pedagogical. [. . .] the
> most I could attain was her not deriding me. On other days,
> it went less well, and then I trembled, awaiting the "idiot"
> she had brought into the world; that affected me the worst
> (*TF*, pp. 68–69).

The result was that Canetti learned to speak German, the condemned "tongue" which had just been absolved. He was able to communicate with his mother in the same secret language that had previously belonged to his father. Finally he succeeded in receiving her praise, "You are my son, after all" (*TF*, p. 70). Canetti then adds, as if he wanted to preempt doubts about the Oedipus complex he so ardently denied:

> It was only later that I realized it hadn't just been for my sake when she instructed me in German with derision and torment. She herself had a profound need to use German with me, it was the language of her intimacy. [. . .] Her true marriage had taken place in that language. She didn't know what to do, she felt lost without him, and tried as fast as possible to put me in his place. [. . .] So, in a very short time, she forced me to achieve something beyond the strength of any child, and the fact that she succeeded determined the deeper nature of my German; it was a belated mother tongue, implanted in true pain. The pain was not all, it was promptly followed by a period of happiness, and that tied me indissolubly to that language. [. . .] *the language of our love—and what a love it was!—became German* (*TF*, p. 70, my italics).

The letters of the German words flow with the blood of the language. To teach and to learn in such an atmosphere of terror is also the source of a bitter jouissance that can be read in every line of the text: the profound nature of Canetti's language can be found in the pain with which the boy, furious and impotent, scours the dictionaries and enters the labyrinth of words pertaining to the Other, the deceased father, in order to share with his mother the omnipresent ghost. ("The awareness of the death of my father entered me and would never leave me.") Thus we are presented with the mother's final confession: before publishing *Anschluss*, Elias Canetti had just published, his novel *Auto-da-Fé*, during Vienna's dark period, 1935, a chilling story and a masterwork of German literature.

There had been long, heavy struggles between us, and she had often been on the verge of disowning me forever. But now, she said, she understood the struggle that I had waged for my freedom [. . .] The book, which she had read, was flesh of her flesh, she said, she recognized herself in me, she had always viewed people the way I depicted them, that was exactly how she would have wanted to write herself. Her forgiveness was not enough, she went on, she was bowing to me, she acknowledged me doubly as her son, I had become what she had most wanted me to be. [. . .] The thought of her bowing to me because of this novel [. . .] was unendurable [. . .] When I saw her again, she may have felt my shame, embarrassment, and disappointment [. . .] she let herself go and finally told me the whole truth about my father's death. Despite her earlier versions, I had occasionally sensed the facts, but then always reproached myself that the distrust which I had inherited from her was leading me astray (*TF*, p. 60).

Elias's victory is definitive: his mother rewarded him with a certain degree of liberty. How did he accomplish this feat? By adapting to the language and his mother's wishes. His mother had to pay a price: she had to admit to a sin that would put his doubts to rest forever. Was Elias more at ease having learned the truth or because the mother had humiliated and mutilated herself by loosening her tongue and confessing her secret? Was he calmed by having softened the incurable trauma of his father's death or because he had managed, through writing and his recognition as a writer, to gain a name that he had earned, coming from a Bulgarian town and from having grown up amidst a pandemonium of languages? Canetti's writing, he confesses is tranquilizing, a vaccine against madness. The frightful aura of war hangs over his books, the mother against her son, the husband against his wife, which can only end in sacrifice. The titanic battle between the spouses: of Teresa against Kien, of Kien against Teresa, is a desperate struggle around which his books revolve and culminate in the *Auto-da-Fé*, the great burning at the stake from which the novel takes its title.

Perhaps no one would fail to suspect that Canetti, like his father, knew the truth of what happened at the sanatorium. It is not common to hear a militant anti-Freudian say that "I always tried to repress" that truth. It was not rewarding for him to hear his mother tell him "the whole truth"; what was important was that she had given in and humiliated herself. The sadistic game between them had lost sense (and it was displaced to his relationship with his wife, which led him, once again, to identify with the personal drama of Tolstoy; Veza was a very possessive woman whose traits appear, disguised, in the uncanny Teresa of the novel). The ghost of his father, like Hamlet's father wandering on the walls of Elsinore Castle, can find peace thanks to the effective, though symbolic, vengeance of his son.

Between his remote memory—that of Carlsbad when he was two years old—and his most durable memory—the one that he cannot leave in the past, from Manchester when he was seven years old—there is a correspondence and an affinity which couples them. What was he told by the young couple who copulated in his presence in their incomprehensible language? What is the mystery of sex, that mystery that Canetti could not admit until a ridiculous age because his mother continued to deny that children are born after the parents do what the rooster and hen do? Why were they going to cut off his tongue if he told anyone about what he knew was going on between the young man and the Bulgarian maid, between Matilde and Jacques, his parents, between the doctor and his mother in the sanatorium at Reichenbach—which his mother never openly admitted? What happened that night in his parents' bedroom behind doors that were closed to the curious? Why did his father really die, if one doubts that he died from overreacting to the news of the day, as reported in the daily newspaper? Why did everyone who knew Elias suffer from the torture of his compulsive jealousy? How was the recurring threat of his first memory manifested, implacably, in that child of letters whose genitals mattered so little to him because they were never recognized as forming part of his anatomy or of the other's? He could not have been unaware that he possessed unspeakable intimacies that could lead to mutilation—and not just of his tongue: "I know he's going to cut it off." Which knife condemned his tongue (the tongue?) to mutilation every day but "Not today, tomorrow"?

I would like to clarify my ideas in this regard: it is not very plausible (as is always the case with childhood memory) that a two-year-old child would have remembered with such precision a complex dialogue like the one reproduced in this recollection. The first component could be genuinely mnemic (if this adverb and adjective do not constitute a contradiction, accepting the oxymoron): the color red, the stairs, the two lovers, the contrast between the smile and the threat, the dread knife. The second element, which adds coherence to and frames the first, emerges from the mother's story in which "red" recalls Carlsbad, 1907, where a Bulgarian girl was dismissed for carrying on an illicit love affair. The third element is the manner in which this "recollection," which is a phantasy (the "union of things seen and heard," Freud said), became part of what the child knew without having been able to know it, the adultery of his mother, revelatory of the sexual nature of the distant memory. In this way, the first memory is the result of a construction that is doubly *a posteriori*, doubly *après-coup*. The episode of the knife that was pointed at his tongue, the dubious word of his mother and the death of his father establish three facets of the window from which Elias Canetti would view the world.[146]

Returning to our questions: Can the tongue—*Zunge*, in both senses of the word—be considered as the phallus? How did Canetti manage, despite his imposed ignorance of the German language— the intimate language of his parents, prohibited to their son—to

---

146. In this argument I have summarized elements of a fruitful discussion with Daniel Koren, who contributed the essential aspects. My grateful acknowledgement is due to my friend and collaborator.

become a poet and essayist who was awarded the Nobel Prize for his command over the forbidden language?

In addition, the boy's feelings of guilt should be considered, and the means employed to save himself from his feelings of remorse. The best thing for the boy, the adult writer recognized, was not to have recognized any reason for the death of his father (57) and, nonetheless, he was capable of writing an entire book with successive explanations for his incessant investigation. What did he feel when he saw his father stretched out on the floor, close to the fireplace? In the narrative, it would seem that he felt nothing; minutes later he was outside playing with a friend. However, we should not disregard our method of intertextual analysis and, consequently, we find in *The Conscience of Words* (op. cit.):

> The terror at the dead man lying before one gives way to satisfaction: one is not dead oneself. One might have been. But it is the other who lies there. [. . .] It is the feeling that very swiftly takes the upper hand; what was only just terror is now permeated with satisfaction. [. . .] These facts are so dreadful and so naked that they are concealed in every way. Whether a person is ashamed of them or not is crucial for evaluating him. But it changes nothing in the facts themselves. The situation of survival is the central situation of power (pp. 15–16).

The two memories, the distant one and the one with greater impact, join together and form a secret harmony. I believe that both Canetti's life and work derive from the threat against his tongue (a threat that made it possible for the otherwise mediocre Spanish translation of the autobiography to claim to its credit having translated *gerettete* as "absolved": *La lengua absuelta*). His questionable "liberation" is brought about by closing himself up in accordance with the apparent wishes of his mother and his relentless fulfillment of the other's wishes. I would venture to propose that Elias Canetti's "most distant memory," which confirms Cortázar's hypothesis, may be understood in light of the confusion between the two meanings, or senses, of the word "tongue." The first memory, retroactively constructed in relation to the second, is the key and functions in the writer's imagination—an imagination that he would have us believe, like Martha Robles's astute intuition, is an oracle. He will go on to become a writer, he will write in German, he will keep his mother tongue ("ladino"), he will hold his tongue and not speak of many things that he comes to understand, he will keep his tongue silent and express himself through writing, overcoming his phantasies through the letters of the alphabet. The sentence will become sententious. Unrestrained, it will fill thousands of pages of journals, calming him and saving him from self-destruction. He will enjoy writing as a means of keeping his dread at a distance and his tongue safely behind his teeth. Safe from the knife.

11

GEORGES PEREC HAS NO CHILDHOOD MEMORIES[147]

1. The Story of an Orphan, a Child of Words

I think it appropriate, before exploring the twists and turns of
Georges Perec's first memory and the Cortazarian echoes contained
therein, to propose that the reader accompany me on a tour of the
writer's biography and literary production. Perec was a French
novelist who wrote texts that could be difficult and challenging
for even the most assiduous and adept readers. The child of Polish
Jewish immigrants, he died at the early age of 46 (Paris, 1936–1982);
in that brief lifespan, he managed to write some of the most
creative books in post-war French literature (or, dispensing with
superfluous temporal and spatial restrictions, in world literature
of all periods). Perec lost his father on the battlefronts in 1940 and
his mother, arrested in 1942, was deported almost certainly to a
death camp, where her death was undocumented. Both disappeared
without his seeing their bodies or participating in their funeral
rites. The early and virtually unnoticed "disappearance" of his

---

147. In this chapter, in addition to the texts by Perec, I have cited from
articles in the magazine *L'Arc*, no. 76, 1979, and *Magazine Littéraire*,
no. 193, March, 1983, and no. 316, December, 1993, dedicated to
Perec. I have also consulted the extensive and recommendable biography by David Bellos, *Georges Perec: A Life in Words*. Boston: David
R. Godine, 1993.

parents would be recorded in his memory as the crucial event of his life and work. In 1956, in a military cemetery, as an adolescent, he looked for and found a cross bearing his father's name; in that moment he describes his feelings:

> . . . wanting to say something, or to think of something; a muddled see-sawing between unmanageable emotion on the verge of incoherence, and indifference at the absolute limit of what can be willed; and underneath that something like a secret serenity connected to this rooting in space, to this writing on the cross, to this death which had at last ceased to be abstract.[148]

If there was a cross with his father's name on it—we could conjecture—then the forgotten father "must have lived." The dead root of a tooth's nerve that the future writer never had was planted in that gravelly plot.

The orphan was cared for by his mother's relatives in the south of France until he could return to Paris once the war had ended. In the years that followed, years of lonely aimlessness, he took courses at the university, worked as a librarian and "earned a living" (?) preparing crossword puzzles for various newspapers. Literary success arrived shortly before his premature death from lung cancer, although he had already been recognized and rewarded as an innovative novelist with the publication of his first story: *Things* [1965].

His preoccupation with defining himself on the basis of these blurred origins and with revealing the mysteries of his ancestry and name pervades every line, and even between the lines, of his extensive body of work. Perec, who History had deprived of memories and roots, was logically and paradoxically, obsessed with memory, a passionate detective of all the strands of a past from which he could not escape. He lived a life afflicted by a meticulous

---

148. Perec, Georges [1975]. *W, or the Memory of Childhood*. Translated by David Bellos. Boston: David R. Godine, 1988, p. 38.

recollection that he cultivated, that obsessed and distracted him and that at one time he would have liked to have lost in order to have become part of a hypnotic present, far from all projects, far from the world of the others, like the protagonist of his second novel, *Un hombre que duerme* (*A Man Asleep*) [1967].[149] The peculiarity of this novel, a barely disguised segment of the narrative of his childhood years, is that it is written in the second person. We find revealing sentences in this novel in which the author tells himself: "You are not dead. You have not gone mad [. . .] Stop talking like a man in a dream" (220–221). In his "self-styled" autobiography, *W or the Memory of Childhood* [1975], a central work in his overall production which will be commented on further in the second section of this chapter, he says enough of himself to make it clear that *the man asleep,* who speaks as if he were dreaming, is indeed himself. When he speaks of that period of his life, as narrator of his own experience and not any longer as the protagonist of a novel, he employs impersonal conjugations rather than the second person singular. He lives without allowing himself to feel, he is a sleepwalker.

> No beginning, no end. There was no past, and for many years there was no future either; things simply went on. You were there. It happened somewhere far away, but no one could have said very precisely where it was far from, maybe it was just far from Villard-de-Lans. From time to time you changed places, went to another boarding house or another family. Things and places had no name, or several; the people had no faces. [. . .] The only thing you do know is that it went on for years and then one day it stopped.[150]

Like Elias Canetti, as we have seen, he believes he would have gone mad if he had not written in his diary. Like so many

---

149. Perec, Georges [1967]. *Things: A Story of the Sixties.* Translated from the French by David Bellos. *A Man Asleep.* Translated from the French by Andrew Leak. London: Collins Harvill, 1990, pp. 220–221.
150. Perec, Georges. *W or the Memory of Childhood.* Op. cit., p. 69.

others: Cortázar, Nabokov, and Kafka (and Joyce?), he seeks to trap memory—to brandish it—in order to distance himself from intolerable reality, to save himself from the terror of the daybreak roosters that took his parents away to a country of no return. In the short piece, "The Gnocchi of Autumn," he painted his self-portrait in words:

> Writing protects me. I advance beneath the rampart of my words, my sentences, my skillfully linked paragraphs, my astutely programmed chapters. I don't lack ingenuity.
>
> Do I still need protecting? And suppose the shield were to become an iron collar?[151]

This confession of the "prophylactic" value of writing appears in the context of a literary "self-portrait"; the title of the text in question, "Les Gnocchis de l'automne," is a play on the well-known Greek saying: *gnoti te auton*, or 'know thyself.'[152] Perec "gets to know himself" by interposing a wall of sarcastic witticisms, incessantly doubting the legitimacy of his project. Like a caricature of a language laboratory technician, he juggles with language; he writes "crossed words."

The amorphous being of childhood and adolescence, the man asleep, toils through life trying to avoid the ghosts of his disappeared ancestors and, at the same time, trying to objectify them, examining photographs, interrogating his relatives, patiently reconstructing his apparent "memory of childhood," which will become the title of his autobiography. Perec struggles in pursuit of a past that evades him, that has been snatched away from him, one which he wishes to capture and enclose in a tight cage of metallic letters which, owing to their rigidity, will not give way to chance or caprice. He argues that he can say nothing even

---

151. Perec, Georges. "The gnocchi of Autumn" ("Les gnocchis de l'automne") in *Species of Spaces and Other Pieces*, from *I Was Born* (*Je suis né*). Translated by John Sturrock. London: Penguin Books, 1997, p. 119.
152. As noted by translator John Sturrock.

though he does not know if he has anything to say, if he does not say what he could say because what he would say is ineffable. The impossibility of expression is the fine powder of anguish that permeates his writing. What can he speak about? What can a hole "tell"? What could he tell himself of that incomprehensible origin for a child who History (with a capital H) has deprived of a history (with a lower-case h) and whose course in life it has altered? The depersonalization of his writing reflects that of his being. He knows that anything he is capable of saying will be inane, colorless, a sign of total nullification. Thus he forces his words onto the page, surrounding History, drawing circles around it with rigid lines as if the words themselves were bound by the electrified barbed wire of a concentration camp. He is, like the prisoners, a number without substance. "If This Is a Man." He cannot console himself with pretty images or by questioning his blocked out memories or by concentrating on trivial details like the length of his father's clothing or by analyzing his own sentences, "certainly finding in them convenient resonances of Oedipus and castration." He lives and writes in order to distance himself from the ghosts that haunt him.

> I will never find, by grinding up my words, anything other than the final reflection of a word that is lacking from my writing, the scandal of its silence and of my silence. [. . .] I write: I write because we have come to live together, because I was one among them, a shadow among their shadows, a body close to their bodies. I write because they have left in me some indelible mark and its trace is writing: in writing, its memory dies. Writing is the memory of its death and the affirmation of my life.[153]

At all times Perec's written word, in addition to being an intriguing literary testimonial, is essentially his mourning the death

---

153. Perec, Georges. "Les lieux d'une ruse," in *Penser/classer*. Paris: Hachette, 1985, p. 63 (my translation).

of the parents he lost at the hands of the Nazi-fascists. It is not just that he was deprived of his parents; something even worse happened to him: he was deprived of their deaths. He invokes the spirit of the vanished parents at the same time as he drowns them in ink. He does the same with his Jewishness: it is not a sign of belonging for him but rather another form of silence and of emptiness. The only certainty he has is that of having been marked as a Jew and, in this way, condemned to live in exile, estranged even from himself, different, not only from others, but also from members of "his own people," whose language, memory and traditions he cannot share because they were not passed on to him. Nonetheless he wonders:

> I don't know exactly what being a Jew means, what it does to me (*ce que ça me fait d'être juif*). It's an obvious fact, if you like, yet a mediocre one, a mark, yet a mark that links me to nothing either precise or concrete. [. . .] It is an absence rather, a question, a throwing into question, a floating, an anxiety, an anxious certainty behind which there is the outline of another certainty, abstract, heavy, insupportable: that of having been designated as a Jew, and therefore as a victim, and of owing my life simply to chance and to exile. My grandparents or parents might have been able to emigrate to Argentina, to the United States, to Palestine . . .[154]

We may conclude that Perec—like Canetti and in contrast to Kafka—did not want to have anything to do with the identity he had been offered and chose to refuse. It is also evident that he took this identity seriously when he planned to write and direct a filmed history of Ellis Island, the arrival point for immigrants in New York City (sixteen million people passed through Ellis Island between 1892 and 1924) but, with total self-assurance, he could also

---

154. Perec, Georges. "Ellis Island: Description of a Project" ("Récits d'Ellis Island") in *Species of Spaces and Other Pieces*, from *I Was Born* (*Je suis né*). Translated by John Sturrock. London: Penguin Books, 1997, p. 132.

make fun of his Judaism in one of the most brilliant beginnings to a "potential autobiography" ever delivered to a printing press:

> I was born on 25 December 0000. My father was a jobbing carpenter, so they say. Shortly after my birth, the gentiles weren't so gentle and we had to take refuge in Egypt. That's how I found out I was a Jew and the origin of my firm decision not to remain one has to be seen as lying in these dramatic circumstances. The rest you know . . . (1997, 95).[155]

He writes to populate a void with doodles, to fill a pure hole, to occupy a house without windows or some windows without a house. He fulfills a mission of tracing signs on paper which enables him in the end, to find the keys to a life that was stolen from him. Perec pursues Perec and tries to moor him with a writing mania that is characterized by compulsion. In 1967, with Raymond Queneau and François Le Lyonnais, he founded Oulipo (*Ouvroir de literature potential*), a writer's workshop aimed at promoting literary creation through counter-traditional practices of twentieth-century artistic license based on the principle that every writer is autonomous and has the right to do what he feels like doing. The writers of Oulipo decided they would obey constraints as stated by certain arbitrary laws that they themselves invented; they were workers in a factory (*ouvroir*), laborers who followed rules that surpassed ordinary language codes—those governing vocabulary and syntax—and even went against the pretensions of transmitting *meaning* through writing, with its inescapable overload of imagination. Following, I will provide some examples of the self-imposed constraints that are exemplary of Perec's unusual writing: all sentences must be written with letters that remain inside the upper and lower parallel lines, thus the prohibited letters would be i, j, p, q, l, d, f, g, h, b, y, t and all letters that require accents (for example, one could

---

155. Perec, Georges. "I Was Born" ("Je suis né") in *Species of Spaces and Other Pieces*, from *I Was Born* (*Je suis né*). Translated by John Sturrock. London: Penguin Books, 1997, p. 95.

write 'ass' but not 'mule'); or, to have to write in palindromes (as in the work of the Argentine writer, Juan Filloy, an Oulipo of the pampas); or, to compose poems that must contain eleven verses of eleven letters each, using only the ten most frequently used letters in the French language (E S A R T I N U L O) plus one additional letter; or, to submit the succession of words and phrases to mathematical laws and equations. The formulas proposed for these oppressive "lipograms" by the members of Oulipo are infinite. The slogan guiding their work is almost Sartrean: only within the prison walls (of words) can there be liberty for artistic invention. There is an evident kinship between this program and the forced compositions of dodecaphonic music that left their mark on the twentieth century.

In his extensive novel, *Life, a User's Manual* (*La vie mode d'emploi*), a masterpiece of Oulipo literature, Perec scrutinizes the lives of his characters, confining them to the space of the Parisian apartment block where they live, and also inside the book that describes them, ordering the succession of episodes in a "Graeco-Latin square on the 10th order" (I will forgo the involved explanation). The leaps from one part of the building to another (from one chapter to the next) follow the movements of a knight in a game of chess on a ten-square board, without permitting the piece to land on the same square twice. One might expect the result to be a book that is practically illegible, a hermetic work only accessible to lunatics who are capable of going along with the capricious rules set by the novelist. This is not the case at all: the writer produces a fascinating game of mirrors that draws the reader into a captivating labor like that of assembling a jigsaw puzzle of life that culminates in a sensational ending featuring the letter W in the starring role, the quintessential stranger, *his* letter. Throughout the text there are quotations, not specified as such, from a multitude of authors: Borges, Stendhal, Calvino, Freud, Leiris, Perec himself, Nabokov, Kafka, García Márquez, Verne, Proust, Rabelais, Thomas Mann, Melville, Joyce, Agatha Christie, Unika Zurn, and others. *Life . . . is a compendium of world literature.*

An instruction manual for entering the labyrinth is unnecessary because the book itself is the manual.

Furthermore, *Life, a User's Manual* is an inventory of inventories that brings together in six hundred pages over a hundred (107) fascinating stories and intimates another one hundred eighty unwritten stories whose plots appear on one or two lines such as: "48. Dodéca's owner's son preferring the porn trade to priesthood," or "179. Lonely Valène putting every bit of the block onto his canvas" (229, 333). The collection of novels is structured like a jigsaw puzzle whose theme is the art of putting together jigsaw puzzles according to a rigorous system of organization of things that seem fortuitous. However, nothing is gratuitous, starting with the title itself: *Life, a User's Manual* and the epigraph, taken from Jules Verne, "Look with all your eyes, look."[156] One artful critic wrote that the five hundred pieces of the puzzle in this great novel formed part of a somber story of vengeance, using the jigsaw puzzle as a weapon against his psychoanalyst, Jean-Baptiste Pontalis.[157] Perec's analysis with Pontalis ended in June 1975, days after the publication of his autobiography: *W or The Memory of Childhood*, which will be both object and tool in the following section.

We should recall that Perec pursued his unconscious ghosts not only in his constrained writing but also by undergoing psychoanalysis. He went through from the couches of Françoise Dolto (1949) as an adolescent, Michel de M'Uzan (1956–1957) as a young man, and finally Jean-Baptiste Pontalis (1971–1975), when he was a prize-winning author. Even more interesting—fascinating, in fact—is to examine the many clinical vignettes that Pontalis

---

156. The phrase seems innocuous. It is from Michael Strogoff which, it may be recalled, passed himself of as blind.

157. It should be recalled that Pontalis, a disciple of Lacan, was already famous when Perec visited him for having written (with Jean Laplanche) *Vocabulaire de la psychanalyse* (Paris: PUF, 1968) which has been translated into all western languages and is still considered essential for the training of psychoanalysts. All words in the field are clearly defined and traced through the history of their use. Perec, a language maniac, had reasons of spiritual consonance to seek the help of a "colleague," J.-B. Pontalis.

himself has left us from the Perec case, attributing to him various pseudonyms (Pierre, Pierre G., Paul, Simon, etc.). As far as I know, there are no precedents of a psychoanalyst who has presented the case of a celebrated patient with information that so readily allows discovering his identity and private life. Certainly there are other, very different, cases of patients, like those of Freud, who became celebrated owing to the analyst's accounts (such as the Wolf Man, the Rat Man, Little Hans, or Dora). Pontalis's comments have a special flavor when read knowing who the patient is, a man who says: "I cannot have any childhood memories because I was so small when I became an orphan," which the psychoanalyst crowns with the following commentary:

Both his [Simon's] parents died when he was still a small child: deported, disappeared. He saw the cause of his 'infantile amnesia' in this double disappearance. He referred often to this: 'I cannot have any childhood memories because I was so small when I became an orphan.' In other words, the parents had drawn the living child into death. All that was left to him was to survive. And what survived in the sessions was an extraordinary machine to produce dreams (not to experience dreaming) to play with words (rather than letting them play), to register daily life (on condition that it remained petrified). He had built himself a closed system of enclosures and separations—a sort of mental concentration camp in which intellectual exploits and a discrete and ironic megalomania had replaced, by turning things inside out, physical cruelty and misery. A system of which I was to be the witness, the guardian and the warrant. Highly talented, intelligent, a brilliant and inventive engineer with a rather sarcastic sense of humor, he appeared to expect nothing from me apart from a strengthening of his 'protective barrier' [. . .] There was in him an obvious division between 'word-presentations' and 'thing-presentations,' between a mental activity without respite and a non-productive psychic life, as if it were encapsulated. His own psyche, just as his mother, had ceased to nourish him.[158]

I cannot help but wonder what would have become of Perec if he had had what his psychoanalyst considered a "productive psychic life."

The central theme of Perec's work is also mine: memory. His was dominated by the horror of forgetting and it was almost Funesian.[159] The idea of writing a "Tentative inventory of all the foods and drinks I have ingested during the year 1974" could have only occurred to him, as well as other attempts at classification of the same sort. His feats of hypermnesia have become legendary.

In another text referring to Perec, Pontalis comments on the characteristics of his memory:

Pierre G. (I keep his name confidential less out of discretion than because the intense and tenacious connection between us could only be established in mutual secrecy) had a vast memory capable of recalling—or, more precisely, of recording—all kinds of information: telephone numbers, the name of a secondary character in a B-movie, the name of a winning horse at Longchamp, the name of a cabinet minister, the address of a restaurant in Yonne were they served leeks au vinaigrette which justified the trip to get there, the call number of a book consulted at the National Library, the exact emplacement of a statue in a plaza of the eighteenth arrondissement . . . an inexhaustible, disorganized data base, a mock computer without utility. Pécuchet deprived of his Bouvard, such was the memory of Pierre. He would go out to visit and explore places, determined to get to know them like a justice of the

---

158. Pontalis, Jean-Baptiste [1977]. *Frontiers in Psycho-Analysis: Between the Dream and Psychic Pain*. Translated by Catherine Cullen and Philip Cullen. New York: International Universities Press, Inc., 1981, pp. 200–202.
159. In reference to the story by Jorge Luis Borges, "Funes the Memorious."

peace or like a lurking photographer. [. . .] Those maniacal
inventories, those interminable lists that included every detail,
caused me a sharp sense of absence. [. . .] In his memory there
were only relics, no people. However, curiously, a hole opened
up in me. I had never felt so atrociously abandoned: forgotten,
launched into a space that seemed to be both desolate and
inflexibly square at the same time.

Pierre's mother had disappeared in a gas chamber. Beneath
every empty room he failed to fill up, there was that chamber.
Beneath every name, were those without name. Beneath all
the relics, a mother who had been lost without leaving a trace.
One day—when was it?—Pierre and I managed to find words
that were not just remainders, words that by some miracle
were directed at their unknown audience.[160]

The psychoanalyst discovered the way to make his invocations
to his disappeared mother audible and to discover the secret that
lay hidden behind his obsession with memory. All names, the
name. All memories, full of an invasive absence, memory. It is not
strange that one of Perec's most provocative books should bear the
title, *Je me souviens* (*I Remember*).[161] The work consists of a series
of 480 numbered memories in an order that lacks any connection
among them. Perec, the writer-librarian, reduced to transcribing
with laconic objectivity a catalogue of memories, displays the
peculiarities that make him an unusual literary figure owing to
the confusing accumulation of odds and ends in a complacent and
expansive memory . . . which is like any other, and any other could
write a similar book; similar, yes, but never the same as Perec. "It's
like in set theory: I share with X memories that I do not share
with Y, and in the large set of our memories each one of us may
reserve for himself a unique configuration."[162] We can hear the
memory mechanism oscillating between individual and collec-

---

160. Pontalis, Jean-Baptiste [1986]. *L'amour des commencements*. France:
     Éditions Gallimard, 1986, pp. 165–167 (my translation).
161. Perec, Georges. *Je me souviens*. Paris: Hachette, 1978.
162. Perec, Georges. *Je suis né*. Op. cit., p. 92.

tive memory. The succession of natural numbers, from 1 to 480, imposes a meandering order on the inventory of memories so that, by virtue of the act of listing, his life is not spilled and wasted for want of a container in which to keep it. Numbering one's memories is an operation that is analogous to cataloguing books, or to creating an inventory of the chaotic animals in Borges's imaginary Chinese encyclopedia. It is an attempt at restoring a semblance of order and meaning to the chaos of a life adrift, unanchored, of an orphan. By compiling the disperse fragments of a memory that is his but also of his contemporaries, he manages to tie his being to "historic" and "collective" memories, in paragraphs such as: "43—I remember Albinoni's Adagio" (one might wonder, do X and Y remember, think and feel the same way when they remember this adagio?); "394—I remember the horse races," but without completely eliminating singular and insignificant memories, such as: "2—I remember that my uncle had a 11 CV with license plates 7070 RL 2" (a pathognomonic memory he surely does not share with anyone). His memory can be, like the memory of Borges's character, Funes the memorious, a garbage heap. Also, favoring the memory of French athletes and their successes in cycling and boxing, a way to acquire, vicariously, a sense of pertinence and identity (for example, "213—I remember the swimmer, Alex Jany").

The being—Perec's being (and everyone's being?)—may be seen as a chaotic cemetery of useless memory, of semantic memory, memory which, in the words of Hegel (*Gedächtnis* versus *Erinnerung*)—who was following in the footsteps of various precursors such as Aristotle (*mneme* versus *anamnesis*)—obstructs understanding. Perec carries out his project of an intelligence that creates an inventory and organizes memories as if the slogan that governs libraries were also valid for the subject: "A book that is out of place is a book that is lost." This eccentric writer's memory is a catalogue governed by numbers that are ordered in sequence and provide a false sense of normalcy to the senseless accumulation of information. The ordinal sequence only serves to cover up the chaos, like the psychiatric classification of "mental disorders," the DSM-V, today's foundation of psychiatric "science." Perec's memory is not the same as Proust's involuntary memory or Freud's unconscious; it is the lava field that commemorates the eruption, the litter of rocks spewed out by a volcano without plan or method, each of which has received a number. It is memory as imbroglio, the capricious gathering of heteroclitic materials that are maintained beneath the yoke of fortuitous mathematics by the writer's obsession with demonstrating the absurdity and imperious necessity of all subjects for endless and unending knowledge.

One might think, recalling Cortázar's classic dichotomy,[163] that Perec was a "fama," the contrary of a "cronopio." It is well-known that *famas* embalm their memories, they wrap them and mark them with black labels bearing their names, whereas *cronopios* leave their memories lying around the house, protecting them from getting hurt. The memories of *cronopios* are left to move freely and cause havoc wherever they go while the *famas* nod their heads knowingly and check to make sure that the labels remain in place. But Perec's situation is quite different. His marvelous and compulsive memory has one purpose which is to protect itself from thoughts that might cause it to encounter something incomprehensible: *disappearance.*

Perec applies formulas governed by the most inflexible whims and he writes surprising narratives, such as *La disparition* (Literally: *The Disappearance*),[164] a 300-page mystery novel in which he never uses the letter *e*; in the Spanish version, translated as *El secuestro* (*The Kidnapping*), the translator did not use the letter *a*, which is the most commonly used letter in that language. The novel staged the "disappearance" of the most common letter in the French language. Subsequently, he published his autobiography (*W or The Memory of Childhood*) which was dedicated to "E," the disappeared letter, which is also pronounced in French as *eux* (meaning

---

163. Cortázar, Julio. "Conservación de los recuerdos," in *Historias de cronopios y famas*. Buenos Aires: Minotauro, 1962, p. 123.
164. Perec, Georges [1969]. *La disparition* Paris: Denoël, Gallimard, L'imaginaire (215), 1987. English translation: *A Void*, translated by Gilbert Adair (London: Harvill, 1994).

them), the *disappeared*. Another text, the honorable brother of the previous text, was entitled *Les revenentes. Texte,*[165] in which, over the course of 60 pages, there are no vowels except the letter *e*. His memory is an antidote, a reactive formation against . . . memory. In Perec there is no repression. The disappearance without a trace of his parents, an event that Perec did not experience, was retroactively transformed into terror and, later, into the cradle of unlimited memory.

2. Fear of Forgetting; The Making of a Memory

I do not believe that in the entire history of the autobiographical genre there exists one that is more original than Perec's (with the exception of certain falsely autobiographical novels: *The Life of Lazarillo de Tormes* and *Tristram Shandy* by Sterne, which we will return to in Chapter 15). I believe Perec's work even stands above Rousseau's *Confessions*, arguably considered the seminal work of the genre, presented by Rousseau himself as "an enterprise which has no precedent, and which, once complete, will have no imitator."[166] In *W or The Memory of Childhood*, two stories alternate, formed by brief chapters that contextually do not seem to have anything in common and to be arbitrarily superimposed. One chapter written in normal Roman typeface, aspiring to be autobiography that is obedient to the rules of the genre, is followed by a chapter written in italics, forming part of an adventure novel that seems to have been written when the author was an adolescent, which lay dormant for twenty years and then was, magically, "retrieved" on a certain day in Venice. I will not pause to analyze in great detail the adventure story other than to observe that it describes

---

165. Perec, Georges [1972]. "Les revenentes. Texte," in *Roman & Récits*. Paris: Le livre de Poche, La pochothèque, 2002, pp. 567–639. English translation: "The Exeter Text: Jewels, Secrets, Sex," translated by Ian Monk in *Three by Perec* (Harvill Press, 1996).
166. Rousseau, Jean-Jacques. *The Confessions of Jean-Jacques Rousseau*. Translated by J.M. Cohen. London: Penguin Books, 1953, p. 17.

a society in a utopian island setting off Tierra del Fuego, which slowly and explicitly evolves into a Nazi concentration camp (or a Pinochetian camp, like a glimpse of the future, the author might say)—and will concentrate instead on the story of Georges Perec's life, his ego, as he himself narrates it. I will acknowledge, however, that the superimposed novel is not a dispensable addendum to the work; indeed, allegorically, it contains the keys to Perec's autobiography. Historical truth, that of the concentration camps, permeates the adventure of the protagonist (an orphan raised by an adoptive family) in search of his true identity which was taken from him and substituted by the false name of Gaspard Winckler. Perec's memory is a two-faced Janus: the imaginary adventure (in italics) of Gaspard W. is superimposed on that of Georges (in Roman typeface), and is filled with information that turns out to be fictitious and artificial—false clues. In his brief preface to the book, the author says that the autobiographical text is "a tale lacking in exploits and memories, made up of scattered oddments, gaps, lapses, doubts, guesses and meager anecdotes." As I said at the beginning of this book, "Life is a novel." And life is more than that; it is an interweaving of novels, a collage of inventions springing from memory in order to escape History, as Perec might say.

Lies, footnotes of doubt and deformations permeate the "true" life narrative in the autobiography of the childhood years, written according to the laws of the genre, posing as a "work of memory" and not the phantasy of a storyteller. Perec bases his falsely authentic narrative on photographs, documents and testimonials that are meticulously and obstinately explored in all their precise details. He presents to the reader two superimposed narratives: the novel, *W*, on one hand, and the life history (bio-graphy), *The Memory of Childhood*, on the other. If neither one is true, which one is less false? The answer: the truth is deposited in the "fragile overlapping" of both, as Perec says in the preface.

Perec, the hypermnesiac—comparable to such legendary figures as Simonides, "Funes," and Sherashevsky, the supposed patient of the neurologist, Luria—begins his autobiography with a powerful statement that at first seems like an unusual lie: "I have no childhood memories" (*W*, p. 6), thus facilitating the identification of the patient identified by the psychoanalyst Pontalis as "Simon" and "Pierre G." Perec would have the reader believe that up to the age of twelve, his life could be summarized in the brief narrative of the disappearance of his parents and that, at the age of thirteen, he wrote a story, *W*, which took the place, if not of *the* story, then of *a* story of his childhood. *W*, the novel, is the story of Gaspard, an autistic child, kidnapped, who was deprived of his identity and is given the responsibility of recovering it. It is worth repeating that immediately after publishing the dual texts of *W or The Memory of Childhood*, Perec terminated his sessions of psychoanalysis (in 1975). Thus, psychoanalysis had served Perec's purposes of rediscovering the identity he had lost with the disappearance of his parents and for the reconstruction of his life history, his true history, characterized by the supposed lack of childhood memories.

The title, *W or The Memory of Childhood* calls attention to the ambiguity of the conjunction *or* (*vel* and *aut*, in Latin). On one hand, the word "OR"—my use of OR in the title of this book is a tribute to Perec's genius—indicates a difference or an alternative (Georges OR Winkler, France OR Tierra del Fuego) that requires a choice between one or the other. On the other hand, "OR" can be an equivalence, indicating that two or more things are the same (Walter Scott OR the author *Waverly*, my grandmother OR my father's mother). The title poses a question: are these two different stories that substitute for each other, OR are they one and the same story? Is there some continuity between the autistic boy who fantasizes about the search for his lost identity and the prize-winning writer who "encrypts" his memories, OR are they one and the same person?

The book, *W or The Memory of Childhood*, poses the question: is it autobiography OR novel? Truth OR lie? Cover-up OR revelation? Memory OR invention? In which of the two stories does one find one thing OR the other . . . ? OR are they both authentic

OR are they both falsifications? How much can one trust a book and, consequently, the author whose name appears on the cover?

In fact, the supposedly "real" part of the double text, the chapters that appear in conventional and respectable Roman typeface, is so full of errors and equivocations that one wonders whether Perec, by leaving clues to be uncovered, was not denouncing the autobiographical genre itself and the validity of childhood memories. His cunning for carrying out deceit in a "novel" that supposedly reveals truth was as superb as his memory.[167] Perec's biographer observes:[168]

Some of his errors are sufficiently flagrant to jump off the page even for readers without Perec's library skills. Did he perhaps make so many mistakes on purpose, in order to humanize himself, since, as everyone knows, to err is to be human? [. . .] In fact, almost every assertion in the memory chapters of *W or The Memory of Childhood* asks to be questioned, and the answer in most cases is that the memory [. . .] has been altered, reworked, decorated or, more plainly, falsified. [. . .] the whole dynamic of the writing of *W or the Memory of Childhood* lay precisely in falsification, in producing *a book that cheats but works nonetheless* (italics in original).

How can the statement, "I have no childhood memories" (*W*, p. 6) be reconciled with the statement, "In any case I still have an extremely detailed memory of my baptism, which was performed sometime in the summer of 1943" (*W*, p. 95)? (The religious ceremony was necessary for entrance into the Catholic school of Turenne and to thus avoid the race laws at the time; he was seven years old at the time.) The reader and commentator (when they are not one and the same person) can easily point out logical

---

167. If anyone doubts his infinite cunning, he or she should read two short narratives produced by this sublime intelligence: *Le voyage d'hiver*, Paris: Denoël-Seuil, 1979, and *Un cabinet d'amateur. Histoire d'un tableau* [1979], Paris: Seuil, 1994.
168. Bellos, David. *Georges Perec: A Life in Words*. Boston: David R. Godine, 1993, pp. 546–549.

fallacies and Perec is a willing companion: "It's the peculiarity of the literary man to hold forth about his own nature, to become mired in a mess of contradictions."[169]

So, how to integrate the denial from the beginning—"I have no childhood memories"—with the detailed description, immediately thereafter, of his first two memories with precise information on the places and time, confirmed as early memories by the presence of the father who died in 1940? Perec himself understands that they are screen memories in the purest sense of the Freudian discovery of 1898. Let us listen to this first memory, prefaced by a warning paragraph (here in italics):

> [O]*bviously, the many variations and imaginary details I have added in the telling of them—in speech or in writing—have altered them greatly, if not completely distorted them.*
>
> The earlier memory is apparently set in the back room of my grandmother's shop. I am three. I am sitting in the middle of the room with Yiddish newspapers scattered around me. The family circle surrounds me wholly, but the sensation of encirclement does not cause me any fear or feeling of being smothered; on the contrary, it is warm, protective, loving: all the family—the entirety, the totality of the family—is there, gathered like an impregnable battlement around the child who has just been born (but didn't I say a moment ago that I was three?).
>
> Everyone is in raptures over the fact that I have pointed to a Hebrew character and called it by its name: the sign was supposedly shaped like a square with a gap in its lower left-hand corner, something like . . . (1988, 13).

[here appears the drawing of a (pseudo) Hebraic letter that resembles a *gamma* cross (*gammeth*, *gammel*) rather than the rather far-fetched interpretation proposed by the biographer, David Bellos, who relates it to an inverted "G," derived from

---

169. Perec, Georges. *Les gnocchis de l'automne.* Cit., p. 116.

the name, Georges, and to a supposed affirmation by Perec of his Jewishness. In any case, the letter in question does not correspond to any letter in the Hebrew alphabet and Bellos says that this "alleged" first memory is the "falsification that has been most studied by French scholars."[170]]

. . . and its name was apparently gammeth, or gammel. The subject, the softness, the lighting of the whole scene are, for me, reminiscent of a painting, maybe a Rembrandt or maybe an invented one, which might have been called "Jesus amid the Doctors". [In footnotes, after the drawing and naming of the Hebrew letter, the author adds the following comment:] Excess detail such as this is all that is needed to ruin the memory or in any case to burden it with a letter it did not possess. There is in fact a letter called "Gimmel" which I like to think could be the initial of my first name; it looks absolutely nothing like the sign I have drawn which could just about masquerade as a "mem" or "M". My aunt Esther told me recently that in 1939—I was three then—my aunt Fanny [. . .] used to take me from Belleville to see her [. . .] one of my games consisted of making out, with Fanny, the letters not in Yiddish but in French newspapers. [And in relation to Jesus and the doctors, he also clarifies:] In this memory or pseudo-memory, Jesus is a newborn infant surrounded by kindly old men. All the paintings entitled "Jesus amid the Doctors" depict him as an adult. The picture I am referring to here, if it exists, is much more likely to be a "Presentation in the Temple" (*W*, pp. 13–14).

David Bellos's comments on Perec's falsification of memory are quite severe, asserting that it is no wonder that Perec found his work to be such a heavy burden since his sleight of hand was so brilliant as to even mystify himself.[171] "The entire passage is a masquerade. [. . .] It is a diabolical game to play with the *memory*

---

170. Bellos, David. Op. cit., p. 552.
171. *Ibid.*, p. 553.

of a Jewish childhood [the Hebrew letter would be a deformed *mem*], and perhaps the most devious example of Perec's simultaneous assertion and denial of his Jewishness."

For my part, I believe—and I am sure that Perec would agree with me—that here lies a paradox: there is evidence of sufficient memory and of sufficient clarity for the subject of an alleged total infantile amnesia. He therefore shields himself by emphasizing and reiterating his remembrance for anyone who is disposed to listen to him. Previously he had said, with evident sarcasm and disqualification of literary autobiographies whose authors boast—as we know—of "authenticity" and "sincerity" that:

> Like everyone else, or almost everyone, I had a father and a mother, a potty, a cot, a rattle, and, later on, a bicycle [. . .] Like everyone else, I have forgotten everything about the earliest years of my existence. My childhood belongs to those things which I know I don't know much about. It is behind me; yet it is the ground on which I grew, and it once belonged to me, however obstinately I assert that it no longer does. For years I tried to sidetrack or to cover up these obvious facts, and I wrapped myself in the harmless status of the orphan, the unparented, the nobody's boy (*W*, cit., 12).

We can clearly see the quadruple movement operating in this unique book, *W or The Memory of Childhood*: 1) *I have no childhood memories*; 2) *everyone has completely forgotten what happened to them during childhood (everyone lies when they narrate their memories)*; 3) *I have many memories, but I don't want to know anything about them*; and 4) *I have very clear memories; in them I appear as the Messiah, like the center of a large family, like the man of letters I have become, like the marvelous object of an immaculate love, like the recently born (three years old!) child with the dignity of a wise man, like the tender model for a Rembrandt painting.*

Where the biographer and common sense discover flagrant contradictions and diabolical games, the reader, who is not so

ingenuous as to be deceived by the false rigors of logic, can appreciate the operation of poetic devices pertaining to the unconscious,
the deliberate use of contradiction, the challenge to formal logic,
the affirmtion of different strata of memory and its three faces—
which, we may recall, are *what is remembered* (false, falsified), *what
is forgotten* (which is constituent of the subject, the nucleus of the
person in relation to what is real), and *what is repressed* (which
can only be known after lifting certain barriers of resistance and
in the relationship between the narrator and the other involved
in the transference, listening to the narrative—who might be the
analyst, depending on the case). Renouncing the tricky conditions
of the genre, Perec writes the most truthful (that is, the most
fictional) of all autobiographies and denounces the deceit hidden
behind the protests of sincerity and the pretension of unifying
the vital narrative that governs all the rest. Perec challenges that
artificial "genre" in the way he narrates his own life, overloading
it with modalities of doubt (like Leiris in his dramatic "childhood
memory"),[172] writing different variants of the narrative of "the"
memory in such a way that all of them become questionable (like
the sublime narrative of Louis-René des Forêts),[173] highlighting—
without correcting—the contradictions ("I was three years old—but
didn't I just say that I was a newborn?"), inventing a letter that
does not exist, fabricating false etymologies and meanings for his
surname, narrating possible memory—memory that he might have
had if he had been born somewhere else, of different parents, etc.
The implicit message of so many rhetorical procedures becomes
explicit at a certain point: "The work of writing is always done in
relation to something that no longer exists, which may be fixed
for a moment in writing, like a trace, but which has vanished"[174]
(1997, 129). Memory oscillates between traumatism and nostalgia.

---

172. Leiris, Michel. " . . . reusement," *La règle du jeu.* Op. cit., pp. 3–8.
    See Chapter 12.
173. Des Forêts, Louis-René. "Une mémoire démentielle," *La chambre des
    enfants.* Paris: Gallimard, L'imaginaire (117), 1960, pp. 91–132.
174. Georges Perec. *Species of Spaces and Other Pieces,* from "Le travail
    de la mémoire" (*Je suis né*). Translated by John Sturrock. London:
    Penguin Books, 1997, p. 129.

Perec would not subscribe to Cortázar's view regarding the conjunctive relationship between "memory AND dread." For Perec there are two disjunctive paths: EITHER the negation of memories, "I have no childhood memories," OR the affirmation of a completely falsified and embellished memory in order to protect oneself from a horrifying reality. He maintained, with absolute certainty, that he had no childhood memories and he refused to answer questions on the topic because he felt excused from the question: "a different history, History with a capital H, had answered the question in my stead: the war, the camps" (*W*, p. 6).

For Julio Cortázar memory begins with terror; for Georges Perec terror begins with History and memory attempts to cap off the well of original anguish, proceeding from the irrational brutality of the Other who tears the child from the maternal bosom. EITHER compassionate memory OR merciless history. Perec, in a similar way to Nabokov—but in other circumstances—takes refuge in happy memories (in his first memory, completely manipulated, we see him as a boy in warm family surroundings) which contrast with *the story of terror* that he would come to understand later—only later—when he is able to work on *"the memory of childhood,"* the only "true memory" he has of his mother. All that he has left of her is her birth certificate, a few other official documents, five photographs jealously guarded and scrutinized and the dubious memory of the farewell in Paris, in the Lyon train station, without knowing that he would never see her again and that the farewell was, in fact, a "disappearance," becoming smoke . . . in the ovens of the crematorium. The moment of saying goodbye is the trumpet call announcing the concentration camp. Auschwitz? Theresienstadt, . . . ? That universe (*W*) that can only be sensed, revealed, produced, years later, when he and the rest of the terrified world know enough to reconstruct a history that lies beyond memory. The terror of the "memory of childhood" is retroactive and remains, for Perec—and for everyone?—masked by screening details. For example, Perec remembers very well that before boarding the train, his mother bought him a comic book, *Charlie and the*

Parachute. Clearly, it is totally unrealistic that such a comic book about the director of the Great Dictator would have circulated in France in 1942. All the details become equally dubious when the different versions that Perec wrote of this memory are compared. As Philippe Lejeune comments:

> The departure from the Lyon train station, surely tragic for his mother who could sense that she would never see her son again, only assumed this nature for the boy retrospectively, two or three years later, when he could grasp the idea that he would never see her again. It was then that he began the work of reconstruction in order to erect a monument in that nearly empty space.[175]

He must either erase the terror of an unspeakable history or save in his memory an unlikely accumulation of superfluous and screening information (*Je me souviens*) or—as a third option—painfully reestablish the absurd puzzle of life on the psychoanalyst's couch. All this in order to finally find that, at the moment of concluding (the novel, the analysis), the black hole of the only piece of the jigsaw puzzle not yet filled in has the almost perfect shape of an X, while the only piece he could not place . . . and that was "foreseen long ago, is that the piece the dead man holds between his fingers is shaped like a W."[176]

We could say that Georges Perec's "first memory" is the pleasurable mystification of original happiness, invented from start to finish, anticipating his fate as a writer, a "man of letters." Furthermore, we might suppose that Perec, after having affirmed that he has no childhood memories, contradicts himself by describing in detail his recollection of the family scene, adding associations as if it were a dream and not the memory of a "real"

175. Lejeune, Philippe. *La mémoire et l'oblique. Georges Perec autobiographe.* Paris: Hachette, 1991, p. 83.
176. Perec, Georges. *La vie mode d'emploi.* Paris: Hachette, 1978. *Life: A User's Manual.* Translated by David Bellos. London: Vintage, 2002, p. 497.

episode. He further aggravates this contradiction when he narrates with meticulous precision the details of the day of his baptism and so many other episodes of his childhood. Bellos, the biographer, takes precisely the preceding view and adds his own associations: if *mem* corresponds to the letter M, which is the letter of memory and the letter that characterizes the vampire of Dusseldorf in Fritz Lang's film, and if M is the letter for mother in all languages, and if M, inverted, becomes W, the title of the autobiography, the name of the island that is a concentration camp, the letter with which the book of instructions for living life closes, and if W is, in both French and Spanish, the quintessential foreign letter, and if . . .

For my part, I think we should not forget Freud, the Freud who would completely agree with Perec and who illustrates *avant la lettre* and in brilliant fashion Perec's affirmation that, indeed, he has no childhood memories for the simple reason that Freud provided in 1898 and which no one seems to remember (frequently not even Freud): *NO ONE HAS CHILDHOOD MEMORIES*. Repression begins long before the first remembered episode and *it is already active in the construction of that memory*. In psychoanalysis a recollection is not the beloved son of memory but rather of its opposite: repression. Its function is not to facilitate the restoration of the past but rather to prevent it. Textually:

> [T]he falsified memory is the first that we become aware of: the raw material of memory-traces out of which it was forged remains unknown [*unbekennen*] to us in its original form. The recognition of this fact must diminish the distinction we have drawn between screen memories and other memories derived from our childhood. It may indeed be questioned whether we have any memories at all *from* our childhood: memories *relating to* our childhood may be all that we possess. Our childhood memories show us our earliest years not as they were but as they appeared at the later periods when the memories were aroused [retrieved]. In these periods of arousal, the childhood memories did not, as people are accustomed to say, *emerge*;

they were *formed* [encoded] at that time. And a number of motives, with no concern for historical accuracy, had a part in forming them, as well as in the selection of the memories themselves (Freud 1899, 322).[177]

Returning to Perec, now in the company of Freud, it is surprising to find that only he knew how to understand the essential distinction between memories *from* our childhood—those that he does *not* have—and memories *relating to* our childhood, which are those that germinate in the pages of as many autobiographies as are written and which will soon culminate our discussion with the example of Michel Leiris. The original memories have been recorded and constitute the essential aspect of the human being's life. However, they lie buried beneath the vaults of infantile amnesia and from there they govern the distortion of early memories. *There is no history of early childhood, only novels, inventions and fables.* Which of the authors we have studied thus far constitutes an exception to this rule?

In summary: *W or The Memory of Childhood* proposes a disjunction: EITHER dread OR memory. If there is conjunction, then: *Memory AND Dread;* the conjunction changes place: *Memory and Dread* OR *The Memory of Childhood.* In order to escape from dread which is, in this exemplary case, the disappearance of the mother—which is the nightmare of history for Stephen Dedalus—it is necessary to wrap oneself in a cloak of memories that will screen it. Memory, knowledge of the world, is to forget the self as *geworfen*, thrown into the world.

Memory is cultivated. One knows what one needs not to know. Or one knows it so well as to be unable to exorcise the curse of returning over and over again to the painful event, the historical remains, of a persistent memory.

---

177. In this quotation the words in italics are Freud's. I added the words in brackets to highlight how, at the end of the nineteenth century, Freud made a clear distinction, consistent with today's psychophysiology, between "arousal" of a memory (retrieval) and its formation (encoding).

And—even before Perec or Freud—the conclusion was foreseen by the gaucho, Martín Fierro:

Know ye that to forget what is bad
Is to yet have memory

—José Hernández (*The Return of*) *Martín Fierro* [1879].
XXXIII, lines 7203–7204 (my translation).

12

MICHEL LEIRIS: THE FORTUNATE FAILURE OF AUTOBIOGRAPHY (. . . *TUNATELY!*)

The word is not a sign, but a nodal point of signification. When I say the word "curtain" [rideau] . . . *Metaphorically, it is a curtain of rain* [rideau d'arbres]; *forging plays on words, it is when I am being curt and sweet or can curr tangentially with the best of them* [les rides et les ris de l'eau], *and my friend Curt Ans off* [Leiris dominant] *these glossological games better than I do.*[178]

1. Presentation of the Author, the Narrator and the Character

No writer has understood so well as Michel Leiris (1901–1990) the difficulties and risks of autobiographical writing, to which he dedicated his efforts during his sixty-odd years as a man of letters. To begin, it will be helpful for us to review his biographical information, as we did in the case of Perec, since it is lacking in his writing. Indeed, I have just referred to one of Leiris's most striking peculiarities: dates, empirical information about identity, the proper names of parents, friends, brothers and tutors, social

---

178. In *Écrits: the first complete edition in English.* Translated by Bruce Fink in collaboration with Héloïse Fink and Russell Grigg. New York: W.W. Norton & Co., 2006, p. 136.

and political references, official documents—all are absent or appear in fragmentary ways and out of chronological order in his writing. The historiography of his life, as it would appear in an encyclopedia, has little to do with his concerns and is contrary to his project. The narrative of his life's peripeteias permits dispensing with social, temporal and geographic coordinates—the commonplaces of the genre. Leiris's copious autobiography is post-Freudian, more in the conceptual sense than the temporal, and the expressive flow is more akin to the narrative dispersion of a psychoanalytic session than the delight of an ego asserting its place in the world and affirming its singularity. The signature that presides over and precedes the text seems superfluous; the proper name could be dispensed with. The author's style utilizes and indulges in the anarchic rigors of free association. He accumulates heterogeneous materials and composes them in a disorganized way rather than cultivating the usual detailed and meticulous exposition that passes itself off as authenticity by filling all the holes and responding in advance to all questions. He offers an incomparable autobiography! For example, amidst the pandemonium of his seemingly random thoughts, we immediately learn, as soon as on the second page of *L'Âge d'homme* (*Manhood*)—his first and most celebrated autobiography—that when he is alone he tends to scratch his anal region, though he does not take the "care," previously or anywhere else in the book, to specify who his parents were or the date of his birth. Leiris prefers to begin with the creation of an implacably written self-portrait and to state that, when he finds himself unaware in front of a mirror, he is horrified to see his own humiliating ugliness. His writing might be considered an attempt to throw caustic liquid on his facial features, *prosopoclastia*[179] is the term I use for autobiographers who write *against* their own image in the mirror. The beauty of the prose must combat the horror of the *prosopon*, of a gaze that is ashamed to land on its own face.

Since he so sparingly provides information about himself, we must resort to the encyclopedia, ever replete with information,

---

179. See below, Chapter 14.

to transcribe certain details that help orient the writer for us: he was born in April 1901 not far from—and in the same week as—Jacques Lacan, who would become his friend after they met in 1935 in the house of Marie Bonaparte. As a young man he frequently attended meetings and was a member of the surrealist group of painters and writers. In 1922, entering his twenties, he discovered and read some of Freud's writings and from that time forward he kept a detailed diary in which he recorded his experiences over nearly seventy years, writing that was directed at an imaginary and future interlocutor. This diary would serve as a data base for his autobiographical writing. In 1926 he married Louise Godon, stepdaughter of Daniel-Henry Kahnweiler, dealer of Picasso, Matisse and André Masson. Fatherhood terrified him: they never had children. In 1928 he was a witness at the wedding of Georges Bataille and Sylvie Maklès, who would later become Sylvie Lacan. In 1929, he broke away from Surrealism and decided to dedicate himself to ethnology, sociology and Marxism. Feeling himself prisoner to an insurmountable physical and intellectual impotence, he followed Bataille's advice and began psychoanalysis with Adrian Borel (1886–1966), one of the first psychoanalysts to introduce Freudianism to France. His first experience on the analyst's couch lasted two years; he resumed analysis for an additional year in 1935–1936. His friends in those years were Picasso, Bataille, Queneau, Jouhandeau (with whom he would have a falling out when Jouhandeau declared himself an anti-Semite), and Breton. In 1942 he met Jean-Paul Sartre and they formed a strong friendship. With Sartre, Merleau Ponty, de Beauvoir and several others, he was founder of *Les Temps Modernes* (1945). Years earlier, in 1929, he finished writing his first novel, *Aurora*,[180] which was not published until 1946: the protagonist of the narrative is named Siriel, rather than Leiris. The palindrome suggests that the novel is a markedly autobiographical fiction (ultimately, are there any that are not?) Siriel's first name is Damocles; Leiris-Siriel always

---

180. Michel Leiris. *Aurora*. Translated by Anna Warby. London: Atlas Press, 1990.

finds himself with his head beneath the sword. From 1933 to 1935 he dedicated himself to writing and in 1939 he gave to the publishers *L'Âge d'homme*,[181] a clearly autobiographical essay that fulfills the requirements that define the "genre": the *author* coincides with the *narrator* and with a *protagonist* who speaks in the first person "I"; the three are one and the same. The first edition of the book did not have a prologue but, following the end of the Second World War, he inserted an initial chapter, written during the intervening years, at the beginning of the second edition entitled, "De la literature considérée, comme une tauromachie" (published in the English translation, *Manhood,* as "Afterword: The Autobiographer as *Torero*"). The prologue was, in many ways, a tacit correction and even a retraction with respect to the book that it introduced. Subsequently, from 1948 to 1976, he successively published, volume by volume, the central work of his literary output, a torrential autobiography, *La règle du jeu* (*Rules of the Game*),[182] which generously exceeds a thousand pages and, in 2003, was published in its definitive form.[183]

A quick summary before moving ahead. In all, there are three autobiographies: a) a novel, *Aurora,* in which Leiris introduces himself as Damocles Siriel; b) Leiris's first "formal" autobiography, *L'Âge d'homme,* published in 1939, which was republished in 1946 with a prologue in which the author, through the audacious exposure of personal intimacies, compares himself to a bullfighter; and c) a second "formal" autobiography, *La règle du jeu,* which was published in four volumes from 1948 to 1976, although, in fact, the writing of the first volume predates the taurine prologue to *L'Âge d'homme.* Indeed, Leiris worked on this first volume, *Biffures,* from 1940 to 1946. Previously, in 1938, he had published another

---

181. Leiris, Michel. *Manhood: A Journey from Childhood into the Fierce Order of Virilit.y.* Translated by Richard Howard. Chicago: University of Chicago Press, 1992.
182. Michel Leiris. *La règle du jeu.* Paris: Gallimard, La Pléiade, 2003. Translated by Lydia Davis. Johns Hopkins University Press, 1997.
183. Leiris, Michel. Respectively from now on: *Aurora, AH* and *La règle du jeu, RJ,* followed by the page number.

text where he idealized and revealed his fascination with the bull-fighting event: *Miroir de la Tauromachie*.[184] Literature—as Leiris conceived of it—is laying one's life on the line. Thus, in his imagination, writing, like the bullfight, is charged with transcendental connotations: it is a date with death impaled upon the sharp tip of the bull's horn. It is hand-to-hand combat. The artistic model of the bullfight thus dominates the writing of this monumental body of work which is of interest to this study because it contains *not one but two* "first memory (-ies)" from childhood.

Leiris died in 1990; by that time he was an award-winning author, celebrated by French intellectuals (not to mention the *intelligentsia*). Leiris did not limit himself to speaking only of himself: he left behind a vast output of books of poetry, ethnographic essays, studies on painting and literature, political texts (we should recall, to gain a more complete understanding of him, that he was a member of the Communist Party, an active resistor during the worst of times, a follower of Castro, an enthusiastic participant in the protest movements of the sixties and supporter of the successful presidential campaign of Mitterand in 1988). At the time of his death, his meticulously kept diaries remained unpublished, for the moment, but he had already achieved fame for the shameless epic *L'Âge d'homme*, as well as the four volumes of *La règle du jeu*, the monumental autobiography that most concerns this study. Nowadays Leiris is an indispensable reference in the history of the "genre" of autobiography, to which he dedicated his life, convinced that he was a passionate pursuer of the truth and a bold torero. The secondary bibliography surrounding his work is beyond the scope of this study. It includes such outstanding names as Michel Butor, Maurice Blanchot, Claude Lévi-Strauss, Jean-Baptiste Pontalis, etc. This psychoanalyst, who treated Perec, we may recall, described Leiris as an "ethnologist of his personal institutions"—an ethnologist of the self—and he stated, fairly and accurately:

---

184. Leiris, Michel. *Miroir de la Tauromachie*. Paris: Fata Morgana, 1981. Illustrated (marvelously) by André Masson. In English: *Mirror of Tauromachy*. Translated by Paul Hammond. London: Atlas Press, 2007.

We must admire the unequaled honesty with which Leiris carries out his project and refuses to dissolve the antimonies between life and death, myth and reality, work and speech, literary language and everyday prose, thus suffusing his writing with an incomparable tension.[185]

This is an "exemplary case" of the intersection of autobiographical writing and psychoanalysis. Leiris communicated—certainly in keeping with his own wishes—more than he intended to transmit as he nurtured his project of "to tell the whole truth and nothing but the truth is not all: he must also confront it directly and tell it without artifice" (*Manhood*, 160). Inevitably the word says more (and something else) than he wants it to. He (the author) *wants to tell* the truth and he does not know that, by failing in this attempt, he *makes* truth, and in this way he captures it. The truth is situated where it should be: not in the place of he who says "I" but rather in the place of the listener or reader. Indeed, what is authentic about one's life—and this is the great secret of autobiographical literature—resides in the Other.

What are the labyrinths of the phantasy of a man who, it seems to me, rather than "living to tell the tale" seems to be motivated by an urge towards "telling the story *instead* of living it," who subordinates his personal existence to the literary transubstantiation of life? In what follows, I will put some order to the five panels of this screen, which tells the story of his odyssey.

First: the question of the first memory, which is twofold, as we have already discussed and seen in other cases that we have analyzed (Perec, Nabokov, Woolf, etc.): a memory that contains the seed of dread and that is the first because it appears on the first page of the narrative and another, the "second first memory," dream-like and ideal, which is evoked many pages later, more distant and previous in time to the first that was recorded. One

---

185. Pontalis, Jean-Baptiste [1955]. *Après Freud*. Paris: Gallimard, NRF (237), 1968, p. 313 (my translation).

that begins the autobiography and another that has chronological primacy.

Second: the attempt to escape from chronology and to set in motion writing that, no matter how corrected it is—and how good!—is sister to the method of free association implanted by the analyst which obliges the author to practice a reading of his or her own text that is governed by its counterpart: the "free floating attention" of the reader, tacitly invited to sit on the analyst's couch, to listen while suspending all prejudice and maintaining the interpretive prudence expected of a Freudian.

Third: the strange, though frequent, ghost of the author's literary survival through the work and grace of autobiographical prose, the desire to live on through writing, the demand on the part of Leiris that his reader confer upon him immortality, the constant manner (the mania) of invoking and denying death in the story of life, the thanatophobic justifications that he confesses for the exhibition of his "*me-me-me*" egocentricity which he supposedly unmasks, the ego condemned to perpetual agony, endeavoring to "put on a show" (*faire semblant*) of being alive. As if writing were a safe-conduct to escape death.

Fourth: what the intrepid writer can "confess" about his sexuality, exactly as it emerges in his analysis—in this respect we can compare him to another well-known psychoanalyzed writer: Hermann Broch—and the contrivances he resorts to in order to reveal (as well as to hide) what, for the majority of men, continues to be the enigma of the relationship with women and with the "other"—the feminine—sex.

Fifth: the result of the autobiographical adventure for anyone who investigates his or her own life to the most extreme limits and consequences, trying, at the moment of self-exposure before the world, to establish a "subjective etymology," demonstrating that the self is embedded in language and that, as an artist, s/he has resources inspired by psychoanalysis, for retrieving memory from oblivion, from censorship and repression.

Five ports of call, then, shall be the itinerary of our flight.

2. The Twofold First Memory: Beatitude and Un-Fortunate Fall

In the narrative of a life story we should distinguish between three starting points, or moments, which are options available to the autobiographer: a] the *notarial*, which is commonly used whenever performing transactions and filling out forms: name, date and place of birth; this is a simple resource for beginning an autobiography (I was born . . . *Je suis né*, my parents were . . . , etc.); b] the *psychological*, a first memory that is lost in the nebula of time, caught in the long night of infantile amnesia, like that told by Leiris evoking the warm presence of his mother; and c] the *literary*, which is a memory that begins the narrative and may be identical to the psychological beginning, as in the case of Elias Canetti, who begins *The Tongue Set Free* with his first memory, or it may be a "pre-natal memory" as in the case of Nabokov's *Speak, Memory*, which, as a further exception, was even attributed to another subject ("a young chronophobiac"), or, as in the case of Leiris, a memory that seems arbitrarily selected by the writer to appear on the first page of the autobiography, preceding, by as many as a hundred pages, one which will later be declared the oldest memory.

Up to this point, I have discussed at length the importance of the first memory and the reasons for its preservation and, moreover, for many people, its idolization as a source of identity. I have set aside the ingenuous notion that its transcendence depends on the *reality* of the remembered event and I coincide with Freud that such childhood memories are no more than retroactive and arbitrary reconstructions in the service of interests that the self represses because they are its own, they are disavowals of unbearable truths. We know that these memories are, in every case, *screen* memories. Both the people who surround the child and the subject him/ herself and, later, those who hear the narrative or who eventually read the autobiography, are destined to carry with them this original episode—hybrid of memory and imagination—with its halo of decisive keys into the life and work of the adult, if not also the prestige of foreshadowing what is to come over the course of succeeding years. How easy it is to be a prophet of the past! The first recollection, the presumed core of memory, is a mythological construction. Is it, therefore, unworthy of interest? On the contrary: because it is a product of the unconscious (like a dream or any creation of fantasy), because it occupies for the subject the place of foundational myth for identity, the first memory contains, as Freud said, the key to the wardrobes of mental life. I would venture to say: albeit a falsification, it is the carrier, the messenger, of truth: the truth of the ghost, the backbone of subjectivity.

Leiris was well aware of this: he sets out in search of memories like a detective. He is more interested in the hunt than the prey, in the pursuit rather than the pursued. His autobiography is "a type of mystery novel." He does not want to recover the original emotion but rather to vividly feel the impact produced by undertaking this investigation. His writings are not "memories" since he takes it for granted that they are all contrived. He does not want the event exactly as it happened but rather as he finds it now: deformed. He is only concerned with measuring the distance between what might have happened in the past—which is definitively lost—and the image he now perceives of the original event. He gives himself over without modesty, and without deceiving himself or the reader, "to the imaginative reconstruction, to the reinvention of the event" (*RJ*, 1120, my translation). What he would like to transmit, in any case, would be authentic, given that "I could not alter, by so much as a comma, my past" (*AH* 19, *Manhood*, 162). The words of the writer, "however he may arrange them on the page, will always be the truth." He commits himself to telling truth, and does so in his writing, and the reader is in the position of demanding that he carry through on his commitment. A pact is entered into between the author and the reader in which the aforementioned (the owner of the copyright), Michel Leiris, becomes the protagonist of his story and offers it up for the approval of whomsoever it may concern: the Other. For him to have been able to alter "a comma" of the past, it would have been necessary for the past to be somewhere, already written. As it happens, it is nowhere: the past comes into being when it is written and filled with commas and other punctuation marks. It is a child of rhetoric.

The mature, post-war narrator offers, as previously indicated, not one but two "first memories": the psychological (in chronology) and the literary (on the page). The oldest and more distant has a sacred aura, enveloped by the marvelous, a halo of chivalric romances and fairy tales, as remote as it is obscure, emerging from *prehistory* rather than the remembered past. Leiris sees and feels himself ensconced precisely in that mythical and inaccessible past, even though he knows that it is something he could not possibly remember. He places the germinal memory in a distant spring, possibly when he was "three-and-a-half years old" ("Impossible!" we might protest, playing at detectives: if it was in May, he would necessarily have been either three or four, but the half year is impossible since he was born in April—nonetheless, we know that this is not "material truth" in a text that aspires to be biographical, but is finally more novel than history.

The initial memory—the oldest—could not be more trivial; moreover, it consists in a commonplace that only accrues meaning when related to "the other" first memory, the one involving the word that is un-for-tunately shortened and corrected by an adult—an adult that is always waiting, always lurking and ready to impose the strict laws of language upon the passage of the *infans* towards the word. We hear, we read the elemental memory, the mother cell of this and so many other autobiographies. We can agree that it is a commonplace: the child is with his mother, in an empty room that smells of dust and insecticide powder. With this evocation in mind, the adult writes, he is always awestruck by things that appear to say to him "Once upon time . . ." (*RJ*, 167–168, *Scratches*, 153). If the scene evokes sacred history, if the memory, rather than smelling of dust smells more of sanctity, it is not owing to what it says but because it is the first and, therefore, the most exotic within grasp. He explains:

The sacred quality attributed to childhood memories may be explained in the same way that exoticism is explained, considering that *archaism* is in time what exoticism is in space: my memories are more sacred to me the more distant they are from me (*RJ*, 1119, my translation).

The "first" memory is not important for the child that was, but rather for the tourist of the autobiography who lives now, discovering virgin lands and recapitulating the mythical past. One minute before—it seems to say—"I" was not here; now, miraculously, I have arrived out of nowhere. The main theme of this short narrative is an instant: the "authentic" birth of the subject, if we accept (with John Locke) that identity is consubstantial with memory. And in that place of calm and sunlight the indelible presence of the mother is notable, the source and origin of all certainty. However, the perfection of the idyllic coalescence with the mother does not reside in this beginning. There is a memory only because before there were not two beings—one and the other, she and I; the union with her is mythical; it is reached after a laborious narrative that begins with the consciousness of the divorce between the self and the other. Personal history is always that of an "unfortunate conscious" in the Hegelian sense, separated and *à la recherche* of itself, determined to recover a jouissance that never existed, a jouissance of being prior to language. Is there any other?

Of great importance, therefore, are the dissociation and the confluence between this early memory of happiness (lost) in the company of the mother and the other memory, the trauma of his initiation into language, the initial moment of his existence, a delineated moment, on a par with the first memory for its multiple signs of uncertainty. The first memory was trivial, common to many autobiographies, closer to an epiphany, because it is a moment situated outside of the narration, an instant and not a sequence, a sensation and not an episode; the second memory is exceptional, a veritable jewel in the literature of the "genre." Let us examine it, albeit with less attention than it deserves.

Biffures (*Scratches* or Erasures), the first volume of *La règle du jeu*, begins with a brief chapter, ". . . *reusement*" (*RJ*, 3–6) that can be translated loosely as ". . . tunately" (the ending of the word "for-tunately"). Leiris's writing is so masterful that this short episode should be an essential selection, without equal, just like the beginning of Rousseau's *Confessions*, for any anthology of autobiographies. I would gladly reproduce the four pages here but conciseness demands that I provide only a narrative sketch. The supposed event takes place in an unspecified room in the house where the child lives and plays. Suddenly a toy soldier falls to the floor but he cannot say whether it is made of lead, tin or painted cardboard, he does not know if it is new or old, nor what color it is, nor does he know what a soldier really is, for this is long before he would have been the proud owner of a collection of toy soldiers. What is important is not that it was a soldier but that it was one of his toys, something that belonged to him that slipped from his clumsy little hands and might have broken. The little Michel anxiously pounces upon the prized object, he picks it up, caresses it, examines it and confirms that nothing has happened to it. Rejoicing, he proclaims, ". . . *reusement!*" Alas, to his dismay, he is not alone. In that same room, not clearly identified, there is an older person—his mother, sister or brother—who corrects him: "I should say *heureusement* (fortunately)." His happiness evaporates and he feels overcome by a strange discomfort. What he believed was a pure interjection is now linked to the entire language: there is "fortunate" (*heureux*) and there is the adverb "fortunately" (*heureusement*). The child is unable and will never be able to use words freely: they are strange to him and are governed by a law that the adults have already submitted to. His will has been expropriated from him because language is *socialized* (Leiris's italics). He is not in command of the words; on the contrary, he must obey them and they are in command over him:

The lead or papier-mâché soldier had just fallen onto the floor of the dining room or living room. I had cried out ". . . *reusement!*" I had been corrected. For a moment I was dazed, seized by a sort of vertigo. Because this word, which I had said incorrectly and had just discovered was not really what I had thought it was before then, enabled me to sense obscurely— through the sort of deviation or displacement it impressed on my mind—how articulated language, the arachnean tissue of my relations with others, went beyond me, thrusting its mysterious antennae in all directions (*Scratches*, 6, *RJ*, 6).

Lacanian doctrine regarding jouissance states that the subject must renounce initial jouissance, the jouissance of the body without language (*hors-langage*), in which it is submerged in order to filter it through the apparatuses of language, which do not belong to it but rather pertain to the Other. The (mother) tongue is the law that expels jouissance from the body and obliges all future satisfaction to pass through its phonetic, semantic, grammatical and syntactic straits. Owing to this violent intromission of the Other "jouissance is prohibited for whoever that speaks" (Lacan) and there is only jouissance in relation to rules that restrict and channel it. Jouissance ceases to exist as a lukewarm sun that is refracted in nameless dust particles and it becomes jouissance of language outside of the body (*hors-corps*), with speech, obedient to an inflexible legislation. Never has an example of this coercion been illustrated in such an exemplary fashion as in this vignette drawn from the little Michel's childhood, recreated in the imagination of the mature writer.

I have reviewed Leiris's first two memories and indicated that one (. . . *reusement*) is the one that begins the autobiography and the other, 165 pages later, is identified by Leiris himself as the more primitive and exotic. In a chronological sense, one of the two must predate the other. I would like to express my reservations, arguing that, from a logical perspective, the two are simultaneous—two shutters of the same window. The joy of being with his mother, gazing in awe at the flight of dust particles caught in sunlight, the memory of jouissance previous to language, is premised upon expulsion from the maternal paradise and acceptance of "life being somewhere else." Presence can only exist upon a background of absence. The object can only re-present itself through absence, through the experience of its own nonpresence. "Re-presentation" implies the entire apparatus of language with the establishment of the difference between the signifiers and the *socialized* apparatus, the turnstile of words that, in contrast to corporeal apparatuses, is not endogenous, it is not "mental" or "cerebral," except to the degree that the system of language (of the Other) has been impressed on the subject. In that system, the subject is outside the law, it is *criminal*, albeit ". . . *tunately*." Leiris's case is clear and shows that, like Freud's grandchild with his spool which was *his* toy soldier, to have and have not, to appear and disappear in the mirror, *fort* and *da*, are correlatives. What is important is not one or the other position but rather the relationship between the two phonemes: *ooo* and *a*. For this reason, I maintain that Leiris's experience is paradigmatic of the presumed traumatism *for every subject* upon entrance into language: the presence of the first object, the mother, is established through her unpardonable loss. *Fort* and *da*, to be present and not present in the visual field of the other, to appear before and disappear behind a curtain, these are the frames of our lives, this life that takes place in that theater which is the gaze of others. To be seen and recognized it is necessary to speak the "mother tongue" and with it one cannot say . . . *tunately*. Misfortune is programmed. *Unfortunately*.

One can speculate about the degree to which this minute episode of the child's expulsion from his sovereignty over words might have become the impulse for Michel Leiris's relentless struggle with the French language following that star-crossed day. Are these the "rules of the game," "the rules of *I*" (*jeu/je*)? Let us play at accepting them. Let us risk exposing our lives like the two participants in the bullfight in their merciless confrontation.

Let us enjoy the exercise of the word that regulates and modifies the jouissance. Is that what literature is, a bullfight, a game of life and death? Can they—the bull or the bullfighter—defeat death? No; the struggle—having to live within language—is lost before it has begun. For this reason it only makes sense, in life, to risk life. To write about life in order to live, or to give oneself the heroic illusion of confronting death without dying in the attempt, is this not to transform life into a dead letter?

3. Autobiographical Writing and Psychoanalysis

Leiris, together with Georges Perec, Hermann Broch, Samuel Beckett, and not too many others, belongs to a group of well-known writers of autobiographies who have undergone personal psychoanalysis. I have already provided the fragmented dates of his analysis and the name of his analyst, Borel, one of the first Freudians in France, who was also analyst to Georges Bataille as well as other well-known artists. In addition there are practitioners of psychoanalysis who have ventured to experiment with the autobiographical genre: Sigmund Freud himself wrote "An Autobiographical Study" although, as we know, the true narrative of his vital experience must be sought for in his foundational writings on psychoanalysis, that is, in *The Interpretation of Dreams* and *The Psychopathology of Everyday Life*, rather than in that essay which was written at the invitation of third parties when he was seventy years old. Theodor Reik,[186] Jacques Nassif[187] and, in novelized form, Serge André,[188] all provide examples of psychoanalytic autobiography and the strategies adopted by experienced

---

186. Reik, Theodor. *The Search Within*. New York: Grove Press, 1956.
187. Nassif, Jacques. *En Face. Confessions d'un Psychanalyste*. Paris: Aubier, 2001.
188. André, Serge. *Flac*, followed by "La escritura empieza donde el psicoanálisis termina" ("Writing begins where psychoanalysis ends.") México: Siglo XXI, 2000. Translated by T. Francés and N.A. Braunstein.

explorers of the unconscious to escape from the traps of narcissism which have so often been the "curse" of a genre condemned to egocentricity. When the psychoanalyst (or the analysand, which is almost the same thing) writes an autobiography, s/he fulfills the obligation of transmitting what analysis has taught her or him and s/he must try to avoid self-indulgence, exhibitionism, seeking in the reader an accomplice or a benign judge, trying to sanction a problematic "identity" realized once and for all, the systematic and documented organization of information that hides life more than revealing it. As I have already commented, psychoanalysis divides in two the history of this problematic genre, which straddles novel and history, regardless of whether or not autobiographical writers have submitted to psychoanalysis. Since Freud it is necessary to take into account the unconscious and no one can lay claim to "sincerity" and transparency with respect to themselves when they sit down to write "confidential" texts, which appeal to reciprocal "faith" and "trust" between the writer and the reader. The father and mother portrayed by a writer are not the same after the enthronement of Oedipus as the fountainhead of subjectivity. The "childhood memory" lost some charm but gained in mystery following the recognition of the universal validity of "screen memories." The theory of narcissism and the discovery of the spectacular nature of the mirror stage with the consequent alienation of the subject into an "ego" which represents it there where it is not, has complicated the subject of the statement who, since St. Augustine and Rousseau, has taken comfort in the deceptive first person singular: it is no longer an option to take comfort in the illusion of being transparent to oneself. The unconscious is "the discourse of the Other" present in the autobiographical setting when the interlocutor, the object of the transference, is a constitutive part of the discourse it receives; for this reason, the reader comes to form part of the autobiography.

The psychoanalyst's bidding for the patient—the "fundamental rule" or law—following Freud, is the opposite of that which guides the traditional life narrative: "Say whatever goes through your mind, even if it seems disagreeable, trivial, nonsensical or impertinent." When this rule is observed, the result is an abundance of equivocations, dreams, doubt and lack of confidence in speech itself, the unexpected appearance of memories that were believed lost, the phantasmatical return of objectified people and personified objects, the reanimation of former longings and fears, the upheaval and collapse of certainties that were considered immutable. "I thought that . . . but now I understand that . . ." The story of one's life is not constructed; rather, it is deconstructed and "all that is solid melts into the air."[189] Still more Goethe: the Mephistophelean spirit of denial exercises its solvent effects on the fair soul that is unaware of its participation in the misadventures of those who complain. No one's autobiography could ever be the same following this Freudian discovery. Jouissance, since then, is not found by hiding from oneself or from others in consolatory deceit but rather in unmasking the impostor who speaks in the first person "I" and in forcing open the avenues so that desire, which is unconscious, becomes the avenue of access to jouissance that was lost when it was first prohibited to say ". . . tunately" and the rigid laws of good speech were imposed. "Writing begins where psychoanalysis ends," according to Serge André. Once the analysis is terminated and the illusion of the ego is dissipated, the challenge is to proceed to the writing of the book that every subject carries inside (Proust), which has been falsified in response to the demands of accommodating the rules—never approved but always enforced—defined at the convenience and by the demands of the Other. An autobiography that provides evidence of the battle fought by the ego as a slave to three severe masters: the id drive, the internal despotic superego, and external reality that imposes limitations. An autobiography, when it is truthful, exorcises the ghosts of autonomy. It is an epic poem depicting the adventures and shortfalls along the avenues of liberty.

---

189. Marx, Karl and Engels, Friedrich [1848]. *The Communist Manifesto*, introduction by Martin Malia. New York: Penguin, 1998.

Free association is the part that corresponds to the writer and presupposes a counterpart: the free-floating attention of the reader. Such writing stimulates the reader of different memories, not through the linking of sentences, but rather through incalculable leaps, consisting sometimes of hundreds of pages, in the sequence of the narrative, linking, for example, the precise memories from Perec's early years with the initial affirmation that he has no childhood memories, or the revelation of the profound solidarity between Leiris's two first memories (the euphoria of being with his mother and the traumatism of his language use being corrected), or unifying Nabokov's collection of "perfect" memories with the collection of his precious moths and butterflies and the dream in which his mother teaches him to anesthetize the insects, or connecting Borges's terror in front of mirrors with the entire body of his literary work which ultimately fails when he tries to unify "Borges and I." Subsequent to Freud there is a new approach to autobiographical writing . . . as well as a new approach to its reading which brings to light topics of genre and permits bright leaps of interpretation which go against the grain of the manifest content. Perhaps I should add that, because the reading of autobiography is now different (following the advent of the psychoanalyst), the writer finds himself encouraged to write against himself and his "spontaneous" inclinations. Life cannot be written without the rope of suspicion of the Other, the reader, tightening around the author's neck.

I should add, in light of these changes regarding the auto-biographical "genre" owing to the irruption of Freudianism, that Leiris was never a tremendous enthusiast of psychoanalysis and was always reticent regarding psychoanalytic discourse and the use of its vocabulary. At a certain point in his diary, in 1929 (October 28), he wrote in capital letters, PYSCHOANALYSIS, and he quickly clarified that it was a slip and not a play on words. Many years later, in 1946 (March 10), he explained that this word, with the letters misspelled, refers to the fish and fishing in the murky waters of the unconscious. He does not hesitate to affirm—and not just to insinuate—that he only sought "psychological treatment which my inner anguish had obliged me to undertake in spite of my repugnance for anything claiming to cure ills other than those of the body" (*AH*, 39, *Manhood*, 14). It is appropriate here to review the dramatic conditions under which he decided to enter analysis on the same couch as his friend Bataille had been analyzed and that, according to Bataille himself, had enabled him to write *Story of the Eye*, which was the object of Leiris's admiration. In 1929, in a state of complete inebriation and after an episode of impotence with an African-American dancer, Leiris arrived at the door of a friend at five o'clock in the morning and asked him for a knife with the intention, "more or less sham," of castrating himself. His friend evaded the request by informing him that he only had an electric razor. Following this episode Leiris had to admit that disease played a part in his mental state and he decided then to undergo psychoanalytical treatment. Failing in everything, destroying himself, and anxious about not being able to submit his articles on time for a periodical, he saw himself more as a clown than a tragic actor. He was tormented by a "hideous sense of impotence—as much genital as intellectual" that he still suffered as he wrote *L'Âge d'homme* (*AH*, 196, *Manhood*, 138). He resorted to psychoanalysis to "free myself from this chimerical fear of punishment" without understanding, it seems, that he was applying to himself the punishment that he hoped to escape. He seems to demand punishment when he writes:

> In a general way of speaking, sadism, masochism, etc., do not constitute "vices" for me, but only means of attaining a more intense reality. In love, everything always seems too gratuitous, too anodyne, too lacking in gravity; the punishment of social disgrace, of blood or death must intervene to make the game worth the candle (*AH*, 197).

He underwent treatment "for about a year with various results," finding it at first to be "salt on my wounds" (*AH*, 138–139). Here, certainly, we hear echoes of the slaughter of the bulls. Borel, his analyst, suggested that he take a long trip as a member of an ethnographical expedition and, to this end, Leiris took advantage of an offer of exile "for scientific purposes" that would enable him to calm himself down through chastity and emotional weaning (*AH*, 199, *Manhood*, 140). Upon his return from the "sad tropics" he no longer considered travel as a means of escape and he only went "back to therapy twice, once for only a brief period of time" (*AH*, 199, *Manhood*, 140). Thus he discovered, through various manifestations, that "one always finds that one is oneself . . . and that everything leads back, whatever one does, to a specific constellation of things which one tends to reproduce, under various forms, an unlimited number of times" (*AH*, 200, *Manhood*, 141). In 1934 (July 2) he noted in his diary the main reason for his hostility towards psychoanalysis: for having taken away from him all his mythological resources, for punishing him for lifting the veil of Isis.

Taking the mythological artifact away from Michel Leiris is no small thing; as an ethnologist of himself, as Pontalis described him, he could not renounce his personal myths without objecting: his jouissance was apparent when he could aestheticize his stories, and the memories he was able to embellish with a stroke of his pen were his favorites. He discovered in himself the tendency of memory to retain "in the prodigious sum of things that have happened to me, only those that are sheathed in a certain way so as to provide foundation for a mythology" (*RJ*, 304, my translation). In fact, the results of his psychoanalysis, replete with myths (*Lucrece*, *Judith*, and *Holofernes*) is the first version of what would flow into *Manhood* and later *Rules of the Game* without forgetting that his first short bout with analysis was preceded by the novel *Aurora*, featuring the palindromic Siriel. If every neurotic organizes an "individual myth" (Lacan), then psychoanalysis, the cure for neurosis, implies, necessarily, a demystification. The process, carried out with no anesthesia, may be quite painful. Leiris does it on the couch and extends into his books, inventing for himself a memory.

After "submitting" to psychoanalysis, Leiris's writing, converted into poetry, implies a compromise between the drive to say whatever one feels like saying and consideration of the demands of the "rules of the (autobiographical) game" imposed by the Other.

> Thus, showing that through the exercise of poetry one addresses the other as an equal, I returned to the truth that I had first discovered: when I learned that one cannot say . . . *tunately* but rather *fortunately*, I learned that language has two faces, one turned inward the other turned outward, and when—later discovering the altruism of dedicating two or three volumes to my own person—I came to affirm that a poet cannot be disinterested in the fortunes of others, I conceived the argument that justifies it according to this double nature [of language], as if what is essential had already been included in my old experience. Thus I find myself back where I started (*RJ*, 772, my translation).

The discovery made on the occasion of the first experience with relation to the word, the one in which the child is corrected by an adult, is one in which language supposes a transference such that "the transmitter receives its own message from the receptor but in inverted form" (Lacan). For this very reason and as a necessary consequence, it is never a question of "applying" interpretations of a psychoanalytic nature to texts in which the terms author, narrator and the character who speaks in the first person singular "I" are equated. In *The Life of Henri Brulard*, by Henri Beyle, alias Stendhal, we do not find the Freudian Oedipus complex, but rather, on the contrary, it is in the psychoanalyst that we find the theoretical and universal understanding of what was already apparent in a concrete way in Stendhal's text. Freud could not psychoanalyze Stendhal; he had to limit himself to listening to him and allowing him to listen to himself as he linked his discourse together. Stendhal is not the precursor of Freud; instead, he is the necessary outlet for Stendhal . . . and many others, both before and after

Freud. Leiris is a product of the work of psychoanalysis, certainly, but not less than the conceptions and practices (automatic writing, oneiroid aesthetic, etc.) of the surrealist movement of which he was a member for many years and the stamp of which he carried with him throughout his life.

In Leiris's first autobiography, *AH* (*L'Âge d'homme/Manhood*, 1939) the dominant theme is that of the trials and tribulations of his sexuality and his phantasies, activated by contact with various women, following the twofold model of, on the one hand, the absolute test of fidelity—constructed on the model of Lucas Cranach the Elder's *Lucretia*—and, on the other hand, the castrating betrayal of a woman who begins by prostituting herself—based on the model of Cranach the Elder's *Judith*. I will return to this topic when I compare Leiris to Broch. In the second autobiography, *RJ* (*La règle du jeu/Rules of the Game*, 1948–1976), which begins with the ill-fated . . . *reusement!*, the story focuses on an unusual non-memory, on his pursuit of the memory he would have liked to have but does not have—the moment of being invaded by the consciousness of death. I will also return to this later. It is possible to say that, of the two formal autobiographies, the first (*AH*) is *Freudian* in terms of both content and method, whereas the second (*RJ*), following the same parameters, is *Lacanian*.

Little has been said on the strange incongruity between Leiris's two autobiographies because it has been preferable to see both texts as if one were the continuation of the other. Literary critics have shied away from considering the self-critical quality of *Biffures* (*Scratches*) (written between 1942 and 1946) in contrast to *L'Âge d'homme* (*Manhood*) (begun in December 1930 and completed in November 1935). The self-critical tension can be seen clearly in the taurine prologue he added ten years later not as a confirmation but more of a challenge to, or a retraction of, the book he was prefacing. In this sense, *La règle du jeu*, whose first pages are those of *Biffures*, (. . . *reusement!*) refutes the project of the first autobiography and its aspirations to gain the confidence of the reader-witness. *L'Âge d'homme* is a text governed by the messianic illusions of "truth," "authenticity," "sincerity," "that objective gaze turned upon myself" (*Manhood*, 156), "the negation of a novel" (*Manhood*, 158), and other expressions intended to preempt criticism. The rectification, written against the grain in the prologue, is clear:

> What I did not realize was that at the source of all introspection is a predilection for self-contemplation, and that every confession contains a desire to be absolved. To consider myself objectively was still to consider myself—to keep my eyes fixed on myself instead of turning them beyond and transcending myself in the direction of something more broadly human. To expose myself to others, but to do so in a narrative which I hoped would be well-written and well-constructed, perceptive and moving was an attempt to seduce my public into being indulgent, to limit—in any case—the scandal by giving it an aesthetic form (*AH*, 13, *Manhood*, 156–157).

Notwithstanding the preceding, *Biffures* and subsequent writings that would make up *La règle du jeu* all constitute the paradigmatic example of a Lacanian autobiography prepared to consume every last illusion of the self, whereas *L'Âge d'homme* is the indispensable (Freudian) precursor of this Cyclopean, occasionally involved—in honor of the truth—work, which would reveal Leiris over the course of forty years. Of course, Leiris does not want to be considered Lacanian or Freudian but rather nothing other than Leirisean, an archeologist of memory, ethnologist, ornithologist and etymologist of that exotic tribe of disperse memories which is himself. He aspires to "justify his existence" through literature in the strictest and narrowest sense: he renounces being a poet, a mythological hero or an imaginative novelist; he is satisfied with having become "the author of honest autobiographical essays that could become a defense and an illustration of that particular literary genre." He recognizes that the project that motivates him is not so exciting, it is the same as a confession of defeat, but he justifies it by alleging that the final word on the question of moral professionalism is that he must "*do what only I am in conditions to do*" (*RJ*, 763, Leiris's italics) and—why not?—it must be acknowledged, no one would be so cynical as to dispute that only he is in the appropriate position to write his autobiography. There remains but one question: In what way does his writing continue the psychoanalysis that was terminated?

4. The Presence of Death in Leiris's Literary Project

It is astounding how many different strategies Michel Leiris experimented with in order to distract and mock death, his irreconcilable enemy (his and everyone else's)—an enemy that met in this author a most devoted admirer and a most combative warrior! I will try to list them: to write about past life in order to conserve it, to revive memories and to cling to them, to deny the debilitating effects of forgetting, to idolize childhood memory by securing it and embellishing it with the magic of rhythm, to dismantle the traps of language through evocation that aspires to the resuscitation of buried events, to embalm emotions, to continuously publish volumes of fictitious and authentic autobiographies, to live by exhibiting himself like a painting in a gallery, like a torero in a bullfight, writing his story until he reaches the extreme of preferring literary invention to suffering a life tormented by impotence, attracted at all times by the imminence of suicide.

For everyone death is an event yet to take place, the prototype of something that is impossible to remember. We are born without knowledge of the event itself; we enter language, . . . *tunately*, until one day, necessarily later, knowledge of language enters us. From the stark future—where it resides—the news that death awaits us reaches the being who has just begun to feel alive, the news that sooner or later it will overcome him or her and put an end to consciousness and the imaginary revelations of mirrors. Certain knowledge is traumatic, unacceptable, irreconcilable with the self, yet it accompanies us during our entire journey through this world.

Knowledge of the end is endless. Against this knowledge, even more than against death itself—which is invulnerable—humanity has erected all kinds of barriers: religion, technology, medicine, policies of social regulation, passions, images for posterity, genealogies and descendants (classical ideas of the family tree + the child + the book), philosophical systems, conceptions of eternity, infinite dressings applied to sores that never heal and constantly ooze. Most people create a road map of life that ignores their destination, consoling themselves with the idea that death only happens to others. The Freudian unconscious—which for Lacan is one of the many names for God—is unaware of and denies death. Many people feel its dark attraction, they avoid it and they summon it, they worship it, they court it and often precipitate the date they already have to meet it, once and for all, face to face. To imagine it is possible, to live it is not, or, at least, it is not possible to live through it and remember the experience. That does not prevent heavens and hells, Lazaruses, immortal souls and *revenants* of all types to populate the mental landscapes of those who speak of it. Some enjoy seeing it up close, touching it, finding the tangential point at which to make contact with it and still be able to draw away at the crucial moment and observe it from a distance feeling that one has escaped it, mocking it. The orgasm as an (almost) repeatable "little death" at will is a pale imitation. War and bullfighting are more serious games, the former being anonymous and the second bathed in limelight. It is no coincidence that it is called the *fiesta* of the bulls, characterized by the bullring where eroticism and death converge, which fascinated this thanatophobic fanatic of death, Michel Leiris.

The writer accumulated, interrogated and carefully organized his memories without concern for chronology. Like a stamp collector with an album in which every stamp in its place, he is devastated when he discovers that a crucial item is missing, the most valuable, that completes the page of his childhood: the coming to consciousness of his own mortality. He cannot "possess himself in his totality" because there is a lacuna, an amnesia, that obsesses him in the very center of his memory and that he would give anything to fill. Since when?:

> The paramount event that I have always been incapable of recapturing (for the simple reason that it must never have occurred, either because there isn't even the possibility of such a discovery, otherwise than in a purely formal manner, as long as one is not up against the wall, or because it acts only by degrees and in a surreptitious way as the end approaches) is in fact that which would have been constituted, for me, by my sudden awareness of death, or, more precisely, of the fact that my own life—that life which I cannot believe is subject to the same laws as the lives of others—would inevitably end, abruptly, in a complete collapse (*RJ*, 304–305, *Scraps*, 17, see also *AH*, 28).

Leiris lives a fight to the death against death and he thinks that, if he could recover his memory of that moment, something fundamental would change in him. In that gap in his memory he produces a screen memory—insignificant on its own but of staggering beauty—regarding the intense fear he felt one night (when he was four years old?) as he was walking with his father along an empty street in Viroflay, a vacation spot. The "very banal anecdote" (*RJ*, 311, *Scraps*, 23) is that of having heard the noise of the trail of an insect, a distant noise that frightened him, that has him evoke the King of the Alders. Who does not hear, at this point, the chilling ballad of Goethe with the music of Schubert (and of Loewe) that Leiris omitted from his narrative? The father shudders, he runs swiftly, carrying the child who whimpers, and arrives anxiously at the castle: in his arms the child was dead, which leads Leiris to interrogate his father about the nature of the sound and to listen to his answer which only increases his terror. "It's a carriage (*voiture*) that is very far away, very far away" (*RJ*, 306, *Scraps*, 18). Leiris doubts the authenticity of the memory but still believes that his father lied to him to hide from him—so as not to explain to him—*something else* that the child should not know. He interprets his father's statement as a merciful lie meant to hide something truly frightening, knowledge that is forbidden to him:

> . . . I have retained a very vivid memory of that fear. An imprecise, even fantastic memory of how my father might have been involved. A real memory of the fear provoked by that slight buzzing heard in the night, a noise the anguish of which resulted perhaps exclusively from the fact that it manifested the state of wakefulness of something infinitesimal or distant, the only sound present in the silence of a more or less country place where I imagined that at such an hour everything had to be asleep or beginning to fall asleep. Fear of the night. Fear of the dark (*RJ*, 306, *Scraps*, 19).

Leiris states that his memory is faint at this point and that he has to substitute for it with constructions, reasoning, conjecture and relentless rumination in order to retroactively ("*après-coup*") fill this lacuna and he wonders why he needs to relate this vague memory of a visit to the countryside with the consciousness of death. He compares his work to that of the Dutch drying out the Zuider Zee and he suggests that art has a responsibility "to organize or colonize certain parcels of land that are vitally important to protect us from the nameless thing in us whose flood threatens us" (*RJ*, 308, *Scraps*, 21). He pursues this memory over the course of several pages and concludes that the "car" (*voiture*, the father supposedly said, when this word did not yet necessarily mean automobile, in 1905, but which is indeed the word the writer remembers when he evokes this nocturnal memory, like music by Bartok, whose screen-memory-like character does not escape him) could be understood metaphorically, for this "car" continues to roll relentlessly in his memory, in this positive or partly false memory, for it deviates from all pretension of authenticity as a memory of a memory: "—a surprising false bottom! somewhat as there exists a theater of theater" (*RJ*, 311, *Scraps*, 24). A memory manufactured from an absent memory, an unreliable photocopy, a graft inserted in place of the missing stamp in the album. Car, automobile, in a period when certain electric vehicles were on the road, manufactured by the Mors brothers. *Mors* is the title of the chapter containing this decisive memory, *mors* which is linked to the zoological *morse* (walrus), to the Morse code, to the fateful *mors* (death) that he would come to learn when he studied Latin as a child.

Because death torments him, Leiris cannot be altogether a man or consider that he exists. From the start everything is devalued given that he must die: owing to his awareness of the transitory nature of everything and all action, everything he sees seems empty and senseless:

> Free of all true passion, all vice, and even all ambition, I am, while I am still alive, subject to a torpor similar to that of the museum figures who once intruded into my sleep, and the acts that I perform are scarcely more than the gestures of an automaton or the mechanical works of a zombie, as though fear, by obliterating everything in me, had transformed me here and now into that bodily frame without consciousness that I am so afraid of becoming. The prescience of the sickening moment when everything will vanish—as the ground disappears from under the feet of a person tumbling into the darkness of a secret dungeon—is enough to make me, reduced as I am to the abstraction of a geometric point, the center of a cottony sort of world inhabited now only by vague forms, except for those, all too distinct for my taste, in which I believe I read a threat (*RJ*, 343–344, *Scraps*, 58).

The Leirisian thanatophobia yields to the counterphobic reaction of defying the feared object. It is only worth living when one is confronted by death. The model, as I have already indicated, is the art of bullfighting. Unable to risk his life in this sublime activity—indeed he was incapable of playing any sport other than hiking—Leiris made a decision that would become the guiding principle of his existence: writing would serve the mission of exposing him, line by line, *biffure por biffure*, to the bull's naked horn. The scene of the fiesta in the bullring fascinated him and he searched for equivalents. Still, it should be pointed out that in his ideal scenario he is not always wearing the sparkling suit of the torero but rather, the majority of the time, he opts for the role of the bull, the preordained victim of a programmed sword thrust from the very beginning of the bullfight. The reader follows Leiris through images that portray him as having surrendered to death. He finds the image of Judith to be marvelous . . . yet he identifies with the hero who is . . . Holofernes, the decapitated nocturnal lover. The other figure that delights him, also taken from the elder Cranach, is Lucretia with the dagger piercing her just beneath her nude breast. The longing is clear: to aestheticize death in a vain attempt to make it disappear.

What value can writing have—when nothing is risked in reality—in comparison with bullfighting and its defiant courtship of death? Leiris explains it thus: in order to shed one's mortality it is necessary to differentiate oneself from other mortals, to clearly establish a carefully maintained difference from them relative to death itself, from which one wants to escape. Without raising one's hopes too much. Every time the writer relieved his anxieties by submitting another book to the press he ended up stating, whether it had been received well or poorly, that the book "will have been a gesture in the void" (*RJ*, 1163–1164, my translation). The attempt to kill death always ends in failure . . . and it is necessary to begin again. The book is the saddled horse, mounted by the bullfighter who crazily attempts to win the race with death but ultimately finds that the book itself is a reason to live, not a vehicle that clarifies how to live. In order to write the book the author refers to memory, that exclusive property that differentiates him from others because no one else possesses those memories . . . but the reins of memory are hardly trustworthy: the difficulties are infinite, the past cannot be recovered through the tip of the pen and the meaning of experience evades him "without even attaining the dignity of enigmas" (*RJ*, 297, *Scraps*, 9). For this reason, so long as death does not overwhelm him, unable to rid himself of the idea of death, he feels compelled to put himself at death's service. To this end he appeals to the timid memories of an unrecoverable past, minuscule slices of life where he finds that something resembling Michel Leiris appears to exist; thus, he dedicates himself to the relentless hunt of those experiences in which his face may be a little less strange to him. He affirms and denies at the same time that the pen, held in the palm of his right hand, had become a heavy column of marble whose weight oppresses him to the point of crying out, had someone not suddenly woken him from the nightmare (*RJ*, 354, *Scraps*, 69). To write is to fulfill a vital and essential mission of denying death, which he feels passing through his body and his life. He pours the ink onto the page like a bull (if not the torero) pouring its blood onto the sands of the arena at the conclusion of the struggle. He is aware that his endeavor is contrived:

> . . . liking to play at being a torero but without ever having a real bull in front of me, and at being a Don Juan, without any conquests nor challenge to the Commandant; no longer existing except through writing and, at each instant, attempting to formulate sententious phrases with the distant tone of last words, as though my fingers were already squeezed by the stone gauntlet of death, am I not a proxy unfaithful to the destiny I have dreamed of, in other words am I not that prevaricator (*RJ*, 350, *Scraps*, 64)?

Leiris has various reasons to lack faith in his undertaking. His life, like any other, is marked by singular events and to pour it out onto the page, transforming it into one or many books is the man's undeniable right; to the point that not even the historic Declaration of 1789 considered it necessary to mention it. It is also certain that every life consists in coincidences and banalities that do not deserve special attention, especially when they lack special achievements or feats to report. Shakespeare's memory, as Borges liked to say, consisted in the same trivialities as other men's. Narrating one's life is, in any case, an innocuous and anodyne, albeit tempting, undertaking as we can appreciate by taking into account the vast quantity of intimate diaries, journals, collected letters, memoirs, confessions and autobiographies that are written, published and even read. Leiris was aware of the current state of his existence and of the possibility of erecting it as a monument through the literary act so as to perpetuate his being beyond the inevitable event—also trivial—of his death. How can one transform the narrative of one's memories into a heroic deed and convert the faded traces of one's life into an event that is not only memorized but also memorable? How can one justify the project of dedicating one's life to writing an unfinished symphony in Me-sharp major, as if it were Schubert's in A? How can one avoid the suspicions—both one's own and the readers'—regarding vanity, narcissism, self-indulgence, the search for alibis and complicities to respond to unspoken accusations, to simulate a sexual power which is fading away?

Leiris knew that all these clouds cast shadows on his literary activity and consequently he resorted to a heroic model that could justify the hodgepodge of an autobiography that was virtually interminable, despite the fact that there were no special events to relate and he even omitted the conventions of the traditional genre with the trite accumulation of information and memories of meetings with remarkable friends and celebrities, people who were not lacking but are fortunately absent in both *Manhood* and *Rules of the Game*. In order to defend himself from these eventual accusations he formulated the analogy between his work and the life-or-death exhibition performed by the torero, without forgetting that:

. . . to write and publish an autobiography does not involve, for the man who undertakes such a thing (unless he has committed an offense whose admission makes him liable to capital punishment) any danger of death . . . Undoubtedly he risks suffering in his relations with those close to him, and risks social opprobrium if his avowals run too counter to accepted ideas; but it is possible, even if he is not a pure cynic, that such punishments may be of little enough consequence for him (may even please him, should he regard as salubrious the atmosphere thus created around him), so that he is dealing with an entirely fictional risk. Whatever the case, a moral risk of this kind cannot be compared with the bodily risk the *torero* faces (*AH*, 16–17, *Manhood*, 159–160).

Nonetheless he insists on extolling his literary gesture by glorifying the risks he exposes himself to: thus, according to the bullfighting model, it is necessary for him to utilize his technical sagacity to the utmost in order to overcome danger. What attracts him about psychoanalysis is, precisely, whatever can grant him a mythical status since the Freudian experience "affords every man a convenient means of achieving the tragic level by seeing himself as a new Oedipus" (*AH*, 20, *Manhood*, 158). The theatrical role of the bullfight in the lives of the spectators does not escape him either: Leiris offers himself as craftsman for the struggle. The public can identify with him. He can bask in their approval, their shouts of *olé!* It is Leiris who will "allow them to discover in themselves something homophonous to this content I had discovered in myself" (*AH*, 20, *Manhood*, 163). He aspires to the universal through the particular and through poetic magnification. In his attempt to defeat death with the pen and eraser (*biffures*), without accepting that in the face of an invincible enemy the best one can do is admit defeat, will he not end up writing the most moving of hymns, the most rigorous of apologies, at the last, supreme moment?

5. Sexuality Analyzed: Michel Leiris and Hermann Broch

The trial by fire for Leiris—the would-be "torero"—is the exposure of certain reserved aspects of his sexual life, "the cornerstone in the structure of the personality" (*AH*, 18, *Manhood*, 161). Imbued with Christian morality, he considers the confession of his carnal acts to be the most dangerous task, one in which he runs the greatest of risks, in which he submits to the most intense—and the most difficult—demands of authenticity. Perhaps in 1945 imparting his little sexual secrets seemed indecent; however, in light of literature, film, poetry, theater and other visual arts over the last sixty years—from Henry Miller to Catherine Millot, not to mention their precursor, the divine Marquis—Leiris's brazen acts may appear to us as rather ingenuous today, even as we recognize in his autobiographical enterprise a (nearly) pioneering spirit for confessional literature. His memories and phantasies could be those of anyone and they even seem to lack the supposed charm that is so common in the perversion exhibited today for the voyeuristic jouissance of the other. The value of his testimony resides more in the style he invented for narrating his intimacies than in the facts themselves—his art of intimating what remains beneath the veil, in the same way that the torero hides the sword behind the cape—and, above all, in his analysis of the subjective mechanisms of his actions. The question that characterizes the obsessive subject: "Am I alive or dead?" is illustrated in exemplary fashion by Leiris when he relates his counterphobic attraction to death which we have already seen and that led him, at certain points in his life, to suicide attempts that were almost successful, followed by tracheotomy and days and days of sleep, topics which supplied material for new pages of memories. However, the strategies, anxieties and doubts of the obsessive subject relative to sex, perhaps more so than death, are the ones that the writer exposes for the reader. With respect to those dangerous "acts of the flesh,"

Leiris does not derive jouissance from exhibiting the corruption of his self so much as from exhibiting his *virtue*, always understood from an Augustinian and neo-Platonic perspective of sex at the risk of castration and condemnation—the supreme sin of the flesh that will lead to perdition, ever so much worse depending on the intensity and level of desire.

> As an adult, I preserve a constant longing for ideal friendship and platonic love beside what some will regard as ignoble immersions in vileness and vice. As a child, I was enthralled by those fabulous adventures filled with wizards, knights, and impossibly chaste damsels, at the same time that the confusions of puberty stirred within me (*AH*, 136–137, *Manhood*, 90).

Once again the idealized silhouette of the torero emerges in this portrait, here converted into the faded image of a challenge that hardly masks his avoidance of a "danger," personified in women, a hazard that is artificially provoked and imaginarily confronted. For Leiris the art of bullfighting is a reenactment of coitus (unless it is precisely the contrary) and the act of writing aspires to be an equivalent or a substitute for both. Not without a degree of sarcasm, I would characterize his effort as well as the result—evoking Nabokov—as "pale fire."

Delving into his past, Leiris recalls his amazement on various occasions: when experiencing his first erection while witnessing the seemingly innocent spectacle of some poor children climbing a tree barefoot (*AH*, 107, *Manhood*, 67); in his infantile sexual theories he believed that babies were not born through the sex of the mother but rather through the navel, "that navel which I had been so startled to learn (at an even earlier period) is, after all, a scar" (*AH*, 62, *Manhood*, 32); the writer describes terror, resulting in chastity and asceticism sustained for long periods of his adult life; he comes to think of himself as someone virtually possessed of impotency because of his fear of sharp instruments and, as mentioned previously, sees this reflected in his attraction to Judith and Lucrece; in his phantasies, organized around the ribbon on the neck of Manet's Olympia, which led him to write a beautiful essay dedicated to that detail of the painting; in the repulsion he felt at the age of nine when he saw his sister's new-born daughter (*AH*, 26, *Manhood*, 5); in the anticipation of the impossibility of making love if he contemplated the possibility that the act was something other than sterile and without anything in common with the human instinct of procreating (. . .), as a result of which:

> It has been some time [. . .] since I have ceased to consider the sexual act as a simple matter, but rather as a relatively exceptional event, necessitating certain inner accommodations that are either particularly tragic or particularly exalted, but very different, in either case, from what I must regard as my usual disposition (*AH*, 26, *Manhood*, 5).

For Leiris having a son represents an ominous possibility that leads him "to the point of having for a long time made sterility a moral position: the refusal to propagate life, because life is too great an evil" (*AH*, 348, *Scraps*, 62). To move to the rank of father is to descend one step toward the grave, to carry to an extreme the incestuous nature of marriage which has the function of turning amorous relationships into family relationships and which, in turn, culminate in the transformation of the man into a husband, a domestic variant of lover, reduced to the exhausted condition of "the father of my child," which is to say, merely kin. Leiris notices that he has fallen into a flagrant contradiction: he is opposed to the propagation of life and, at the same time, writing his books, he appeals to posterity and contemplates with disjouissance the possibility of destruction or disappearing into the oblivion of the volumes that he submits to the publisher with such care and constancy. He would like to have a semblance of living on through future generations of readers. If procreation is senseless, literature is no less senseless. If literature proclaims the vanity of the human world, the very denunciation is a boomerang that mercilessly strikes the writer himself: "to speak of the absurd to an absurd world is necessarily absurd" (*RJ*, 349, *Scraps*, 63).

Sex, on which he focuses so much of his writing, is both the cause and mirror of his anxiety. Leiris is horrified by the prospect of having to prove himself a man to a woman. To love is to expose oneself to the sword of the torero, to the sword that cut the throats of Holofernes and John the Baptist, the dagger in the left breast of Lucretia, the scalpel that removed his tonsils when he was a child, to episodes of impotence like the first time he visited a brothel or the first days of a relationship with a woman he has fallen in love with (*AH*, 173, *Manhood*, 113). For Leiris poetry is an alibi that allows him to escape from the sword hidden behind the woman's red cape. He enjoys the "weight and savor of words," which he lets melt in his mouth like ripe fruits, more than "any strictly erotic delights" (*AH*, 184, *Manhood*, 128). Faced with the panic of sexual penetration he consoles himself with the knowledge that, from a sentimental perspective, he is satisfied with the friendship of a woman and when he finally decides to get married he feels that he has "committed a kind of treason or at least made a bitter renunciation" (*AH*, 187, *Manhood*, 130).

He finds his attitude towards women comprehensible strictly (and conventionally) in psychoanalytic terms, that is, in terms of castration: he feels at once horror and desire over liberating himself from the curse of having to present himself as a desirous man when "proposing sex." He views coitus as an act that is not only guilt-filled if one surrenders to it very quickly, but also painful and dangerous. The inversion of the masculine and feminine roles is conspicuous; he hysterically plays the part of the woman, although he never displays or describes fantasies of homosexual encounters. On a night of drunkenness he went to the home of a homosexual friend. Leiris narrates the episode saying that he "slept with him after having humiliated my mouth and his own in a reciprocal frenzy" (*AH*, 146, *Manhood*, 97). His erotic ghosts always have a feminine (phallic) object that terrifies him in the double figure of Judith and Lucrece, the women with swords. After narrating short descriptions of no less than fifteen episodes of impotence, he concludes: "For a woman, to me, is always Medusa or the Raft of the Medusa. By this I mean that if her gaze does not freeze up my blood, then everything must ensue as if we compensated for that by tearing each other apart" (*AH*, 147, *Manhood*, 99). To this may be added the following, for greater detail:

> . . . even now I cannot love a woman without wondering, for instance, into what drama I might dash for her sake, what torture endure—a grinding of bones or a rending of flesh, drowning or roasting over a slow fire—a question I always answer with so exact an awareness of my terror of physical suffering that I am perpetually crushed by my shame, my whole being corrupted by this incurable cowardice (*AH*, 49, *Manhood*, 22).

Cowardice is notable and underlies the literary project that substitutes for his vacillating sexuality at the same time as it illuminates the reasons why, with veiled self-confidence, he narrates the details of his love life. Leiris writes in order to escape from the truths about sex and death that envelope and terrify him. He recognizes that "I am a specialist in confession" (*AH*, 155, *Manhood*, 105), which is something all his friends know, because his shyness leads him to reveal intimacies that convert him into a dramatic person who increasingly suffers feelings of inferiority the more he is gripped by anxiety. For this reason he cannot express himself as a male who desires a female. Rather, it is always necessary for the gesture of erotic advance to originate from her towards him. In this way he understands that, in the erotic joust (an imaginary struggle, I would say, and I believe Leiris would agree), he does not occupy the position of the conqueror but rather the "subjugated element" (*AH*, 156, *Manhood*, 106). Thus he heightens his feelings of inferiority believing that he must always be content in the passive role, he must be the one who is chosen, at the mercy of the woman's desire, having fallen into a trap that shames him whenever he finds himself in circumstances of loving and being loved.

His autobiography enables him to expose himself as a child who does not seek jouissance but rather, from the woman, absolution and a consolatory gesture, a soft breast on which he can cry in comfort. At the same time they are all Judith and she fascinates him and paralyzes him with terror, as well as soft Lucrece, faithful until death, who is the only woman he could conquer while dreaming of Judith. Because every Lucrece presents herself as a consequence of his cowardice in pursuit of Judith, he has no option but "in order to love Lucrece better, to make her into a martyr" (*AH*, 151, *Manhood*, 101) and then to try to compensate to her by introducing into her daily life a moral laceration expressed as pity.

> For if I examine the nature of this pity with sufficient exactitude, I perceive that the intoxicating confusion I suffer from it derives above all from the remorse attached to it because it is I myself who have behaved in a cowardly fashion, and cruelly enough to occasion such pity (*AH*, 151, *Manhood*, 102).

At this point it seems appropriate to refer to a testimonial, in large part concurring with Leiris's, provided by one of the major figures of the twentieth century, Hermann Broch [1886–1951], the acclaimed author of *Sleepwalkers*, *The Death of Virgil* and other master works. While under Freud's influence and also under self-analysis (with Paul Federn, while living in exile in the United States), in his curious *Psychic Autobiography*[190]—the text is an incomparable epiphany of the sexuality of the obsessive—he attempts to explain to his friends why he is not able to live a normal life. Broch offers a stark portrait of himself on the erotic and sexual level in which he exposes with bold sincerity his neurotic

---

190. Broch, Hermann. *Autobiographie psychique*. Translation by Laurent Cassagneau. Paris: L'Arche, 2001.

particularities with women after having discovered over the course of psychoanalysis certain phantasies of sentimental and mental life. The literary project he undertakes, using himself as guinea pig, as he indicates from the beginning, is a search for truth and, therefore, a *philosophical work*. For my part, I prefer this affirmation to the dubious and forced analogy with the bullfight scenario that guides Leiris's work. Broch lives overwhelmed by a terrible feeling of inferiority that he attributes to having received less love from his mother than she gave to his brother. This (a common Oedipal complex) is not what is of most importance, but rather the consequences he suffers: he cannot see himself as a man; his fundamental characteristic is impotence, including physical aspects of the condition, impotence that is counteracted through excessive compensation that lead him to prove his virility by multiplying his amorous relationships. Aware of the falsity of his efforts, he denigrates himself and seeks a peaceful return to ascesis as a form of life that better suits him. These exaggerated performances later awake an implacable demand to dedicate himself to the truth and to humanity as a whole which, always insufficient, only reinforce the feeling of inferiority. What, we might ask, lies along this avenue of insatiable and disgraceful sexuality? Nothing less than *The Death of Virgil*, "a strictly esoteric book, begun despite myself as a private affair concerning the salvation of my soul."[191]

The accumulation of consummated failures and of suspicious successes in his relationship with the opposite sex produces a result that is similar to Michel Leiris's; in good measure Broch's analysis would have been of use to Leiris for discovering unusual aspects of his erotic psychology and, in this sense, of the literary sublimation to which he dedicated his energies and his life in the infinite autobiographical project that absorbed the French writer. Broch admits his timidity and weakness and goes on to discover that, because of that impotence, which is the effect of his cowardice, he has no right to court a woman but rather he has to wait to be—like Leiris—chosen by her, such that, if

191. Broch, Hermann. Op. cit., p. 100.

impotence is manifest, the responsibility falls to her; thus, his shame is diminished because he knows that, in fact, he has possessed the woman, a woman that was not even the object of his desire. However, he cannot ignore that he got the woman, via the strategy of playing the part of one who lets himself be seduced, and therefore guilt and responsibility fall on him, and he enters servile and oblational relationships which are moral rather than erotic commitments. They culminate in the pathetic figure of a genuine moral masochist, expressed in "the grotesque obligation to consent to every consenting woman—at least in theory and on principle—but also to devote my life to her. In this way I have constructed a feminine role" (*ibid.,* p. 14). Broch goes on to say that his virility is not natural: it is exhibited overcompensation and hypertrophied sublimation. With his acts of polygamy he proposes denying the stealthy infantile reverie of a relationship consisting absolutely in dependence, in total and mutual commitment, in a miraculous mystique that is always defeated by the sad lasciviousness of his relationships with women. It is obvious to the reader that the precocious and Oedipal ghost of chivalrous love appears in the same terms for Broch and Leiris. Because liberation from such a cumbersome and impractical ideal ("human reality does not countenance such a relationship between myself and another self") does not happen, another solution takes its place: that of turning away from sentimental relationships and seeking refuge among prostitutes. It is understood: the payment of money permits escape from guilt and consequent moral obligations.

Broch's erotic life, both real and fantasized, is degraded, dissociated and split, just as Freud anticipated much earlier in a theoretical text, and as it emerges in Leiris's text, such that we find two contrasting tendencies oriented towards two different types of women. Freud spoke of the opposition between the mother and the prostitute, and Leiris addresses the opposition of the mother to Lucrece and Judith. In contrast, Hermann Broch sets up the opposition between older, beautiful, Jewish women who enjoy privileged economic situations, "decorative" women, who know how to carry themselves, who satisfy him regarding his erotic vanity and in the social dimension but do not attract him; they terrify him as they fall into a class that is prohibited by the incest taboo; with them he can consummate a "white marriage," like the one that existed between his parents as he recalls it in his infantile memory, and he contrasts these women with fast women, maids, women of low social status with whom he can display a pseudo-virile sufficiency in relationships that, in any case, must remain hidden from the mother's and the broader world's sight, to be carried out in the shadows, in hiding and shame. In such relationships he does not play the valuable role of the father but rather of the child who needs to be looked after and, therefore, demands attention: "In summary, the first type corresponds to my superego, the second to my id-drive and if the former permits me to live my masochism, I situate all of my sadism in the latter" (*ibid.*, p. 55). The obsessive *impasse* is manifest: whatever he does and with whomever he enters into a relationship, he will always be indebted and he will always feel that he is not doing what he should or would like to be doing. Satisfaction is always condemned and, therefore, in one case or another, jouissance is guaranteed through doubts that feed on the guilt that his choices lead him to suffer. Who can liberate Broch? He knows and denies the solution: successful analysis, its continuation until it reaches a proper conclusion of the process that was begun and interrupted. However, if he should decide to complete it, he will have to face another hell: if he submits himself to this analysis, he will be committing a twofold betrayal that will cause moral conflicts and obsessive attitudes to reemerge, that is, the betrayal of each of the women he could love and another betrayal regarding the literary project to which he has dedicated himself by permitting that "analysis shall be the only lover that reigns." The conclusion is astounding: "To state it in a paradoxical and grotesque manner: my neurosis seems to impede any analysis" (*ibid.*, p. 78).

Leiris's taste for analysis is just as anemic as Broch's. He invites and incites "modern explorers of the unconscious" to speak of

Oedipus, castration, guilt, narcissism and whatever else they care to because—as he understands it—nothing will be learned from it about the essence of the problem which, for him, is always linked to the unsolvable enigma of death (*mors*) and, therefore, concerns metaphysics. He finds that, in the end, there is a substantial relationship between beauty and fear. Thus he can identify with Apollinaire's verses: "Cette femme était si belle / Qu'elle me faisait peur." ("That woman was so lovely / She terrified me.") (*AH*, 152, *Manhood*, 103). The most intense anger Leiris ever felt towards his father sprang from when his father characterized these two lines as incomprehensible and absurd.

Sex and death, Eros and Thanatos, death and sex. Leiris discovers the intimate connection between them, as we see in these two eloquent fragments from *Fourbis / Scraps*:

> *Our death is bound up with the duality of the sexes. If a man were male and female at the same time and capable of reproducing alone, he would not die, his soul being transmitted unadulterated to his posterity.*
>
> *The instinctive hatred of the sexes for each other comes, perhaps, from an obscure knowledge that their mortality is due to the differentiation between them. A violent resentment, counterbalanced by the attractions toward oneness—life's only number—which they try to satisfy through coitus* (*RJ*, 346, *Scraps*, 59, italics in original).

Thus Leiris confesses to his phantasy, his *bisexuality*: pertaining to the two sexes at the same time could dissolve the opposition and the *impasses* that he perceives between the beast and the torero, man and woman, life and death, ink and blood, fact and fiction, Judith and Holofernes, desire and jouissance, and, finally, between "love and terror." To be a man who was also a woman, surrendered to an interminable coitus with himself: would that be an autobiography?

6. Methodical Ego-Graphy and the Perpetuation of Memory

As I have already stated, Leiris's entire work, although at times embarrassing and even against the grain, is nonetheless a symphony in Me-major with mystical pretensions and a hunger for eternity, for perpetuation beyond death.

> If I bring together all these facts extracted from what was my daily existence when I was a child, I see emerging, little by little, an image of what for me is *sacred* [. . .] Insofar as one of the most "sacred" goals that a man may set for himself is to gain knowledge of himself that is as intense and precise as possible, is seems desirable that everyone, scrutinizing his memories with the utmost honesty, should examine if he or she can discover in them some indication that would enable discerning the *color* of the notion of sacred for the person ("The Sacred in Daily Life. The Man without Honor" [1939], *RJ*, 1118, italics in original, my translation).

Leiris's project has biblical features. Its title could be, *The Gospel According to Me*.

> I imagined that I had, still more than a vocation, a *destiny*, for the state of exaltation in which I found myself seemed to me an irrefutable proof that my life had something mythical about it. Conscious as I was of the mediocrity of my literary means, I regarded myself as a kind of prophet, and I derived a great deal of pride from a messianism which seemed to me inherent in the fate of any poet (*AH*, 190, *Manhood*, 132–133).

The narrator in this case presents himself undisguised as preordained, a demiurge, the forger of a real universe, capable of reaching the absolute and possessing it. Here it would be easy to appeal to morbid notions of megalomania and narcissism. But Leiris is not raving; he knows very well that the color of what is sacred has faded due to the uncertainty of memory and by the indefinite aspect of his own ending. For good reason the title of the first volume of *La règle du jeu* (which, it should be noted, is also *La règle du je*, or, *Rules of the I*) is *Biffures* (*Scratches*). This heading is a play on words: each moment of life, every line of his narrative, is susceptible to being narrated in different ways because it presents a *bifurcation* like a railroad track. Choices must be constantly made. However, once a choice has been made, it is necessary to decide what and how much to say: the text must be submitted to scratch-outs, amendments, erasures which leave an imprint of what was written, that is, a trace of the original text. *Biffer* is the French verb meaning the act of crossing out by drawing a line through what has been written; *biffures* are the lines themselves that are drawn through the words. Thanks to the ease of correcting with electronic word processors which have made both crossing out and rubber erasure obsolete, this action is one that we are no longer accustomed to. Memory is recorded, then, from the raw material of memories through the selection of narrative avenues, at the crossroads of the discursive lanes, using ink lines that invalidate first compositions in favor of others that, as palimpsests, hide the subsistent imprint of what one wished to eliminate.

When I write *egography*, my word processor automatically, without cross-outs or warnings, corrects and alters the order of the first letters to spell *geography*. Perhaps it is not so wrong: *geography of the self*. It could also—but it is not so wise—write *geology*, the study of the superimposed layers of the self. I am interested in Leiris's method for exploring and writing himself and, eventually, deceiving himself about the result of his tireless autobiographic effort. He has let his pen run free for seventy years, from the moment he began his intimate diary. He has rummaged through his memories and has produced indelible pages such as the infantile discovery of having to submit to a language that does not belong to him: *heureusement/fortunately.* Perhaps—and this is my impression—he never resigned himself and does not trust this discovery which makes him dependent on the Other for language. He has passed his life trying to challenge it, sustaining that his omnipotent word is capable of forcing the Other to concede that indeed one can say . . . *reusement /* . . . *tunately.* At some point in his vast work, fleetingly, humbly, hiding it even from himself, in *Aurora* (a play on the words *aurora* and *horror of*), he recognized that he was writing *novels*, fictions. The ambiguity regarding the genre of his writing is one of the keys to his work. The more carefully he composes his texts, the deeper he delves into his past; the less he wants to be taken as a fabulist, the more he surrenders himself to the task of *encrypting memory.* He is like a torero trying not to know that what he does is a representation, a performance, a spectacle conceived to garner applause by protecting one's own skin. That, by exposing himself to the naked horns, he fulfills a decorative function for the approval of the public.

When I visit a bookstore in the United States I notice that the books offered to readers are organized in two broad categories: fiction and nonfiction. In a way that is not as obvious as it might appear, biographies and autobiographies are on the nonfiction shelves; it might be supposed that these books are "truer" than the others because they take care to exclude the imagination and invention of the author in the presentation of the text. The difficulties of classifying texts into genres—since Derrida—are well-known. I would venture to say that there is no law but rather an *aporia*, an impossibility of genre. As an example, if we read on a book cover, *The Martian Chronicles*, we immediately understand that we are faced with a fictional work. However, immediately thereafter we encounter the word "Stories." Does the word "stories" pertain to the group of stories that make up the volume and that take place on Mars or is it a nonfictional addition that externally characterizes the narratives, fixing their destiny internally and sending the reader a message: "Do not believe that what you are about to read is *true*." A self-referential exception would be

Lope's sonnet about sonnets where the word "sonnet" does not form part of the sonnet itself. Here the proposed analogy is to bullfighting—is it fiction or nonfiction? How often have novelists presented their fantasies as representations of life in its most attractive or crude reality? How often have we wondered if what we were reading was a true story?

Serge André[192] resolved the dilemma when referring to the novel of his childhood, his narrative, saying that it is "one thousand percent" autobiographical, that is, "one hundred percent autobiographical plus nine hundred percent that I added." He explains that the elements contained in the first hundred percent "would not have been of interest to anyone, including myself, if they hadn't been inflated by the nine hundred percent that I added." What has he done? He has taken what was confusing and enigmatic in his memories and he has worked the remains of the shipwreck of memory into a poetic form that could rescue them and make them interesting for a reader who would become judge and executor of his words and sentences, but not of his life . . . because no matter how much one writes it is not life but rather . . . literature. If something is *graphy*, life (bios) is absent.

The more an author asserts the authenticity and sincerity of an autobiography, the more artificial it seems. This is the deceit of which Leiris is more a victim than a perpetrator: there is no "genre," particularly in the field of narration, that does not fall into the category of fiction because a "natural genre" does not exist. No one can narrate without the use of artifice—particularly if they are attempting to produce a lasting work and feel that they are putting their life into it or that with the pen they are emulating the torero with his sword—and "the truth" transmitted by the text is secondary, it is retroactive to what is written, it is pronounced by the audience, the reader. In this type of text, what is verifiable is usually anecdotal and secondary, it is more confusing than informative, it *rationalizes* more than it discovers *reason* in what has

---

192. André, Serge. *Flac, suivi de "L'écriture commence où finit la psychanalyse*. Bruxelles: Que, 2001.

been lived. Nothing is more mistaken in an autobiography than the invocation of truth "without altering so much as a comma of the past."

Let us consider two not-so-random examples. Before writing *Remembrance of Things Past*, Marcel Proust wrote an enormous draft of 700 pages that he never gave to the publishers and which only appeared thirty years after his death (in 1952) under the title (invented by scholars of the manuscript), *Jean Santeuil*,[193] the name of the protagonist of this narrative written in the third person singular. It is clear to everyone that for Proust this text, brimming with incongruities, was directly replaced by the very different one he wrote later, the great novel that brought him fame, narrated in the first person singular by a character named "Marcel." Nonetheless, *Jean Santeuil* begins with this brief introduction:

> Should I call this book a novel? It is something less, perhaps, and yet much more, the very essence of my life, with nothing extraneous added, as it developed through a long period of wretchedness. This book of mine has not been manufactured: it has been garnered (p. 3).

Jean Santeuil is a narrative about the author's own life but all the personal information has been modified in service to the literary project. Would it be any more "true" if the protagonist were "I, Marcel Proust" instead of "Jean S." and if it were filled with verifiable information? No; there would only be an appearance of objectivity and, therefore, the fictional component, far from being lessened, would be more evident. I will argue in the final chapters of this book that, whatever the subject, it is impossible for a text not to form part of the autobiography of the author and to allude to the moment and the setting of writing—we embellish, we exaggerate: even when copying the telephone directory.

---

193. Proust, Marcel [1896, first published, 1952]. *Jean Santeuil*. Translated by Gerard Hopkins. London: Weidenfeld and Nicolson, 1955.

Let us take the second example: the highly original Austrian novelist, Joseph Roth (1849–1939) also begins his novel, *Flight Without End*,[194] with a brief foreword:

> In what follows I tell the story of my friend, comrade and spiritual associate, Franz Tunda. I follow in part his notes, in part his narrative. I have invented nothing, made up nothing. The question of 'poetic invention' is no longer relevant. Observed fact is all that counts (p. 5).

Ingenuousness or an attempted ambush for the reader to wander into? If option and enigma are valid for the two novels, this is also the case, for the same reasons, for all autobiographies, for every attempt at telling a human life "au natural." Fiction, including the Martian Chronicles, is what we call the world in which we live, what we call the author and even what we call ourselves as we read (ourselves in) those very works. The *egography*, of course, of any writer, politician or scientist also speaks of all this . . . but it does so in a deceptive way, on the pretext of "authenticity." The fabulous *Tristram Shandy* by Sterne is as "true" as Rousseau's *Confessions*, Rousseau is as "true" as Stiller in the novel, *I'm Not Stiller*, by Max Frisch, which denounces the pitfalls of identity. "*Yo soy*" ("I am") is a deceitful palindrome: no predicate could make the "I" true, and then the verb "to be," conjugated in the first person singular, consummates the deception. The claim of "naturality" is an alibi into which both author and reader often fall. Here I will propose an analogy, once again as a question: Can flowers in a house be "real" and be distinguished without problems from "artificial" flowers? Cut and placed in a vase or in soil in a flowerpot, bought or picked in the garden, arranged in a certain place with care, in water or sprinkled with water, they always obey laws of language that govern their owners who "happily" believe they are using them. How is this different from the case of a

---

194. Roth, Joseph. *Flight Without End*. Translated by David Le Vay and Beatrice Musgrave. London: Peter Owen, 1977.

book, whatever its qualities, plot or genre? Who could narrate his or her memories without cultivating them, discarding some and tracing some so that they become more visible, trimming them and framing them, grouping them and arranging them carefully for the gaze of others, enclosing them in a vocabulary that cannot avoid that the differences between the lived event, the memory and the narration will be highlighted? Is a book not like a flower vase with printed pages? All of us willfully participate in the deception of the illusion: flowers that are too perfect seem artificial and artificial flowers, if they are well-made, seem natural. It is not unusual to find oneself touching flowers to test if the petals are made of plastic or if they are natural.

Leiris did not inspire this comparison but the analogy may be seen in a certain "documented" way in the warm temptation of the quotation when one, with considerable surprise, finds it in the final moments of his monumental autobiography. The thanatophobia reemerges in the last lines of the last volume of *La règle du jeu*. Leiris narrates the death of this brother, a clear foreshadowing of his own death; on the day he writes that page, he describes the horrible image of the deceased person and he anticipates how that face will be materially hidden by the last *toilette*. He then wonders if he himself is not proceeding towards a *final toilette* by attempting, "in order to make the thing more tolerable, to impose with the pen some order on what is a horror without a name" (*RJ*, 1054, my translation). Following the concluding lines of the last volume, *Frêle bruit*, he feels it is appropriate to add a brief epilogue in order to reflect on the whole of his life which he confuses with the act of having made it public, combining—in my opinion—the functions of notary and poet. Thus he reviews his tactics in order to consider "the snows of days gone by with the spirit of the present, removing them from the pages or the drawers of his memory in order to mix them with things of the present" and he wonders, feeling hurt:

But, does one obtain a view of eternity by mixing the periods, multiplying the points of view and joining or opposing the tonalities as one pleases? It is a question of arrangement, as in Japan where one patiently arranges a few flowers—without merging them into the profusion of the bouquet—for the jouissance—or the peace—of the gaze, in any case, leaving something hidden. A floral arrangement, then, limited by absences in an even more unpardonable way than any deliberate choice: what I have not discovered, what I did not know how to formulate or what I have refused to bring to light (*RJ*, 1055, my translation).

And now *La règle du jeu* (*du je*) is finished. He does not conclude by affirming the primacy of the word but rather by touching the limit of the indescribable, that which exceeds the limits of knowledge or of disgust. The task of writing autobiography culminates in the artificial composition of life like an ikebana, center of the dream that communicates with what is real that no typographer could print. It is what is exposed at the end of the autobiography as well as at the end of psychoanalysis: not the primacy of an interpretation without defects, but rather the arrival at a goal that is recognition of the defects in knowledge. Leiris—like Broch, Beckett or Perec—passes from his psychoanalytic experience to the exhibition of his phantasies, he passes from the word to the discourse, capriciously organized in the analytic sessions in search of a definitive and impossible construction of a rigorous writing that attempts to surround the indescribable nucleus of existence, limited by the invincibility of death and sexuality, this conjunction that is condensed for Leiris in the combined figures of Lucrece and Judith, imagistic representatives of that (reality) which cannot be known. In this sense—as proposed by Lacan for Joyce—writing (always more or less autobiographical, as we now know) fulfills a function of a *symptom* that enables the subject to navigate the choppy waters of what is called "life," albeit precariously and albeit when the image of suicide meanders through the fantasies of so many writers.

As Serge André used to say, "it is not psychoanalysis that interprets literature" (as has been believed with the ingenuousness of enlighteners in the arrogant attitude of psychoanalysts addressing writers to inform them of the secrets they have discovered in their pages—and Freud himself is not exempt from this sin of "application" if we recall his paper on Jensen's *Gradiva*) "but rather, on the contrary, it is writing that clarifies psychoanalysis" (*Flac*, 184, my translation), especially with respect to the central cavity in the column of life which we have tried to fill with an "all-encompassing word," with a language containing the truth about being. Leiris's writing, and that of all autobiography since Freud—for which reason it is more revealing for whomsoever has some experience of psychoanalysis—is a disillusioned writing that highlights, . . . *tunately*, the limits of language. Leiris would not achieve immortality with the pen, nor would he compensate for his sterility by thinking that the poetic endeavor—as if it were maternity or birth—could provide a substitute for the paternity that horrified him; he could not consummate that perfect union with himself that would defy the difference between the sexes nor could he achieve his own true image, unless the true image were his death mask, necessarily in the hands of the person who performed his *final toilette*. Is that the reader's function? I believe it is: indeed, that is one of my theses.

13

AUTOBIOGRAPHIES AND SELF-PORTRAITS

1. On All That Is Written as Autobiography

The legal documents that certify the "person," the accumulation of recollections in memory and the perceived continuity of the image in the mirror are the founding elements of the subject's "identity," expressed with the personal pronoun "I" (or "we," in reference to the subject's community). My analysis of the texts dealing with the beginnings of memory—renouncing interpolations that are foreign to the text—confirms that childhood memory as a cornerstone of identity, is a dubious witness. "I," the *subject of the statement* (" 'ego' is he who says 'ego,' " according to Benveniste's powerful dictum),[195] scarcely or never wonders about the *subject of the enunciation*: do I know who is speaking when I say "I remember"? And even less about the *subject of the annunciation*: what is the desire and aspiration motivating the "I,—ego,—me," ignorant of the subject of the enunciation, to present itself with these statements? What is the goal of the *"autobiographical"* exposition? What is the hidden jouissance, what is the phantasy achieved with the manic reiteration of *me-me-me*? Where is the amusement in exposing

---

195. Benveniste, Émile. [1946 and 1958]. *Problèmes de linguistique générale*. Paris: Gallimard, 1966, p. 259. *Problems in General Linguistics*. Translated by Mary E. Meek. Coral Gables (Fla): Miami University Press, 1971.

remembered intimacies, even the most painful ones? The one who calls himself "I" betrays an unconscious desire that manifests itself in e(qui)vocations and lapses of memory, all directed at the other, who is responsible for giving credence to his/her discourse. The other being this anonymous figure that appeals to the author (or that the author believes appeals) to tell his story. Ultimately, this "whoever" takes the place of the judge that is expected to sanction the narrative that "I" produces with *me* as the main theme. All autobiography, whether acknowledged or not, is an appeal for acquiescence founded on a promise to tell "sincerely" "the whole truth." One of the commonplaces of the "genre" (in quotation marks because I will dispute its existence) is the beginning that entails a declaration of sincerity, of spontaneity, of rejecting artistic cosmetics. The ideal of authenticity could be developed further through the psychoanalytic method of free association, but we can see the path it takes and how very quickly it is betrayed: "I am letting myself be carried away, I am wandering from the point, I will be unintelligible if I do not follow the sequence of time and, besides, the circumstances will not come back to me so well."[196] On the other hand, this character I have just quoted: *Henri Brulard* (a name that does not coincide with the author's (Henri Beyle) or with the pseudonym he used (Stendhal) and is also the name of the book (a novel or an autobiography?)) reveals, with a sincerity that would have made Freud recognize him as his precursor, his sexual desires for the mother (who died when he was seven years old) and his hatred of his father and even of God himself, all of which is spine-chilling for anyone who believes he has found something new in the Oedipus complex.[197]

It cannot be reiterated enough that it is from the precarious certitudes given us by the mirror—the imaginary guarantor of the "I"—that the subject attempts to establish itself through writing

---

196. Stendhal (Henri Beyle). *The Life of Henri Brulard*. Translated by Catherine Alison Phillips. New York: Alfred A. Knopf, 1939, p. 10.
197. I resist the temptation to work on Stendhal's concise "first memory," but I nonetheless highly recommend reading it in the above-cited novel.

a narrative called *autobiography*. The autobiographer is caught in a dispute between two contradictory objectives: to confirm or to repudiate the specular image. The mirror is the stage, not of the autobiographical "pact" but rather the autobiographical *struggle*. The reader is called upon to act as referee.

We have already examined Borges's testimony and his misadventures with mirrors, and in three women writers we have found the narrative of the difficult relations little girls have with the mirror; we saw how they link the uncertainty of defining who they really are through a comparison between what they could see of themselves in such a mirror and the message that they received from the first and other enigmatic reflecting surface: the image vaguely glimpsed as it is reflected in the eyes of the mother. Who is that "she" that gazes at me from the other side of the mirror? That which she sees is me? Am I like my mother? What am I and who am I? What will I be? A question that goes beyond the peculiar behavior of schizophrenics in front of the mirror, or of Snow White's mother, longing to have her beauty confirmed. The perplexity of Narcissus extends to the whole of humanity: specular alienation or flight from the prison cloister that the mirror offers to whoever gazes into it—whether along avenues of activity or through the path of writing. The quicksilver in the glass seems to hold prodigious keys that will inform the subject how his or her relations with others will develop. The subject wants to know how he or she is seen and thus make the pertinent changes in the figure it presents to the audience. It would be "normal" for there to be a convergence between the figure in real space and the image in virtual space presented to the other. However, this convergence is not random or mechanical; it is a laborious task to be performed. One learns to see oneself just as one is seen by the Other; just as the Other commands one to see oneself. This identification is not spontaneous; it is induced; it is an effect of language; an inlay of the imaginary, grafted into the symbolic order. "I" is whoever can produce a narrative in the first person and find reason in the continuity of his/her existence subsequent to the statement, "I was born" (*Je suis né*—Perec). The profound-ness of the mirror is due to the words that name what one sees reflected there. The self confronts and contrasts itself with that imaginary dimension that is imposed on its will and recognizes in the "I" *that others see* ("maculated by guilt") an actor that either pleases or displeases him. That pleases and displeases him. That exaggerates, falsifies and conceals. That remembers and forgets, believing in the phantasy of himself.

The mirror provides the first opportunity for the division of the subject to be grasped by the subject itself. What is the sub-stance of "the thing I am and that makes me live"?[198] Does this "substance" coincide with what I scrutinize and try to decipher and what others see? Autobiography and self-portraiture are two attempts to illustrate through writing the results of the exploration of the self—painting is also writing; the canvas is as appropriate for bearing lines or imprints as the blank page; to describe and to draw oneself are parallel operations. In these self-referential works there is always some kind of an allegation; a sort of bowing to the other in order to illustrate who one is. They tend to be rhetorical exercises for transmitting, modifying or obviating the images that the other invariably constructs and imposes on us. The self hopes to cover itself with a Veronica's veil and to show the world its "veritable" image. It may also be done as a private exercise, for example in the countless self-portraits by Rembrandt or Egon Schiele, which show, in the comparative succession of so many images, the gradual changes between one and another and, at the same time affirm the continuity of a single ontic substance. Others follow the path of Paul Valéry, who wrote twenty-nine thousand pages for no one except himself, never imagining an eventual reader, with "nocturnal stealth" as I mentioned some time ago.[199] Valéry

---

198. Shakespeare, William: Borges was captivated by the statement by Parolles in *All's Well That Ends Well* [1602–1603], act IV, scene iii. Parolles is a despicable character who begs his supposed enemies to spare his life, saying "The thing I am shall make me live."
199. Braunstein, N.A. "El amor en *La llama doble* de Octavio Paz y en los *Cahiers* de Paul Valéry," in *Ficcionario de psicoanálisis*, pp. 166–196.

wrote and kept these infinite notebooks as exercises of thought or, better yet, as "gymnastics of the pen." The architect of the marine cemetery was an experienced detective who pursued Paul Valéry, the slippery prisoner who fled from every page: "Writing demands that the writer divide himself against himself. It is only in this way that the whole man can become an author."[200]

To create one's own image, whether it is recognizable to others or not, is the *task of the autho*®. I will use this strange spelling (*graphy*): "*autho*®," to indicate the legal and forensic nature of *autho*®ship, an essential element today whereby the artist is only considered as such if s/he has assured the ©*opyright* for his/her material. This is another way of saying that art is a product whose fate is determined by the Other and it is from the Other that the creator receives his/her re-cognition. The *autho*® must be ®egistered. He himself is the "trademark."

The auto-biographer / self-portraitist[201] attempts to capture the representation of him/herself, entering into competition with the photographic camera. He attempts to portray life-in-motion as a still. We see this very often with some exceptions—such as in the case of Virginia Woolf. She aspires to demonstrate the persistence of being despite change by making of her own (*auto*) life (*bios*), a book (*graphien*).

To state and to state voluptuously like Rousseau; to address God himself in a defiant tone:

> . . . I have bared my secret soul as Thou thyself hast seen it, Eternal Being! So let the numberless legion of my fellow men gather round me, and hear my confessions. Let them groan at my depravities, and blush for my misdeeds. But let

---

200. Valéry, Paul. *Cahiers*, I. Paris: Gallimard, La Pléiade, p. 474 (my translation).

201. Translator's note: It is interesting to note here that the words in Spanish for "autobiography" and "self-portrait" are, respectively, "*autobiografía*" and "*autoretrato*"; in German, they are "*Selbstbiographie*" and "*Selbstbildnis*." One might be tempted to say, in English: "self-biography" and "auto-portrait."

each one of them reveal his heart at the foot of Thy throne with equal sincerity, and may any man who dares, say "I was a better man than he" (Rousseau, 17).[202]

As I write this page—as I quote Rousseau and so many other authors—I become aware that these moments "are impressed on me" as memories of my own writing, as future memories of this writing scene. As I press the keys of this word processor, the present is transformed into the past and becomes part of my memory, sustained by the movements of my fingers and the letters that appear on the screen. I will become the book I am writing. The scene of this writing conceals a parthenogenetic phantasy. I appear and disappear with every key I press: *fort / da*. Like Proust with every awakening and relapse into reverie and darkness, like Virginia Woolf with every wash of the waves, like every time we open or close the wardrobe of our memories. Or every time the rooster crows. Rummaging through myself, depositing my secretions on the page in a movement of alternating diastoles and systoles.

Examining the "paper scraps" of so many others who have written about themselves, I carry out acts that are recorded in my memory store. I write myself. These moments form part of my life and, therefore, extending the reflection to others, I must acknowledge an *auto* dimension in all acts of expression, whether or not the "I" appears as the subject of the statement. My memory constructs my memory . . . in the other, the auditor or the reader . . . to whom I address myself for confirmation. On the rebound, from the unpredictable response, memory is constructed in me. Only science can pretend that the subject of the enunciation disappears in the act of formulating its statements and that it does not matter who says what so long as what is said can be confirmed by the other. This presumption is suspicious if not altogether false. Whether I write, for example, on the production of ornamental gourds and

202. Rousseau, Jean-Jacques. *The Confessions of Jean-Jacques Rousseau.* Translated by J.M. Cohen. London: Penguin Books, 1953, p. 17.

silverware in eighteenth century Peru, or on a clinical case I once treated, or on the novels of Thomas Mann, without necessarily knowing it—throwing the stone while hiding my hand—indirectly, I will be writing a fragment of my own life. The choice of topic, the way in which I approach it, the references and footnotes, the allusions to the authorial "I" of the text, the phantasmatic construction of the other to whom I address myself, the attempts to disguise the subject of the enunciation by removing it from the statements and replacing it with the impersonal "one," the appeal to the reader to approve "my" statements, the ostentatious use of the royal "we," the use of rhetorical and heuristic resources as evidence of "objectivity," all of this, all that the artist and scientist do when they write, demonstrates the undeniable truth that the writer—every writer—is an effect of his or her writing plus the reception it elicits. In writing there are no innocent personal or impersonal pronouns. "The sender . . . receives from the receiver his own message in an inverted form" (Lacan).[203] This specular production is called "©ommunication." One receives the message from the other, but retains the legal and commercial rights on its reproduction: the ©*opyright*. The ideology of liberal individualism is present: "I am the owner of myself and I can sell and distribute this product that issues from my self; it is possible and very legitimate that I transfer my being to writing, which is mine and obeys whatever designs I propose for it."

This is a Derridean theme: the author's name, as well as the title of the book, the date, the place, the name of the publisher, etc., all of which do not form part of the text, are nonetheless components that are decisive to and inseparable from it. It is no wonder that the evolution of the "autobiographical genre" (if indeed a text can *pertain* to a "genre"[204]) followed in the wake of the French revolution and its consequences—with various notable previous exceptions, such as that of St. Augustine, at the service

203. Lacan, Jacques [1956]. "Le séminaire sur *La lettre volée*." In *Écrits*, Paris, Seuil, 1966, p. 41.
204. Derrida, Jacques. "La loi du genre." In *Parages*, Paris, Galilée, 1986, p. 264.

of the evangelical mission and his mother's memory. Rousseau is a precursor and Romanticism, beginning about two hundred years ago, would emphasize the self-definition of the subject through the preservation of memories. Freud is an epigone of Goethe—albeit a subversive one, considering that he introduced the unconscious.

In this sense, all writing—and painting—is autobiographical. On a certain occasion, while observing a painting by van Gogh entitled "Rain" in the Philadelphia Museum of Art, a painting that shows a disordered series of diagonal lines and a blurry landscape in the background so that one has the impression of rain beating against the windowpane through which the painter gazes, I had the distinct sensation of viewing an X-ray of the artist's inner state; the painting, "Rain," was a self-portrait that was just as genuine as any of the others that went by that title and whose "object" was the face of the artist. Certainly we have all visited the home or arrived at the office or the library of a friend to find that the arrangement of the objects, the order and disorder, the harmony and anarchy, the distribution of what is essential and what is ornamental, everything that we see, all of it seems to be a marvelous unconscious self-portrait! Sometimes, in the kitchen or the bedroom, we find a mirror of the inhabitant that reflects as much as, if not more than, the made-up face—a flower of rhetoric—that the person presents to the world. All that surrounds us is our own creation and speaks of us. Autobiography flows in spurts, like blood from a severed artery, whenever one opens a book. It is not necessary for it to be expressed as "I" or for it to be transparent; more often it remains veiled and confused, as if glimpsed through a glass, darkly (*Corinthians*, XIII: 12). However, without the hope of Saint Paul: the self will never come face to face with the truth. It is in direct opposition to the truth: no autobiography will ever escape this fate.

Nonetheless, all that speaks, all the eloquence of words and objects, speaks of the subject . . . to the subject appealing and invoking him. One lives—one writes—for the other. There is no text, no painting, that is not animated by the movement of the existence that produced it. The usual insistence on the "death of the author" conflicts with the evidence of a subject who insists on proclaiming him/herself "present!" Horace [65–8 BC] is, in this respect, relentless: *Mutato nomine de te fabula narratur.*[205] ("Change the name of the fable and it applies to you.")[206] *Quod spiro et placeo, si placeo, tuum est.*[207] ("For if I am inspired to please, if please I do, the merit is all yours.")[208] I will resist the temptation to continue quoting from Horace's *Odes, Epistles and Satires,* which are so apropos to the topic that I will refer to as *heterothanatophony.*

Autobiography is performative; it is a promise. The author, in an explicit or tacit way, at the moment of ascribing the text to the "genre," makes a commitment to the reader to tell "the truth" about him/herself. Nothing more and nothing less. Lies and concealment, unlike their occurrence in works that are admittedly fictitious, are tantamount to perjury. The writer is supposed to be the only person who has access to the reality of his or her story, who is in a position to maintain a discourse in accordance with that "truth" and able to transmit it to the reader without contamination. The writer aspires to trace a fine borderline between the "truth," which s/he exposes, and the falsehoods that proceed from phantasy. Michel Leiris[209] presents his plan:

> . . . it was a question of condensing, in the almost raw state, a group of facts and images which I refused to exploit by letting my imagination work upon them; in other words: the negation of the novel (*Manhood,* 158).

---

205. Horace, *Satires,* I, l. 69.
206. Horace. *The Complete Odes and Satires of Horace.* Translated by Sidney Alexander. Princeton: Princeton Univ. Press, 1999, p. 193.
207. Horace, *Odes,* IV, #3.
208. Op. cit., p. 159.
209. Leiris, Michel [1939]. *L'Age d'homme.* Paris: Gallimard, Folio (435), 1973, p. 15. *Manhood: a journey from childhood into the fierce order of virility.* Op. cit. in the previous chapter. *Manhood,* p. 158.

The narrator of his/her own story signs a pact with the reader and aspires to credibility as the indisputable authority on the topic under consideration: him/herself. They both participate in good faith, but . . . nothing is more dubious than an autobiographical text, given the inveterate custom of the self to lie to itself on the pretext of sincerity. It is well known that Freud (preceded by Nietzsche) brought the self under suspicion. The transparency that one has for oneself—the foundational faith for the autobiographical "genre"—was rudely shaken by the notion of the "unconscious." The Freudian discovery split the history of autobiographies in two. Regardless of their date of publication, there are autobiographies that are pre- and post-Freudian. Linguists, redoubling in their field the division of the subject, contribute the key distinction between the *subject of the statement*, "I," and the *subject of the enunciation*, which is never completely expressed by any set of statements, but rather is always out of reach.

The interest in autobiographies, nonetheless, resides less in the statements, less in the explicit text, and more in the surreptitious appearances of the subjects of the enunciation, as well as the annunciation, in moments when the narrative consciousness is distracted, moments which permit the truth to filter through the cracks of the discourse and to reveal itself in the receptor, the reader, the invoked countersigner (Derrida) of the autobiography. The reader has the responsibility to interpret the text, to take the bait from the hooks of style (if there are any, and there always are!), to discern the half-truths and acts of self-love.

In the arts, the concealment of the subject of the enunciation is not intended to be as radical as it is in science or in positive historiography, both of which boast of being produced as if there were no subject behind the statement. Artistic works are messages that are acknowledged as such. The spectator must approve of the artist's presence (sometimes obvious, sometimes spectral) in the objects of the artist's invention, in the imitation, in the copy, in the rigorous ascription or disavowal of the laws of the genre, in the original production. On the one hand, an anonymous and little-inspired artist of the Renaissance—who chooses to represent a conventional theme, such as the adoration of the shepherds, without flair either in form or color—and, on the other hand, van Gogh painting a fantastic starlit night or wheat fields burnt by sunlight: both are representing on equal terms an object that, at the level of the statement, is exterior to them, something that is visible and that they offer to attract the spectator's gaze. However, at the level of the enunciation, they represent themselves and their relationship with the world. In the first case, it might be the complacent fulfillment of the responsibility of a pious brotherhood to cover the walls of a chapel, in the other case perhaps a revulsive rebellion against interior demons that compel him to project his delirium and viscera upon the canvas. The style, the choice of colors or words, the audience of the painting-story-essay-sculpture-concert: all is autho®ship and the product, retrospectively, *will have been* the autho®.

The writer, poet, essayist or scientist does not precede his or her work: s/he is rather a consequence of it. This is true for the most formal and abstruse disciplines as well as for the most "creative" and personal arts. Whoever writes, hiding behind his pen or brush strokes, reveals the work of dissimulation to which he is dedicated. We can easily see who is the better liar: he will be the one wearing make-up, the one who pretends to show himself "exactly as he is." Thus, as it is impossible for the autho® to hide, *how can anyone write anything that does not end by being an autobiography?* Every writer, when he creates a character, is a Flaubert floating among Bovaries. Hence, Emma Bovary *c'est moi* inasmuch as "I is an Other."

2. The Disjunction of Philosophy and Memory

The essay is a particularly suspicious genre. All the distinguished examples, beginning with the first ever written, those of Montaigne, and ending—begging the reader's indulgence—with

Derrida's last writings, are marked by the active presence of the autho® in the statements. Not as an author floating in the ethereal above but rather as someone who is *embodied* in every line. There are illustrious insurrectionist examples against this shameless subjective intrusion in novels and essays. The most celebrated, perhaps, is Pascal's denunciation of Montaigne and *the foolish project of describing oneself,* a project that—as Pascal says—is saddening and boring, a vain exercise that suffers due to the lack of a correct method and settles for the saving grace of elegance with a disorganized discourse that jumps around chaotically from one topic to another.[210] The invective of the Jansenist is eloquent and passionate against the unsystematic essayist. There has always been tension and conflict between philosophy—which aspires to eliminate the contingent by giving precedence to the necessary, and thus poses as a "science of the spirit"—and autobiography—which necessarily presents singular, random events, resorting to slippery memory and emphasizing what distinguishes the narrator's "I" from all other "egos." The biographer of himself seeks, through writing, the lost past where he believes he may find that which makes him *Unique.*[211] The reference here to Max Stirner[212] is essential, as this little-known predecessor of postmodern thought knew very well that autobiography was a hopeless avenue for the self:

210. B. Pascal [1660?] *Pensées.* París: Seuil, 1962, #790: *Parler de ceux qui ont traité de la connaissance de soi-même, des divisions de Charron, qui attristent et ennuient. De la confusion de Montaigne, qu'il avait bien senti le défaut d'une droite méthode. Qu'il évitait en sautant de sujet en sujet, qu'il cherchait le bon aire. Le sot projet qu'il a de se peindre et cela non pas en passant en contre ses maximes, comme il arrive à tout le monde de faillir, mais par ses propres maximes et par un dessein premier et principal. Car de dire des sottises par hasard et par faiblesse c'est un mal ordinaire, mais d'en dire par dessein c'est ce qui n'est pas supportable . . .* Translated into English by A.J. Kreilsheimer. New York: Penguin (USA).
211. Stirner, Max [1844]. *The Ego and His Own: The Case of the Individual Against Authority.* Translated by Steven T. Byington. New York: Libertarian Book Club, 1963, p. 320.
212. Stirner, Max [1844]. *The Ego and His Own: The Case of the Individual Against Authority.* Translated by Steven T. Byington. New York: Libertarian Book Club, 1963, p. 320.

Not till I am certain of myself, and no longer seeking for myself, am I really my property; I have myself, therefore I use and enjoy myself. On the other hand, I can never take comfort in myself as long as I think that I have still to find my true self. [. . .] Henceforth, the question runs, not how one can acquire life, but how one can squander, enjoy it; or, not how one is to produce the true self in himself, but how one is to dissolve himself, to live himself out.

Not "living to tell the tale" but a categorical choice: either to write it or to live it. In any case, to have lived it in order to confess it later on; to prevent the character (*auto*) from replacing the being in one's life (*bios*) in the act of writing (*graphy*). Thus it was that Antoine Roquentin, the protagonist of the Sartre novel, *Nausea*, understood it and became the unexpected contradictor of Gabriel García Márquez:

> . . . for the most banal event to become an adventure, you must (and this is enough) begin to *recount* it. This is what fools people: a man is always a teller of tales, he lives surrounded by his stories and the stories of others, he sees everything that happens to him through them; and he tries to live his own life as if he were telling a story. But you have to choose: live or tell (italics added).[213]

Nonetheless they are trivial personal events, which do not seem to have anything philosophical about them yet function as a condition of possibility for philosophy. The *necessary contingency*, this hexed oxymoron, is the avenue that cannot be avoided between life and work both for the novelist and for the lover of pure or absolute knowledge (as well as the "sincere autobiographer") who boasts of abhoring fiction. For example, the trivial coincidence of

---

213. Sartre, Jean-Paul. *Nausea*. Translated by Lloyd Alexander. New York: New Directions, 1959, p. 39.

finding this text by Sartre one Sunday in June 2007, that I read for the first time decades ago:

> Nothing happens while you live. The scenery changes, people come in and go out, that's all. There are no beginnings. Days are tacked on to days without rhyme or reason, an interminable, monotonous addition [. . .] That's living. But everything changes when you tell about life; it's a change no one notices: the proof is that people talk about true stories. As if there could possibly be true stories; things happen one way and we tell about them in the opposite sense. You seem to start at the beginning: "It was a fine autumn evening in 1922. I was a notary's clerk in Marommes." And in reality you have started at the end. It was there, invisible and present; it is the one which gives to words the pomp and value of a beginning. [. . .] For us, the man [who does the telling] is already the hero of the story (op. cit., pp. 39–40).

Sartre's lesson is critical to this study of first memories and the prestige of beginnings. The narrator leads us to feel that all the details of what happened to him that evening constitute so many other annunciations and promises of an unexpected adventure still waiting to happen in the future. Nonetheless, when we are told the story, the future is already past and it is from the ending that the tale encounters its *raison d'être*. There is no other meaning for the gesture of recounting one's own life and of composing a succession of verifiable events and memories that no one else could share. Memory is the servant of the narrato® and obeys his or her whims (*Je me souviens*—Perec).

It is difficult—a genuine challenge for novelists—to imagine an autobiography written by a rigorous philosopher such as Kant, Hegel or Wittgenstein. Not so in the cases of Sir Karl Popper or Sir Bertrand Russell who, at least in the moment of writing them, stopped being philosophers. They were *sirs*. However, returning to Pascal and limiting ourselves to a few of the more common references to his work, are we not reading a veiled autobiography in the "thinking reed" (347, 348), in "The eternal silence of these infinite spaces frightens me" (206), in "the heart has its reasons" (277), in the "bet" (418), in the insistence that "Montaigne is wrong" (325), in the "ease—banality!—of evil" (526), in the "Self is hateful" (455) . . . and in all his other *thoughts*, not to mention the memorial "of the night of Monday, November 23, 1654, between ten-thirty and twelve-thirty at night," when the truth of Abraham, Isaac and Jacob's God was revealed to him instead of the god of philosophers and scientists" (555)? And this is to say nothing of the epitaph he himself wrote in Latin and that I provide here in translation: "I measured the immensity of the heavens, I measured the shadows of the earth; my spirit came from heaven [*mens cœlestis erat*], my body lies in the shadow." In short, Blaise Pascal's epitaph is a concise and highly fatuous autobiography of the man who said: *le moi est haïsable*. Pascal Narcissus? Certainly. Why should he be an exception?

Every autobiographer feels himself called upon to justify his expository method and to explore the disturbing differences between what happened in "reality" and what was recorded in his memory. No one can be certain of how events transpired and the majority aspires to historiographic objectivity that, as is well known, is a dream even for historians themselves: "to recount the past exactly as it happened." The chronicle is limited and the (constant) introduction of phantasy renders the memories suspicious. Marguerite Yourcenar,[214] who refuses to use the pronoun "I" for the little girl born in 1903, recognizes that the child arrived already engaged with Christianity in a Europe just entering the twentieth century. "That the child is in fact myself I can hardly doubt without doubting everything" (*Dear Departed*, 4). In any case, assaulted by a feeling of unreality, she feels driven (as if her memories were those of Hadrian and not her own) to cling to

214. Yourcenar, Marguerite. *Souvenirs pieux* (1974) (English translation: *Dear Departed: A Memoir* translated by Maria Louise Ascher); *Archives du Nord* (1977) (English translation: *How Many Years: A Memoir* translated by Maria Louise Ascher); *Quoi? L'Éternité* (1988).

snippets of memories drawn from others' anamnesis, searching
through documents, letters and notebooks rescued from the fate
of the wastebasket and squeezing those paper scraps mercilessly
until they yield what they do not have, rummaging through files
in which the legal jargon all but negates whatever human quality
they might contain. Why does the writer persist in her mission?

> I am quite aware that such gleanings are deceptive and vague,
> like everything that has been reinterpreted by the memories
> of a great many people; flat, like items written on the dot-
> ted line of a passport application; inane, like oft-told family
> anecdotes; and corroded by gradual accretions within us, as
> a stone is eaten away by lichen or metal by rust. These odds
> and ends of purported truths are, nevertheless, the only bridge
> still standing between that infant and me. They are also the
> only buoy that keeps both of us afloat on the ocean of time.
> Mildly curious, I set about assembling them here, to see what
> the completed puzzle will reveal.[215]

Yourcenar wants to establish and confirm continuity between
the little girl who unenthusiastically came into the world and the
elderly woman sitting down to write her memoirs; to give her (self)
identity, security in the constant sameness of being. The project
is clear: "to fill the joints."

The good autobiographer is both bashful and embarrassed. He
knows that the "genre" he chose is a hybrid, that there are huge
leaps between the event lived, the memory of that event and the
transformation of the memory into words. He doubts his own
"sincerity," he is aware of the inevitable narcissistic traps; aware of
a bad taste in his mouth when he writes the word "I" and tries to
treat his self-absorption as a material entity. He understands the
fallacy of promoting himself as the protagonist of his own novel
with the intention of revealing the true image of the character. The

---

215. Yourcenar, Marguerite. *Dear Departed*. Translated by Maria Louise
    Ascher. New York: Farrar Straus Giroux, 1991, p. 4.

good autobiographer has heard Oscar Wilde's warning to André Gide one sad day in Berneval (as quoted by Alan Sheridan[216]): "From now on, my dear, never write 'I' any more. In art, you see, there is no *first* person." Nonetheless, the autobiographic ambition forges ahead, as in H. Michaux, who seeks to establish bridges between "those that I have been" and the one that I am, feeling that those weary emissaries of the past are stalking him, pursuing him and submerging him in perplexity with their tirelessly repeated questions: What have you done with us? Where are you taking us?

> I am possessed; I speak with those I was (*qui-je-fus*) and those I was speak to me. I am disturbed sometimes by the feeling of being foreign. Now they are an entire society and it has just occurred to me that I no longer understand myself (Michaux, 73).[217]

Philosophers, hunters of universal propositions, driven by a love of geometry, can write a *Tractatus*, but not an autobiography. Once reaching the point of leaving a "personal" testimony, they feel it is impossible to speak; thus, it is better to keep quiet. The coherence of a system of thought is tortured by randomness and, in the life of each person, there are only coincidences, unexpected encounters, peripeteias and mishaps. The philosopher would like to imprison himself in what is *necessary* and valid for everyone, in categorical judgments. The phantasy of the philosopher is that of the legislator. Instead of the longed-for universals, he finds what is *contingent*—that which, because it has already happened, is therefore necessary and, at the same time, impossible to explain. The past, an effect of chance, cannot be modified. It has arrived and will remain in perpetuity; it has left forms and scars that could (poorly) be remembered but not eliminated. What is done is

---

216. Sheridan, Alan. *André Gide. A life in the present.* Cambridge (Ma): Harvard University Press, 1999, p. 148.
217. Michaux, Henri [1927]. *Œuvres completes.* Paris: Gallimard, La Pléide, 1998, p. 73 (my translation).

done and not even God himself can undo it. Nothing is so necessary, nothing is so fatal for everyone, as the fact of having been born by chance at a certain time and place. Yourcenar, the little girl, one hour after having been born, is already "caught, as in a net, in the realities of animal suffering and of human pain" (*Dear Departed*, 37) by the futilities of the period in which she lives, by the consequential and inconsequential news events of the day, by the fashions and routines, by the banal objects that envelope and await her. The universal—in her case—is that her contingencies, although her "own," are comparable to those of everyone else. Memory gathers together the infinite unique trivialities, those of everyone—like those of the fabulous Shakespeare that Borges creates in his fiction on "The memory of Shakespeare"—and tries to give them meaning, if not augurial value.

The philosopher would prefer that her "work" be understood without reference to her "life—*bios*." She knows, from a very young age, that identity is a psychological myth and a requirement of the State. She does not participate in the self-deception of "egography." In order to demonstrate this—via the paradox—I propose an autobiographical example taken from a lecture given by Theodor W. Adorno:

> Identity is the principle according to which something is the same. Thus we can speak of the identity of a man. I clearly remember that when I was a child I was always struck by the thought of a man's identity and I would not be surprised if the same happened to those of you still uncorrupted by philosophy. To say of a man that he is identical to himself seemed to me extremely strange while I had a conscious that was still not deformed; since to say that one thing is identical to another gives rise to the expectation that two different moments might be, in some way, identical to one another. Thus, from the affirmation that I am identical to myself, I pass to the affirmation that I am different from myself. Faced with this concept of identity, one is overwhelmed by the shock of

splitting in two parts, the shock that one is no longer oneself (*selbst*)[218] (my translation).

The biographer of oneself—who, more often than not, has previously published several books and has been acknowledged as an autho®—is a being who mixes and confuses work with life. Many readers, often including even the author himself, endeavor to try and find keys in the autobiography that will serve as bridges that establish continuity and coherence between life and work. To assemble them, conjugate and patch them. From a strictly philosophical perspective, the intromission of the author's personal phantasies threatens the success of the project. The work should emerge untainted from the test of subjectivity, to escape the author's miserable and trivial circumstances, to have value and live for itself. Nevertheless, it always emerges tainted by chance. To purge it of contingencies is an impossible mission in the same way as the insistent attempts to "explain" a work through the psychological or social traits of the author are doomed to failure. *No code—psychological, Marxist, psychoanalytical, neurophysiological, epistemological, aesthetic—can serve as the key to reading the relationship between life and work.* Not even if they are used all together. Restating previous questions: How is it possible that Gabriel García Márquez proceeded from Aracataca to *One Hundred Years of Solitude*? How is it possible that the fall from a horse ("he had been thrown by a half-tamed horse," as Borges says with reference to "a vernacular and rustic Zarathustra" who was Funes the memorious) could have transformed Nietzsche from Prussian hussar into philologist and philosopher? How is it that just one Jew, and a German-speaking one, more precisely *that* Jew from Vienna, and no other, could have invented psychoanalysis? The question of the relationship between life and work underlies and stimulates interest in the autobiographical endeavor. Apart from that, memory—everyone's memory—just gathers banalities, such

---

218. Adorno, Theodor W. [1962]. *Terminología filosófica II.* Translated into Spanish by Sánchez Ortiz. Madrid: Taurus, 1977, p. 100.

as the encounter with one or various mirrors, a crib, or a rooster's crow in an ancestral mansion or in a run-down shack.

If, as some would say, memory is the foundation of identity for human beings (Locke: *Memory makes personal identity*), every essay, poem, novel entails (metaphorizes) mnemic traces pertaining to the writer. An entire voyage is transmitted. It would be a poor essay that aspired to feign the disappearance of the autho®. The genuine essay would be a reflection that recognizes as its raw material what the author previously thought and wrote. For an essay to be truly anonymous it would be necessary to imagine the fiction of an author who is born at the moment of sitting down to write, without any previous readings or publications, without a style consolidated through the hard discipline of sculpting the crystal material of language. I, the autho® of these lines, am in full agreement with Cynthia Ozick:

Essays are expected to make the writer's case.[219] Sometimes, of course, they do; I feel fairly sure the book reviews in this volume incorporate judgments that time and temper will not seriously alter. Yet most essays, like stories, are not designed to stand still in this way. A story is a hypothesis, a tryout of human nature under the impingement of certain given materials; so is an essay. After which, the mind moves on. Nearly every essay, like every story, is an experiment, not a credo.

Or, to put it more stringently: an essay, like a story or a novel, is a fiction. A fiction, by definition, is that which is made up in response to an excited imagination. *What is fictitious about the essay is that it is pretending not to be made up—so that reading an essay may be more dangerous than reading a story.* This very foreword, for instance, may count as a little essay: ought it to be trusted? (Italics added.)[220]

---

219. Meritorious ambiguity of language!: ". . . the writer's case."
220. Ozick, Cynthia. *Metaphor & Memory: Essays.* New York: Alfred A. Knopf, 1989, pp. x–xi.

This goes beyond the imaginary, the traditional refuge of the specular self. The most abstract of paintings (Malevich, Kandinsky, Rothko) is a communication of mirrors between the painter and the spectator. Through the painting the painter queries: "What do you see when you see me?" It is not a symmetrical relationship since, as we know, every painting tells us: "You do not see me from where I see you." And it is for this reason that it functions like a mirror. It is either in our excited state of attention or in our eventual indifference that the work of art is produced. Even when it takes the form of a rusted bicycle wheel sitting on a static and elevated kitchen shelf in a museum pedestal; it also carries the traces of its author's genius, it also forms part of the author's "autobiography." Here I cannot help but mention *"Étant donnés: 1. la chute d'eau 2. le gaz d'éclairage"* whose two elements in the title of Marcel Duchamp's masterwork—on which he worked in secret for twenty years [1946–1966]—textually reproduce the landscape of the square that he saw every morning of his childhood from the window of his house on rue Jean d'Arc in Rouen (the childhood memory!), while, at the same time, the artist was expressing in code his romance with Maria Martins, the wife of the Brazilian ambassador in France.[221] Autobiography is impossible: that is why everyone attempts it; that is why no one forfeits the chance of practicing it; that is why it is impossible to write a text that is not autobiographical.

---

221. Tomkins, Calvin. *Duchamp: A Biography*. New York: Holt & Co., 1996. I am indebted to my friend José L. García Castellano for the precise and indubitable location of the gutter and gas streetlamp in the center of Rouen, contrary to the affirmation of the biographer.

PROSOPOPEIA: APPROACHES TO AUTOBIOGRAPHY

1. The Contradiction Between Words and Mirrors

Jacques Derrida[222] wrote a magnificent essay on the self-portrait, and the theses he presented there are equally valid for autobiography. However, there is one important difference I should not neglect to observe: the self-portrait one paints of "oneself" represents an instant in time, whereas the autobiography is a diachronic narrative that attempts to establish—albeit retrospectively—a temporal continuity of the subject who writes "him/herself" by gathering together disperse fragments. Whoever undertakes the project of constructing his own image stands before himself in the position that *we* occupy, urging us to see ourselves with him, the author, *face to face*. We are the point on which the artist has fixed his gaze, just as one views oneself in the mirror. We substitute for (and we obfuscate) the mirror. Whether the author (signatory, model, subject and object of the painting) seeks admiration in our gaze (*miroir* / mirror), or whether he seeks our terror as is sometimes the case, in any event, he is expressing an appeal: "Look at me. Confirm my identity by countersigning this image I propose

222. Derrida, Jacques. *Memoirs of the Blind: The Self-Portrait and Other Ruins*. Translated by Pascale-Anne Brault and Michael Naas. Chicago and London: The University of Chicago Press, 1993.

to you." Whoever uses himself as model assumes, necessarily, a posture. And what posture is not poised on the verge of imposture? Returning to Derrida and his ideas on the painter of self-portraits:

> We are the condition of his sight, certainly, and of his own image, but it is also the case, as in Hoffman's "The Sandman," that we rub out his eyes in order instantly to replace them: we are his eyes or the double of his eyes.[223]

We can, with our gaze, put him together or tear him apart.

The writer (in a broad enough sense to include musicians who scribble on musical staffs and mathematicians who transcribe equations or draw topological figures) is always someone who, by writing, writes him/herself and addresses his/her writing at some more or less hypocritical accomplice who will know how to read him/her. This has been, from the beginning, the *leitmotiv* of this essay: an investigation of the poet and thinker that seeks traces of the person in the *paper scraps* that narrate childhood memories. The graphologist—is this not, in the end, the *métier* we have adopted?—encounters the subject on any slip of paper that has been graced by his pen. Without touching upon the concept of *projection*, which has been so abused in the past, we should acknowledge that every stroke of the pen or brush participates in the curiosity of the mirror. It reflects the author and contributes to his disappearance before the gaze of his audience. Have I not already said that mirrors strip us of identity?

Occasionally, as we have seen, the writer may feel rage and horror, amazement and fascination, before the image that the mirror returns to him. At this point I will sift through my reflections on this confusion—not always perceived by the authors themselves— between the word and the abominable looking glass.

Let us cast our gaze on the writer—any writer, including myself: how could I not see myself writing?—poring over the blank page or, more commonly these days, over the keyboard with all

---

223. *Ibid.*, pp. 62–63.

the alphabetic characters and a luminous screen framed by icons and extending infinitely downward for as long as I press the keys which leave marks that are easily erased or replaced by me or others on the screen. What does the writer see on the paper or in the glass screen of the computer? Perhaps it would be better for us to highlight *what he does not see*: neither his own face nor that of any other person, reader or otherwise, of that page he is writing. Writing is supposed to transport the body of the writer to the space of a page—neither virtual nor real—from which the specular image has disappeared. Or, in other words, where the writer's image has been substituted by the supposed gaze of a reader or spectator, turned not towards the writer's face, but rather towards a printed book that will reproduce in the future the strokes he now inscribes on the page. All writing proceeds from the future. (If he did not believe that someone would read these lines, he would not compose them. *If on a winter's night a traveler . . .*) Thus Borges's idea may be understood as: whoever scribbles practices a "drastic abolition" of mirrors—which may be precisely what he realized in his own blindness. The author, whether awkward or brilliant, who dedicates himself to the task of constructing a text, must substitute his personal presence with a combination of alphabetic signs that do not resemble either himself or that which he writes about. The word "peach" on a computer screen is more metaphysical than one painted by Cézanne; the word "shoe," written by an industrialist from Guanajuato, is just as useless for walking as the worn out shoes of a peasant woman or of van Gogh himself (we will never know) which he presented to us as oily black smudges on a piece of canvas.

Writing disfigures, it steals the face of the writer, it expels him from all mirrors. It is the enemy of all that is specular. Let us remember that *prosopopeia*, beyond the insufficient definition found in dictionaries, is the construction of a face (*prosopon* = face, *peia* = *poiesis*, generation, poetry). "Prosopopeia is the trope of autobiography, by which one's name [. . .] is made as intelligible and *memorable* [my emphasis—J.D.] as a face" (de Man, quoted in Derrida 1986).[224] *Prosopoclastic* (just as *iconoclast* is one who destroys images) would be writing in general, as it deconstructs the countenance and dissolves it into pen strokes, into bits. *The text, every text, is a mirror that blinds, that gouges out one's eyes.* It overstates. Writing, by definition, is faceless.

By writing, as I was saying, one scratches over a virgin page that does not return an image to the author: he is deprived of and exiled from himself when he gazes at the blank page which incites him to write or draw on it (often the cause and reason for anxiety). In this framework of absence, he may attempt to convoke and restore his lost face through the magic of the word. I would like to propose the hypothesis that the written word permits renewing, taking distance from or correcting, as well as, given the particular case, annulling the relationship with the mirror. Writing "realizes" the specular as a response to a disjunctive option: the choice between the visible image of the painting or the written, faceless word. Either the visage or the word: Mosaic religion knows about this; idolatry is the greatest of sins, writing is both venerated and venerable. In alphabetic signs the face is erased: the visage no longer recognizes itself. Nonetheless, no one would deny that it is possible "to describe," "to paint with words," to awaken the imaginary through verbal linkages, and that this is one of the essential functions of poetry, that which Plato, as if he were a Jew, condemned in *The Republic*. The face, evicted by the word, may return through music and the colors of words. In principle, the text should establish a *prosopagnosia*—the clinical neurological condition characterized by the inability to recognize the faces one sees, the disconnection between somebody's image and the name that corresponds to it. As we will see below, this is not the case for autobiographies, which attempt to "portray the body and soul" of the author, exposing the "foolish project of describing oneself" (Pascal, quoted).

---

224. De Man, Paul [1983]. Quoted in Derrida, Jacques. *Memoires for Paul de Man: The Wellek Library Lectures at the University of California, Irvine.* Translated by Cecile Lindsay, Jonathan Culler and Eduardo Cadava. New York: Columbia University Press, 1986, p. 27.

By proceeding along this avenue we would be heading towards the absorbing topic of the writer's desire. However, I will hold back for now and return to *memory*, as the memory of this project returns to me. Meanwhile, on the relationship between the author and his face (*prosopon*) in the mirror, we may derive a typology of autobiographical texts.

First. There are authors who treat their memories in such a way as to avoid an encounter with their specular image. They achieve this through the signs drawn upon the blank page; they write in order to avoid themselves. On the pretext of exactitude, they restrain their episodic memory and hide in semantic memory, which is supposedly public and shared. They banish from themselves the myth, metaphor and image. They take refuge in the referential function of language; they are "objective" autobiographers who offer information and write "diaries," "journals," "notebooks" and "memoirs."[225] This is like someone preparing their *curriculum vitae*. One's professional career, what an autobiography! This is *prosopagnosia* taken to an extreme. The author is left without representation, he accomplishes a mere bureaucratic transaction with a purpose and a filing cabinet destination.

Second. There are other authors, in contrast, who can write in order to transmit a certain image to a virtual reader; they can enrich it by following narcissistic impulses, embellishing its face and drawing the reader into a peaceful and consolatory recognition. They do not present themselves as they really are or believe themselves to be, but rather in a more or less idealized way, as if wearing makeup. The self is a sublime commodity, all dressed up for the other to admire. These authors—typical of most autobiographies—display themselves as they would like to be seen and, in order to reinforce their project of concealing the fact of

225. This is the case for Sigmund Freud in his "An Autobiographical Study" [1926], cit., which is very different from the revelations he presents in *The Interpretation of Dreams* [1900] and in *The Psychopathology of Everyday Life* [1901]. Combined, the latter two essays approach that ideal autobiography whose impossibility we have already recognized.

their showing off, they proffer "confessions" that simulate seals of authenticity. They represent themselves as role models because they narrate their sins and thus demonstrate that they knew how to escape the pitfalls of the ego. This is the case for the source and origin of the "genre": Rousseau's *Confessions*,[226] which demands recognition, admiration and absolution. The writer reveals his crimes in such a way as to displace the reader's attention and, indirectly, to accuse those who have misunderstood them or caused them harm. Rousseau and his perpetuators profess the strange belief that there is a common thread between the autobiographical self and subjectivity, as if the unconscious did not exist. They are convinced of their own transparency and would like the reader to confirm it in a pact between equals, from one ego to another ego (*des égaux*, Lacan might say, *des egos*). Quite frequently they assume the role of victims unjustly persecuted or mistreated by fate and they aspire to transmit the compassion they grant themselves. Thus, *prosopagnosia*, pertaining to all alphabetic writing, as stated previously, becomes *prosopoplastia*. In everydays words: cosmetic, aesthetic surgery.

Third. In addition to these two—those who avoid and those who fall in love with their own image—we should note those who write to unmake their image, those loathsome authors who loathe themselves and publicly break down before the reader. They do not provide us with a still photograph of themselves but rather a cinematographic description of their daily Samsaesque "metamorphosis," of "the advancing tooth decay" in "a man asleep" (Perec) of the putrefaction of his organs and his physical appearance, of his dissolution "under the volcano" (Kafka in "The Hunger Artist" or in "A Report to an Academy," Perec, Lowry, Samuel Beckett,

---

226. Without neglecting the illustrious Latin predecessors: the *Confessions* of St. Augustine and, later, the autobiographies of Guibert de Nogent [1114] and Benvenuto Cellini [1558], to name only the most typical of the Medieval period and the most accomplished before Rousseau. Nor should we neglect the *Lazarillo de Tormes* from the Spanish Golden Age, a picaresque novel that is a parody of autobiography. We will soon see that the origin of the "genre" in Rousseau is simultaneous with its parody in Sterne's *Tristram Shandy*.

Akutagawa, Thomas Bernhard). In these writers, who were all enemies of their own faces, we find *prosopoclastia*. Their texts are frequently defiant, intolerable and unreadable.

Thus we derive a possible typology of narrators who write pages that are more or less autobiographical relative to their memory and their specular image: 1] Prosopagnosia, in which the authors evade encounters with the mirror and try to be seen objectively, from a distance; 2] Prosopoplastia, in which the authors are content to paint themselves in a favorable light, justifying themselves; and, finally 3] Prosopoclastia, in which authors exhibit terror before their own image. In summary, we have presumed historiographic presentation in the first case, romantic hagiography of the self in the second case, and deconstructive self-dissection of identity in the third case. Some choose to expose their circumstances by presenting themselves as that thing that no one ever knew how to define and therefore is designated by the evasive name of "human being"; others present themselves as heroes, saints or martyrs; the remainders descend into the abyss and do not resist presenting themselves as simians or insects, as discarded waste. Purgatory, paradise and hell embodied in the self-image. Three non-excluding ways of writing (the self): there are many autobiographies in which the narration consists of successive peripeteias that correspond to the three parts of the *Divine Comedy: Purgatory, Hell* and *Paradise*. The majority of personal narratives mix to varying degrees the three types of relationship with the mirror: the objectifying type, the idealizing type and the desubjectifying type.

2. The Gaze of the Other

As an illustration and paradigm of the combination of the three types of autobiography we have the greatest explorer of memory, the most penetrating of all, Marcel Proust, who we could not place within any of our three categories of authors. The fundamental discovery of the author of *Remembrance of Things Past* (a *novel*, we must never forget)—a discovery that was simultaneous with that of psychoanalysis—is that what is essential in our lives cannot be seen by us because it takes place in a space that is inaccessible to us: in the gaze of the other. Marcel, the protagonist, inhabits a gallery of distortionary mirrors where no one is who they believe or say they are and he himself is the result of all the gazes that converge to photograph him. Since the truth of our lives proceeds from the discourse of the Other, it is impossible to hold a discourse about ourselves that could be "true." For this reason the Proustian quest is a profound lesson for neurophysiologists of memory. Where in the brain are the gaze, thought and silent interpretation of the other located? Ex-sistence consists in being seen from the exterior; just as memory is not internal or lodged in some kind of "spirit." Memory is in the very objects that have the property of actualizing the body's experiences: in madeleines, in uneven paving-stones, in the sound produced by train wheels racing over rails, in ancient *grimoires*. Ultimately, it resides in the unwritten book, in the book about to be delivered by the pen, the object of desire for Proust (and for his mother: desire is the desire of the Other). Such is the object of the *recherche* and its crucial moment occurs during the episode when the madeleine is dipped into the cup of tea. The small cake functions as myth of the birth of memory—a recollection that sets memory in motion—the pure point of departure for the narration. As Sartre (Roquentin) showed us a few pages back, a false beginning is involved. Indeed, it is the end of the search for lost time: following the episode of the madeleine, time is set in reverse motion until it reaches the beginning, which is the publication of the novel ["the essential, the only true book, though in the ordinary sense of the word it does not have to be 'invented' by a great writer—for it exists already in each one of us—has to be translated by him," a book "of which the 'impression' has been printed in us by reality itself"][227]

227. Proust, Marcel. *Remembrance of Things Past*. Translated by C.K. Scott Moncrieff and Terence Kilmartin; and Andreas Mayor. New York: Random House, 1981, vol. III, pp. 926 and 914 respectively.

and our frequent readings of it . . . which lead us to believe that it begins with our awakening in the middle of the night and the memory of the blessed madeleine.

Those gazes that rain down on us do not seem to leave a trace but function like lassos, like strange bodies that trap us and appropriate our very being. What is seen by whoever observes us is an unknown; we ceaselessly try to obtain indications of it, confirmations, exact outlines, but they never exhaust our curiosity. Others observe us; they are many, voluble, scarcely trustworthy and they view us with the color deformations and limitations of their own optical instruments. We exist in the concave mirror of their unfathomable and dark occipital cortex, where all retinal stimuli end up. They are mirrors, yes, but multiple, curved and soft mirrors, moved by inscrutable passions. Our unconscious is a reflection of this life developed on a screen that we cannot perceive, a screen that is modified by the phantasy and the desire of the Other. "The subject's unconscious is the other's discourse" (Lacan).[228] Inscrutable, unfathomable, inaccessible.

How can we know ourselves if this knowledge of ourselves passes through the gaze of the other? It is precisely this question that divides the history of the autobiographical "genre" in two stages: before and after Freud. In conventional autobiography, the writer thinks he can enlighten himself in a parthenogenetic way through the text he transmits to the public. Subsequent to Freud, self-knowledge must pass through the other, through a person of whom little is known and who is the object of transference. In the presence of the psychoanalyst the subject reveals heretofore unknown keys to his subjectivity and memory. He is suspicious of his own beliefs and memories and understands the "phantasmatic" impetus that animates and colors the contents of his conscious. Following analysis the subject can deconstruct what he imagined to be his self-portrait and he can understand that his history comes to him from the place of the Other.

---

228. Lacan, Jacques [1953]. *Écrits*. Paris: Seuil, 1966, p. 265 [ed. Norton, p. 219]. He returns to this formula in *Écrits* on pp. 379, 469, 549, 628, etc.

We never come to completely know who we are no matter how much we remember, photograph ourselves and write our memories, whether naturally or novelistically, using a real name or that of a character. *We live naked, exposed in the gaze of others.* No autobiography—and no photograph—can ignore that. The majority of such narratives are written in order to guide the other's gaze and control the way one is seen. The design is to provide unity and continuity to life through writing. That this is what one hopes to achieve indicates that this is precisely what is lacking: to join the body and the soul, the past and the present, social reality and the specular image. This unifying intention is conspicuous, as stated above, in those who choose to write their "Confessions," from St. Augustine and Rousseau onwards, in those who make public recantations with a clear apologetic intention, hoping to correct the errors of their past, showing their defects to be virtues because they have the courage to expose them. Sincerity, as I said at the outset of this itinerary, evoking Sartre, is a form—perhaps the most widely disseminated—of "bad faith."

The gaze of the other can be objectified thanks to the creation of a mirror with memory: the photographic camera.[229] But the image it provides for us is always but a clot in time. In a photograph in which we appear, we see only a "still life," our own. In English, the term *still life* (in contrast to the Spanish, *naturaleza muerta*, loosely meaning "dead nature") contains the word "still," which may function as an adverb, adjective or noun. It may mean "immobile, calm" or "yet, even." In the third instance, which interests us most, a *still* is an image taken from a motion film. It is a *still* image of life. In the photograph, a moment from the past is present although it is not possible to go back. It is fascinating to see how fast the difference between present and past materializes in the minuscule lapse of time from the moment of taking a pho-

---

229. The sensational metaphor of the camera as "a mirror with memory" is almost as old as photography itself. O.W. Holmes, North American doctor and amateur photographer, used it in 1859. Cf. A. Draaysma, *Metaphors of memory*, cit. p. 119. I wonder: Is the brain also a mirror with memory?

tograph and viewing it on the LCD screen of the digital camera to see how it "came out." This is a perfect example of Derridean "*différance*." There is a *difference* between the moment of clicking the shutter and the moment of viewing the objectified result and there is a temporal *differation*. Photography, like autobiography, as we shall soon see, objectifies death while the person is *still* in *life*. Photographs always lie because they show the past as present. Just as memory does.

A totally original autobiography would be one attempting to narrate the life of its protagonist (who goes by the same name as the autho®) without any reference to the "memory of the observer," that is—if we recall a previous reference (see page 48, footnote 46)—erasing all that he has seen with his "subjective camera," immersed in the scenes he remembers. The author would have to write from the field memory of the other, from which s/he would observe his/her own life; to narrate (him/herself) from the point of view of a hypothetical camera that is filming him/her. The story would be read as an adventure of the imagination in the realm of distanced subjectivity in which oneself becomes the object. Not the subject. For example, an autobiography by Odette de Crécy, written by her through the gaze of her three husbands, or of Mme. Verdurin, or of her lovers, or of her daughter Gilberte, or of various of the characters who knew her. This would be a cubist view of the "ego"; the angles of the gaze would be constantly changing. One would try to achieve the impossible "truth" of a life through the combination of subjectivities, points of view, perspectives, multiple mirrors like those that tormented Borges as a child. Falsehood, which we always find in this variant of (diegetic) narrative genre called autobiography, is an inevitable effect in which the author confuses him/herself with the "I," unaware of the fact that "I" is the effect of the other's gaze in which "one" exists. Proust knew this perfectly while Nabokov had no idea. In any case, we know very well that the truth in both works has the structure of fiction. Showing and dissecting the fictitious construction opens the path to a possible truth of being. One has to write the book one carries within oneself . . . it will never become a "true" autobiography . . . and it will never cease to be one.

Oedipus and Narcissus are called upon as witnesses: the former discovers who he is and tears his eyes out; the second glimpses himself in the pool, confuses himself with his own image, drowns himself and is replaced by a flower. The fate of both seems to bear relation to that of autobiographers and to two of the life narrative strategies I have typologized. Oedipus, the prosopoclastic, undoes himself in the search for himself and destroys all mirrors out of blindness; Narcissus is ruined by idolizing his own image and becoming one with the mirror that observes him. Can autobiography save Narcissus and enable him to realize that the image is an illusion? This is the function assigned to the critic and reader, to countersign the biography and certify it as *hetero-* and *thanato-* graphy. If the author, concerned about saving face, engages in profuse falsification, it is the reader who might register and denounce the imposture. The history of psychoanalysis has provided two tools for the task of questioning the imaginary scaffolds erected by the subject to scale the walls of the empty fortress of his autobiographical self: Freud's "Family Romances"[230] and Lacan's "individual myth of the neurotic."[231] Jean-Paul Sartre's autobiography,[232] whose details I will not venture into here, portrays the interaction of both referents, myth and family romance: the novelized version of his family history in the first pages and the conviction that he can send the idea of Salvation to the devil (*au magasin des accésoires*) and change the world, the great man who can respond to Proust's effeminate beginning, *Longtemps, je me suis couché de bonne heure* (*RTP*, I, p. 3), with a virile *Longtemps, j'ai pris ma plume pour une épée*,[233] which leads to another hurried protest:

---

230. Freud, Sigmund [1908]. "Neurotics' family romance." *St. Ed.*, cit., vol IX, pp. 141–153.
231. Lacan, Jacques [1953]. "Le mythe individuel du névrosé ou poésie et vérité dans la névrose." *Ornicar?*, no. 17–18, 1979, pp. 289–307.
232. Sartre, Jean-Paul [1964]. *The Words*. Translated by Bernard Frechtman. New York: George Braziller, 1964.
233. *Ibid.*, p. 211.

À present je connais notre impuissance. ("For a long time, I took my pen for a sword; I now know we're powerless"[234]) I will skip over the significant words "sword" and "impotence"; any interpretation would tend towards caricature.

An autobiographical approach that combines different perspectives foreign to the subject would be very unusual, but one can always, at least, intersperse personal memories with the gazes and gestures of the other that have served to shape one's own life. It is imperative that the author view himself from where he is seen by others, especially when memory is involved. "The only way to preserve memory is to not keep it to oneself."[235] Idiosyncrasy of style is convenient as it may be equivalent to the author's signature, but it is also necessary to intersperse other narrative styles, other vocabularies, in order to preserve the style of the other, the *socius*, the witness.

> I should like in some way to make my soul transparent to the reader's eye, and for that purpose I am trying to present it from all points of view, to show it in all lights, and to contrive that none of its movements shall escape his notice, so that he may judge for himself of the principle which has produced them. [. . .] His task is to assemble these elements and to assess the being who is made up of them. The summing-up must be his, and if he comes to wrong conclusions, the fault will be of his own making.[236]

The other's response gives meaning to the questioning of oneself. As does the other's silence. Neither the word nor the gaze of the other can be omitted from the odyssey of the autho®'s life.

---

234. Sartre, Jean-Paul. *Les mots*. Paris: Gallimard, Folio, 1974. *The Words*. Translated by Bernard Frechtman. New York: George Braziller, 1964, pp. 253–254.
235. Derrida, Jacques, "Être juste avec Freud." *Penser la folie: essais sur Michel Foucault*. Paris, Galilée, 1992, p. 141.
236. Rousseau, Jean-Jacques. *The Confessions of Jean-Jacques Rousseau*. Translated by J.M. Cohen. London: Penguin Books, 1953, p. 169.

The true stage for our lives, the scene of our actions, is always that of an exam that we can neither know nor even control. Autobiographers generally wish to oppose this fatality of alienation through a trial that is likewise beyond control: that which plays out before society and is consigned to posterity. *"Credite posteri."* ("O believe me, posterity!")[237] The essence of paranoia consists in wanting to enclose oneself in the gaze of the other and wanting to appropriate or dominate that which the other sees in us, which may become grandiose in megalomania and atrocious in the delirium of persecution. As the design of controlling the gaze of the other is destined to failure, the other may logically become more hostile and threatening. "Normal" life consists in a wise defense in the face of the unpredictable judgment of someone who could eventually abandon or dislike us. Dialogue is a fencing match. The intersection of gazes is, in a certain way, a bar with which the danger that the other represents can be measured, as well as a medium for presenting a possible challenge; it is a duel. The seduction forces the other to see that our foil has a ball on its tip and is thus harmless, and at the same time it invites the other to blunt his weapon. This strategy also works for oneself. Perhaps we could all say, like President Bush of the United States of (a part of North) America: "That there are people who hate us . . . I simply can't believe it. I know how good we are." If we did not believe that we were good and deserving of the love of others, perhaps we would be unable to engage in the overt and covert wars—the preventive and retributive wars—which seem to be so essential to the scripts of history. The other, in the logic of paranoia, is whoever threatens the values that organize our "goodness." The other is almost always the perverse one whereas it is oneself that would like to preserve the innocent conscience of the pure soul. "To err is human" . . . and to blame the other for our errors is even more human. As if to prove this, many autobiographies have been written. Rousseau is not alone.

---

237. Horace. *The Complete Odes and Satires of Horace*. Translated by Sidney Alexander. Princeton: Princeton Univ. Press, 1999, Book II, Ode 19, p. 87.

The other is, in many cases, the specular double that terrifies and terrorizes, the rival with whom one engages in a lethal relationship. The *Doppelgänger*.[238] It would be a lengthy task to review the anthropological studies and the great variety of literary works that deal with the opposition between the subject and itself in the form of the brother (especially the twin), the homonym (like William Wilson), the shadow that lives independent of the body, the other self, the Mister Hyde, the Golem, the sleepwalker, the hypnotized self, the specular image that is absent or acts on its own, the dead self that returns to exact vengeance, the *Horla*, the oval portrait that comes to life as the model dies, the portrait of Dorian Grey that ages as the model retains its unwilting youth, the mirror that takes control of the body, the "Borges and I," the broken mirrors that kill or bring seven years of bad luck to whoever gazes into them, the rituals that require that all mirrors be covered when there is a corpse in the house being mourned. These phantoms are sufficiently "pervasive" to be considered "human patrimony." A patrimony that is not protected by UNESCO and is much more than the resource of a few writers of fantasy and horror: it is the very structure of the divided subject. The hallucination of the double is a tomography of the author.

This is why I am interested in psychoanalysis and the writers who demonstrate, in the way they approach autobiography, their strategies for relating to the mirror: there is nothing like analysis, nothing like writing, for revealing the pitfalls of self-love that are at the heart of mental illness in normal individuals and that we refer to as paranoia. The limits of the self are imprecise by virtue of being implied in the vision of whoever observes us, in that invasive eye that leads us to put up lines of defense, to dig trenches and string up high-tension wires, producing the result that the "stronger" the self is, the more it depends on the walls of contention it must construct, one after another, relentlessly, protecting the self from the enemy gaze. Thus alienation increases.

238. Rank. O. [1924]. *The Double: A Psychoanalytic Study*. Translated by Karen Christenfeld. London: Karnac, 2000.

Narcissus is weak from birth, and he dies on the mirror's surface. Chained to the mirror.

15

HETEROTHANATOPHONIA

1. The Myth of the Birth of Memory

We imagine our birth without actually remembering it. We imagine it without being able to describe it. We can find a conspicuous example of just such a thing in the aforementioned autobiography by Marguerite Yourcenar,[239] beginning with a colorful description in which she presents herself in the third person: "The being I refer to as *me* came into the world on June 8, 1903, at about eight in the morning, in Brussels. My father . . ." We are provided with the usual information: date, place and circumstances of birth. There is never a lack for witnesses who remember and offer us this information like a clothes hanger to which we can fasten our existence. With a small effort of imagination we can put ourselves in the place of that small bundle of flesh covered in various types of mucous and viscous membranes, traveling through a narrow tunnel without ventilation towards its escape into infinite space, that is, into the celestial body inhabited by speaking simians who, given time, will be considered peers.

About eighty years ago it became fashionable to speak of this

---

239. Yourcenar, Marguerite. *Dear Departed*. Translated by Maria Louise Ascher. New York: Farrar Straus Grioux, 1991, p. 3.

landing as a traumatic event, shared by all humanity, of which each and every one of us retains a dark and inaccessible memory. It is something we know without knowing it, an asphyxiating episode that is impossible to remember, the archetype of what is most horrifying to which we will always return, terrified, on those nightmare nights.

This un-rememberable memory would be the beginning of life, the memory of the destruction of the precarious certainties that one might have sensed amidst the clear, warm and constant liquids of the amniotic cavity. Upon exit from that lost maritime paradise, as our small bodies pass through the funnel-like fish gullet that opens before us, sliding and squeezed along that tunnel to who knows where, with the cranium squashed and deformed by the narrowness of the canal, pinched at the end by a pair of claws much larger than our heads, struck by a stream of cold, searing air that rips into the privacy of our lungs, and a pair of fingernails and scissors sever our only connection to that vessel of previous space-time, screaming out of pain, rage and desperation, hearing our own scream that destroys the virginity of our private eardrums, our little bodies, received kindly or unkindly—who could say and after how much time?—by a certain congregation of animated things who know as little about us as that nothing that we know about them. And, to top it all, they have the arrogance to believe that they know what is best for us from that moment onward.

The traumatism of birth which—as Sandor Ferenczi and Otto Rank[240] said long ago—one never gets over and always returns, even though it is not an object of memory. In any case, it is evoked retroactively in the multitude of painful episodes, separations, losses, abandonments and frustrations that mark subsequent life, expelled as we are from the uterine paradise. Some people propose that we view this succession of painful events through rosy lenses and they describe these bumps and bruises that push us into the world with consolatory words: learning, growth, acquisition of

---

240. Ferenczi, Sandor and Otto Rank [1923]. *The Development of Psychoanalysis*. New York: Dover, 1956. Translated by C. Newton.

abilities, command over the physical and social worlds, gathering forces, skills and autonomy. They are in some way justified: human life consists in abandoning the field of certainties in order to invent ways of conserving it, that is, of surviving by moving among seats and stages, balconies and movie screens, until settling into some kind of box—wooden boxes preserving skeletons, urns containing ashes, residuals that someone will keep or that will be scattered and left to the arbitrary judgment of Aeolus, Neptune or the river and wood nymphs who will know how to use them to fertilize new life. Perhaps (*chi lo sa?*).

Before being born, death did not exist . . . and to be born is to begin to die. On this voyage from life to death various characters and institutions take charge, in their view, of the estimable task of guiding us along paths already blazed and worn. If one is "the one" (countable), they are "the Other": guides, mentors, models, mirrors, judges, executioners, witnesses, captains or artillerymen of the ship on which we sail. Captains and artilleryman. Shipmates on the voyage as well as the shipwreck. They receive us in a world without limits and mark the points of reference, names, addresses, destinations along the way. Among the multitude of others, the maternal figure stands out. She is the one who receives us in her arms, calms our hunger, alleviates the discomfort stirring in our bodies, she instills drops of meaning through auditory channels, notes of song and music, gentleness and roughness of clothing and caresses, rhythms of hunger and satiety. One, two. Now you see me, now you don't. One, two. *Fort—da.* One, two. Waves rolling in, waves rolling out. I love you so much, so little, not at all. One, two.

She, our mother, takes responsibility for us; she takes us in her arms and bears us from the initial silence of the night to the day with its certainties and dangers. She is—following our reference to Winnicott when we dealt with Virginia Woolf's first memory—the first reflective surface, our first mirror. She is there, but not always. When she is not there, we must live in the space of her absence, in the timeless interval, exposed to the risk of her not returning. Is she shut away, like Amalie Freud, in a wardrobe to which we have no key? Usually her disappearance is temporary; she leaves but she also returns and the anticipation of her return transforms life into waiting. The end of childhood is the moment that other women and men take her place and our "own" lives are organized around new points of reference. To live—to truly live—is to continue living even though our mother is no longer there and we are no longer parasites who depend on her comings and goings, on the looking glass of her gaze in which, for the first time and forever, we see ourselves. To look to the past for a reunion (*wiederzufinden*) that will never take place. Nostalgia.

And what happens when she is not there and no other person—no others—fill in for her absence? There are lives of writers that are unimaginable without the long period of living with their mothers for whom their work is a monument to her memory, such as Saint Monica, the mother of Augustine of Hippo. Borges, who never wrote an autobiography,[241] was a writer brought up tied to the apron strings of his mother who lived until her son reached a glorious old age. Biographers will continue to disagree as to whether she was the hand behind the translations that "Georgie" signed or whether the writing of the illustrious narrator suffered when she died—a day on which he was left without his point of insertion. Other literary figures lost their mother at the moment of their birth, such as Jean-Jacques Rousseau[242] and Marguerite Yourcenar,[243] to name just two—or three, adding Leo Tolstoy, whose mother died when he was one and a half years old. They produced a literature that may be read as a scar of initial loss, as

---

241. The extent to which he participated in writing the text that is attributed to him is debatable. It was published as: *Un ensayo autobiográfico*. J.L. Borges. Buenos Aires: Galaxia Gutenberg—Emecé, 1999. It was written by Norman Thomas di Giovanni on the basis of a conference given by Borges in Oklahoma in 1970. The translator of this text into Spanish, Aníbal González, states in his prologue (p. 11) "that another hand intervenes in this text—that of his translator and secretary at that time, Norman Thomas di Giovanni." (My translation.)

242. Rousseau, Jean-Jacques [1782–1789]. *Confessions*, cit.

243. Yourcenar, Marguerite. *Souvenirs pieux*, (*Dear Departed*) cit.

if their pens had to draw the outlines of a mother that would never appear, an absence recognized as a missing element while other human beings are sustained by the very inverse. The mystery of survival amidst maternal absence may be read not only in Rousseau's *Confessions* and Yourcenar's "memoirs," which they have left for posterity, but also in each and every one of their works.

The oft-repeated Cortazarian thesis that has functioned as a *motto* in these pages could be reduced to the alternative of the mother's presence or absence. If she is there, the baby, scarcely able to speak, lives in the continuity of her gaze; so, there is no trauma and, therefore, there is no memory either, but rather sweet evocations. Terror takes possession of the person in the moment her absence is discovered: all the examples presented, including Nabokov's innocent memories, confirm this simple conclusion. This merging with her is at the root of the Joycean and Woolfean "epiphanies" that I have described. I could add other examples relating feelings of warmth, well-being, security, solar heat and light that have led certain writers (Pierre Loti, George Sand, Michel Leiris, etc.) to relate experiences of communion, wonder and the awakening of all that is sacred. They are images like those invented by Georges Perec, as Pierre Loti said, that are "completely confused of the beginnings of life"[244] and that structure a typical way of narrating the beginnings of memory as commonplaces, clichés, that are different from the Cortazarian form we have seen in so many examples. This is the way we can understand the mythical nature of first memories, always objects of reconstruction, screen memories and supposed carriers of keys that will explain so many mysteries of our existence. When one travels up a river in search of its origins one gets lost in the labyrinth of small brooks that sometimes converge and become creeks before they can be streams. Is it possible that the great Danube springs from the water tap in a peasant's home, as Claudio Magris tells us?[245] This is what

---

244. Loti, Pierre [1890]. *Roman d'un Enfant*. Paris: Flammarion, 1998, p. 39 (my translation).
245. Magris, Claudio. *Danube*. Translated from the Italian by Patrick Creagh. New York: Farrar, Straus, Giroux, 1989, p. 17.

happens in the search for that El Dorado of first memories which one hopes to transform into the origin of existence. Its sacred nature proceeds from the fact of being "first": it is of the utmost importance for the adult autobiographer with lantern-like pen in hand who ventures into that original night, but not for the child that he or she was. Its importance comes—and this is no longer a revelation for us—from the future. Leiris acknowledges this:

> Sufficient evidence of this is the following memory, definitely one of the most moving of those I have retained, perhaps only because it is the most remote and remains as ill defined, as problematic, as though I were extracting it from some sort of prehistory (*RJ*, 167, *Scratches*).[246]

Thus begins the hunt for the first memory. It is curious, as I have stated, that so many have made such an effort in this retrospective pursuit and that they take such pride in being able to put an earlier date on this memory than all other memory hunters. I have already alluded to the research results of Binet and Henri (1895) and of the Henri brothers (1897) which Freud cited with broad knowledge of the subject. For my part, I have studied the aforementioned questionnaire and I saw that it contained an absolutely banal series of questions that would be embarrassing to quote textually. Quantitative psychology, based on surveys with up-to-date quantifiable data, remains anchored in this type of "research." The content and text of the questions follow a certain scheme that is . . . the same as the way in which autobiographers have long presented their collections of mnemic puerilities (*anemic*, my word processor automatically corrects the word *mnemic*, knowing that the last is not included in its spell-checking dictionary).

I do not reproach either the writers or the psychologists, but rather the task itself of relating one's life and the method—almost a pandemic in fact—of the egographies, crowned more by Narcissus's laurels than by those of Orpheus. Where to begin?

---

246. Leiris, Michel. *Scratches*. Op. cit., 153.

With the ancestors? With mama and papa? With one's place among one's siblings? With one's place and date of birth? With the astral conjunction? With the house? With the historical circumstances? With the first memory? And, then, how to continue? I was told that when I was born . . . that I first spoke when I was . . . x years old, I learned to read, I went to school, I discovered sex, we moved to, I liked to see, to eat . . . How predictable everything can be in the absence of a great writer, someone brave enough to begin by saying, "For a long time I used to go to bed early!" The beginning is immaterial; the content matters little. The poetry is found elsewhere, in "They made me sleep alone," in "I have no childhood memories" and the remission to the *Freudian* dictum: "Indeed, no one has memories *from* childhood, since they are all memories *about* childhood." Chronological sequence does not help the writer. Rather, it can block him as it brings him closer to prosopagnosia. It is not surprising that the fate of such texts is often the Museum, a far cry from Parnassus. What is important is the style, which is the man, as Buffon said, to which Lacan added: yes; the man . . . to whom one speaks. Or the woman, I am pleased to amend.

I was speaking of the bravery required to begin an autobiography without asking forgiveness for speaking of oneself, without choosing a conventional beginning and without pausing to discuss the ambiguities of the genre. I was reflecting on all the different beginnings elected by different authors, the first memories that have been revealed to me over the course of this essay, the search for supporting documentary sources, etc., when it occurred to me that not one writer had begun by relating an instant that, in any case, should be the true beginning to all auto-*bio*-graphy, the moment when life begins—inaccessible to all memory—the moment of one's conception. As a psychoanalyst I am familiar with the idea, the memory and the phantasy of the primordial scene, the scene of origins, the origin of all scenes, which is the scene of coitus between the parents. What was happening between them, what did they feel, what idea did they have of the child they could engender, what desires, aversions, social commitments were they fulfilling with respect to third parties? I know of the difficult lives of those who cannot conceive of their own conception, the concordance or the discordance of the parents' desires, the love or violation, the engendering of a child as manifestation of longing or the mechanical result of a copulation lacking in meaning. I was wondering about this apparent lack of the primordial scene from the many autobiographies that I have read without, of course, discarding the possibility that there might be an exception, when, finally, I remembered . . . *I remembered Tristram Shandy.*

Amazed, I confirmed the absolute coincidence between the date of the source and the origin of the autobiographical "genre" that everyone, particularly the French, agree corresponds to the *Confessions* of Rousseau (1765–1770) with its grandiose beginning:

> I have resolved on an enterprise which has no precedent, and which, once complete, will have no imitator. My purpose is to display to my kind a portrait in every way true to nature, and the man I shall portray will be myself. Simply myself. I know my own heart and understand my fellow man. But I am made unlike any one I have ever met; I will even venture to say that I am like no one in the whole world.[247]

and the dates of the writing of the brilliant novel by Laurence Sterne, the Irish writer who, during his lifetime, was a military officer and protestant minister. The misadventures of Tristram Shandy were written from 1760 to 1767.[248] I was pleased to discover that the starting point for all autobiographies, the celebrated work by Rousseau, is simultaneous or even subsequent to the parody of the "genre." A caricature that precedes the face! In effect, Sterne's novel is presented as a "life narrative" and begins, precisely, with the scene of parental coitus that I felt was missing from the other

247. Rousseau, Jean-J. *The confessions.* Op. cit., p. 17.
248. Sterne, Laurence. *The Life and Opinions of Tristram Shandy, Gentleman.* Oxford-New York: Oxford University Press, 1983.

"cases" I am familiar with. It is appropriate here to contrast the beginning of Tristram Shandy to the opening of *Confessions* quoted above:

> I wish either my father or my mother, or indeed both of them, as they were in duty both equally bound to it, had minded what they were about when they begot me; had they duly consider'd how much depended upon what they were then doing;—that not only the production of a rational Being was concern'd in it [. . .]—Had they duly weighed and considered all this, and proceeded accordingly,—I am verily persuaded I should have made a quite different figure in the world, from that, in which the reader is likely to see me.—Believe me, good folks, this is not so inconsiderable a thing as many of you may think it;—you have all, I dare say, heard of the animal spirits, as how they are transfused from father to son . . .[249]

While Tristram's parents were engaged in this procedure ("To my uncle Mr. Toby Shandy do I stand indebted for the preceding anecdote . . ."),

> *Pray, my dear*, quoth my mother, have *you not forgot to wind up the clock?—Good G—!* cried my father, making an exclamation, but taking care to moderate his voice at the same time,—*Did ever woman, since the creation of the world, interrupt a man with such a silly question?* Pray, what was your father saying?— Nothing. [. . .] My father . . . had oft, and heavily, complain'd of the injury . . .—*But alas!* Continued he, shaking his head a second time, and wiping away a tear which was trickling down his cheeks, *My Tristram's misfortunes began nine months before ever he came into the world.*—My mother, who was sitting by, look'd up,—but she knew no more than her backside what my father meant,—but my uncle, Mr. *Toby Shandy*, who

---

249. Sterne, Laurence. *The Life and Opinions of Tristram Shandy, Gentleman.* Oxford-New York: Oxford University Press, 1983, p. 5.

had been often informed of the affair,—understood him very well (cit., p. 7).

The hilarious beginning to this "autobiography" is exemplary for making so prominent the one element that I noted as an "omission" to all those autobiographies written in subsequent centuries: that which should be the absolute "first memory." The 600 pages that follow the primordial scene maintain this tone of mocking the "genre" that—according to the experts—was simultaneously commencing.[250] Sterne relates in first person—appropriate to convention—the choice of his given name, his initiation into language and grammar, his coming of age (*Bildungsroman*), his games, his loves, his dedication to the military arts, etc., peripeteias that are not very special in themselves but they are narrated with many of the techniques developed by the literary vanguards of the twentieth century: pages left blank so the reader may draw to his or her liking that woman who is so beautiful that the author prefers not to describe her, unusual temporal leaps, asterisks, typographic inventions that even surpass Apollinaire, enumerations that surpass Borges, socio-historic interpolations that surpass Döblin, inserted sermons and homilies, crossed-out words (*biffures!*), empty chapters, multiple dedications to the book and changes to the dedication in the middle of the text, doodles, *mises en abîme*, self-referential indications, whimsical punctuation, etc. Sterne gives birth to his protagonist and author of this "autobiography" half way through the book and always with a crushed nose; in the final chapter (Chapter 33, volume IX), a conversation is narrated between Tristram's parents and his uncle Toby when the ill-fated Tristram is still in early childhood.

The associative disorder, the lack of narrative plan, the constant

---

250. The novel as parody of the novel is nothing new. All the best works of the narrative genre during the Renaissance and the classical period are extensive, violent and elaborate sarcasms directed at the genre to which they profess to pertain: Rabelais, Cervantes, Voltaire are precursors of Sterne's hilarious work. For a more recent example, I would have to mention Joyce and his two great parodic novels: *Ulysses* and *Finnegans Wake*.

appearance of the unexpected, the wordplay and bizarre ideas, the mixing of genres and languages, the unpremeditated appearance of dreams . . . does not all of this also anticipate—paradoxically—another diegetic subgenre: the free association of the psychoanalytic session and the case report presented by the psychoanalyst in the form of a succession of "clinical vignettes," that lend themselves and are made available for interpretation?

Let me also state that the "cubist autobiography" I anticipated by way of a wish and a phantasy has already been realized in *Tristram Shandy.* The narrator's ego is secondary to the opinions that those around him hold regarding him, particularly his father and his uncle Toby who speak about Shandy and observe his life and his efforts to write the countless chapters of his book. As in the case of Proust (as well as Diderot: *Jacques le fataliste* [1773]), the writing of the book forms part of the book itself. One example that presents the "autobiographer" (Shandy) arguing with himself about the narrative space is pertinent here:

> Is it not a shame to make two chapters of what passed in going down one pair of stairs? For we are got no farther yet than to the first landing, and there are fifteen more steps down to the bottom; and for aught I know, as my father and my uncle *Toby* are in a talking humour, there may be as many chapters as steps;—let that be as it will, Sir, I can no more help it than my destiny:—A sudden impulse comes across me—drop the curtain, *Shandy*—I drop it—Strike a line here across the paper, *Tristram*—I strike it—and hey for a new chapter! (Chapter X, vol. IV, 225.)

2. As I Lay Dying

If it is difficult to narrate the copulation of the parents from whence one came or, for that matter, one's own birth, then, without a doubt, it is ever more difficult to produce a truthful description of one's own death. No one has had the temerity to tell his/her story after having "lived" it; few are those who have succeeded in imagining it. Nonetheless, it is the capital event with which every true autobiography should end. So long as the grim reaper does not arrive, everything one writes is provisional, transitory, subject to future revision. Death is, for each and everyone, the moment that signals the end of our dates with the mirror, the moment when we can no longer see, paint, narrate or write ourselves. The physical body still exists but the cells are dying at a constant and pre-set rhythm, leading up to the final breakdown. The subject subsists in the symbolic, there are funereal rites that will be carried out. One is remembered. One's name persists in certain blood relatives, in documents and signatures that are archived and recorded. All this in the imaginary, only in the imaginary, that realm of the "self" where death carries out an instantaneous and irreversible task.

Following Derrida's ideas,[251] proposed in his superb analysis of Nietzsche's autobiography (*Ecce homo*), we should reiterate that the narration of one's own life is done into the ear of the other (*otobiography*) and that it is from the other that the subject confronts his own message, but in inverted form. The structure of autobiography—as I have indicated—is transferential. Memory always has a cable that is plugged into community history. For this reason the "*auto-*" of biography and the narrative is transformed into "*alo-*" or, into *heterobiography*. It is equally certain that *bios*, or life, is written, as I have also indicated previously, from a blank page, like a shroud that hides the face of the cadaver lying beneath. The written text, always-already-dead inasmuch as it cannot answer questions, will always serve as testimony even if the writer is still alive. The author of an autobiography writes in the shadow of a foretold death, writing as one who is already deceased and substituted for by the text at the very moment it is written, transferring memory

---

251. Derrida, Jacques. *The Ear of the Other: Otobiography, Transference, Translations.* Lincoln and London: University of Nebraska Press, 1988. Translated by Kamuf and Ronell.

to whoever is in a position to conserve it: a peer, a community, a public record. Although not always the case, perhaps, there lives in the author the phantasy, the hope, for escape, through the strategy of everlasting writing from the irreversibility of time and the end of life. It is in this sense that I refer to *heterothanatography*. The subject is playing *fort / da* ("now I see you, now I don't," in the mirror) with his heirs: he leaves them his textual remains. Often, the author writes in order to prescribe how he or she would like to be remembered . . . in accordance with his desire. The narrator "tells of himself" in order to exorcise the specter of death . . . unaware that in this way he is staging it. The book of (one's own?) life is transformed into an epitaph (*epi—taphos*), something that is written on one's tombstone. All memories are from "beyond the grave" (Chateaubriand, 1850).

Ultimately, this is also the meaning of the annunciation made to Maria: the denial of death in the messianic hope for a redeemer who would annul it and provide, in return, eternal life. The dialogue between Gabriel and Maria that we read in Luke (I:28 and I:36) "—*Ave María, Domine tecum.—Ecce ancella Domini*," so often written in the paintings of the annunciation in the late Middle Ages, is no more than a call to an alternative Master (*Domine*) in the face of the supreme Lord which is death. The author writes from the prescience of death:

> Look what thy memory cannot contain,
> Commit to these waste blanks, and thou shalt find
> Those children nurs'd, deliver'd from thy brain,
> To take a new acquaintance of thy mind.
>
> These offices, so oft as thou wilt look,
> Shall profit thee, and much enrich your book.[252]

---

252. Shakespeare, William. Sonnet LXXVII. This sonnet is pendant to another on the same subject (CXXII) whose reproduction I will omit here but that I analyze in *La memoria, la inventora* (*Memory: the Inventor*) op. cit., pp. 22–24.

The mirror shows, mercilessly, how the image wilts and beauty evaporates. The clock's face ticks away the flight of both minutes and memories. The open-mouthed graves demand both corpse and memory. Only the book remains to preserve the imprint of the spirit. From the desperate future one narrates the irrecoverable past. Before birth (into language, which is the only birth that matters in this case), there was no subject to call itself "I" although there was a body in which memory could be stored. In this way memory is what we are made of, retroactively.

> I assume today what in the absolute past of the origin had no subject to receive it and had therefore the weight of a fatality. By memory I assume and put back in question. Memory realizes impossibility: memory, after the event, assumes the passivity of the past and masters it. Memory as an inversion of historical time is the essence of interiority.[253]

In addition to this merited evocation of Levinas—coincident with the course of this study—in these latter paragraphs I have followed in Derrida's footsteps. However, I feel it is appropriate to go beyond these references and add something that arises from the experience of the psychoanalyst. The psychoanalyst rarely reads texts written by his or her patients. Even when he accepts them, he generally sets them aside and asks the patients to *tell* him what they have written. Not only is there no *auto-* or *bio-*, there is no *-graphy* either. The analysand creates a discourse that is his or her *heterothanatophony*. The moment of narrating one's life is submitted to the unpredictable accidents that occur during speech: dreams, errors, slips and unexpected associations expressed in the statement. These will strike the listening ear of the analyst who, playing his cards, highlighting the ambiguities, will give rise to a new discourse that rectifies the former one. For

---

253. Levinas, Emmanuel. *Totality and Infinity: An Essay on Exteriority.* Translated by Alfonso Lingis. Pittsburgh, PA: Duquesne University Press, 1969, p. 56.

as long as the analysis continues, the analyst will aid in a process of constant transformation of the writings that accompanied the subject, a deconstruction of the many formulations (phantasmatic, social, and even psychoanalytic) with which the subject would console himself as well as lie to himself, unconsciously, under the influence of both the ego and of memory. No autobiography (heterothanatophony) emerges unscathed from trial by analysis. Memory should emerge "enriched" by the treatment, like uranium, ready for fission with its nuclei. (*Shall profit you and much enrich your book.*) Does analysis make it possible to gain access to the "truth" of being? No; clearly it does not, because that truth can only exist in discourse, and words always fail in the attempt to articulate that truth.

It is justified to consider ways of narrating life other than those offered by the psychoanalytic experience. In fact, writers who have spent time on the couch produce narratives that differ considerably from those who have not had the experience of analysis or those who have undergone it fruitlessly. The cases of Georges Perec and Michel Leiris, which I have considered in detail, are paradigmatic. A French psychoanalyst who has written a great deal about himself, Serge Doubrovsky,[254] accurately coined the term "autofiction" in referring to those texts that capture the identity of the subject in the interaction between individual events and unconscious multiple determination. The purpose of these autofictional narratives is to broaden knowledge of oneself by challenging and eliminating the barriers that exist between biographical restitution (the life narrative) and novelized transposition (the speech and discourse of the imaginary). As I understand it, the idea of Doubrovsky coincides with one that I expressed several paragraphs above regarding the necessity of going beyond approaches of the singular individual and sociopolitical identities of filiation in order to commit oneself to a transpersonal writing—a "cubist" composition of perspectives, I ventured to say—that takes into account this transgression of the limits of the self. This would constitute a new form of narrative,

---

254. Doubrovsky, Serge. *Fils*. Paris: Galilée, 1977.

that is, writing of and within the limits of language: a borderline writing that is contrary to *egography* and is, rather, *dis-egography*. This is precisely how we could designate the falsely autobiographic works of Perec, Leiris, and perhaps that of Serge André . . . or those of K. (either Joseph, the character, or Franz, the author of the diaries). I am well aware that no text can *belong* to a specific genre, but rather, at best, it may *participate* in one and in others as well: the relegation to a genre does not form part of the text itself:

> Let us take the designation "novel" as an example. This should be marked in one way or another, even if it does not appear in the explicit form of a subtitled designation, and even if it proves deceptive or ironic. This designation is not novelistic, it does not, in whole or in part, take part in the corpus whose denomination it nonetheless imparts. Nor it is simply extraneous to the corpus. But this singular *topos* places within and without the work, along its boundary, an inclusion and exclusion with regard to genre in general. It gathers together the corpus and, at the same time, in the same blinking of an eye, keeps it from closing, from identifying itself with itself.[255]

In light of my research I can affirm that, based on childhood memories (or any other arbitrarily selected beginning), there is no way to distinguish autobiography from novel and the notion of "narrative" embraces both. The participation of memory and imagination is joint, as we have known since Hobbes, even though many try to ignore this. Personal memory constitutes identity: acknowledged. But this identity is not a sacrosanct monument. It is a statue with feet of clay. It is also a prison cell in which the subject is captive but from where he escapes every night while dreaming.

I believe it is possible to distinguish three planes of personal identity and all three are related to memory. One is *identity in the*

---

255. Derrida, Jacques. *Parages*. Op. cit., pp. 264–265. "The law of genre." In Jacques Derrida, *Acts of Literarure*. Derek Attridge (ed.), translated by Avital Ronell. New York and London: Routledge, 1992, pp. 230–231.

real, present in each of our cells, in our chromosomic and genetic maps. Let us call it *Darwinian identity*, preserved (written) in our DNA molecules. The second is *identity in the symbolic*, that is, identity that is embodied in one's name and in documents destined to be recorded and kept in archives; this is memory of the State and for ©opyright purposes, memory that is legal, forensic, Hegelian or Kelsenian. The "I" and the "subject" are legal "fictions," as Bentham[256] said and was later seconded by Nietzsche.[257] Finally, there is *identity in the imaginary*, which enables us to recognize our own face in mirrors and photographs, stating "that's me." This is *psychological* identity that offers continuity from birth until death in spite of the constant transformations that take place among the three identities: cells die and are replaced, the conscious and the manner of seeing one's own past constantly change even though one's name remains the same, the specular image is relentlessly transfigured by the simple passage of time through the gullet of the clepsydra until the last drop of water has run out.

One could propose a fourth type of identity, arising from the discovery of the unconscious. This would be a *Freudian identity*. I would not credit it nor grant it substantiality. Imaginary and symbolic memories may be written and one can imagine the real of death working in them as the pre-written ending that is already present from the very beginning, which sets the autobiographical project into motion. We may recognize in such memories the deleterious action of the repetitive compulsion and the death drive. Nonetheless, the unequivocal conclusion is that the unconscious does not have nor does it confer identity *because the unconscious is the solvent agent of identities*, both symbolic and imaginary. The unconscious cannot be written for the simple reason that it is the unconscious itself the one who writes under the various guises of the "objectivity" of *curriculum vitæ* and the unbridled "subjectivity" of our Hegelian beautiful souls. The unconscious, oriented

---

256. Bentham, Jeremy [1817]. *The Theory of Fictions.* Second Edition. London: Routledge, 1951.
257. Nietzsche, Friedrich [1886]. *The Will to Power.* Translated by R.J. Hollingdale. New York: Random House. Vintage. § 515.

towards the receptor, is the stage for a writing that can be nothing but transferential. Even when the self is split and the writing of journals and notebooks could seem to have no specific audience (for example, Valéry's *Cahiers*, mentioned above, and Franz Kafka's and André Gide's infinite diaries). Written for eventual rereading, they are also manifestations of the split selves of the author. The unconscious is the point of departure for the dispersion and the ruin of the autobiographical project. One self is the writer, the other is the reader . . . of oneself.

If we narrate a dream—the *"via regia"* to the unconscious according to Freudian legend—the narrative is necessarily signed and confirmed by an "I"; it is a "memory of the dream" in which what is important is not the reference to the life of the dreamer, but rather the way in which the "dream-work" has operated a distortion in order to render it "palatable" and "presentable" for the other in the transference, whoever listens to the narrative and from whom one expects an interpretation. The analysis of the dream can have no other objective than that of permitting the subject to discover himself as other than he whom he believed to be thus dismantling the traps of identity and of the presumed continuity of the self. The translation of the dream, its interpretation, is *anti-autobiographical*. We could say that it adheres to Pascal's twice quoted disqualification of the "foolish project of describing oneself." What is that longed for and exact interpretation? One that falls upon the very scene of the dream's narrative, on the hidden teleology that guides the narrator who imposes himself on his listener in his search for a jouissance of which he prefers to know nothing.

It is for a good reason that I speak of dreams at this point in this study: *an autobiography—every autobiography that I am familiar with—has the structure of a dream* (*or a nightmare*). It is a message: it reveals truth in the form of the distortions that memory imposes on the narrative by virtue of the fact that it is a narrative. In it we hear and analyze its imaginary and symbolic components, and the analysis culminates in the discovery of an umbilical cord that communicates with what is real. Real? Yes; with what is real: the terror described by Cortázar, the terror that has been confirmed by other accounts of "first memories" collected here. The cry in the absence of the mother, the cry that finds no consolation in her return.

And life from the perspective of the unconscious? It is not an edifying novel or a novel of formation (*Bildungsroman*). It is recognition, as Goethe (the visionary master of this art) suspected, that life is offered to us by others, just like personal history and the name with which the autho® signs. The image we have of life as a unit is a mechanism of *mise en scène*, a question directed at whoever can ratify that image appealing to the presumption of identity by the other, who is the reader. The naive autobiographer aims at the desire of the other and requests that—between them—he and his hypocritical reader should reciprocally ratify one another. What is more, if the author supposes that it could appeal to his reader, he will dream dreams in order to please him. We are exposed to such deceits by virtue of merely saying "I" and conjugating a verb! Grammatical "statements" are religious "prayers" that implore recognition from the Other. They are addressed to Our Father. As Nietzsche said: "I am afraid we are not getting rid of God because we still believe in grammar" (464).[258] Alienation, as demonstrated by Leiris and Perec without actually meaning to, is basically, to fall into the snares of language which conditions what we can say and, consequently, what we cannot say. And that which we cannot say, that which constitutes what we are, is the language and the desire of the Other. Unspeakable; that which, because we cannot say it, is better left unsaid. Or, as T.W. Adorno said, addressing himself to Wittgenstein: if we are

---

258. Nietzsche, Friedrich [1888]. *Twilight of the Idols; or, How to Philosophize with a Hammer.* Translated by Duncan Large. London: Oxford University Press, 1998. In *The Nietzsche Reader*. Malden, MA: Blackwell Publishing, 2006, p. 464. It is interesting to note that in the Spanish translation of this sentence, the translator uses the future tense: "I am afraid we will not get rid of God . . ." ("Temo que no vamos a desembarazarnos de Dios porque continuamos creyendo en la gramática.")

not going to speak about what we cannot, then what else can we speak about? In his own words:

> Properly speaking, one can only philosophize, in general, when, with consciousness of its impossibility, one tries, none-theless, to express the inexpressible. Whosoever capitulates to this, whosoever does not undertake the impossible with the consciousness of its impossibility, would be better off removing his hands from this task (my translation).[259]

Birth is trauma, yes, but it is one that does not appear in the civil registry. It is birth into language that "humanizes" us by "denaturalizing" us. "Human nature" is language-based rather than biological; it requires that we live in an environment conditioned by the word, which is always the word of the Other. It was not necessary to wait for Freud in order to realize this. Nietzsche[260] already knew this although he did not acknowledge from whom he had learned it. In the same year that Nietzsche was born, 1844, Max Stirner, who has been forgotten today, or is remembered only because Marx and Engels criticized him strongly in *The German Ideology* (1846), published *The Ego and Its Own*,[261] a key work that is the first explicit critique of language. Without Stirner's work, it would be impossible to trace Fritz Mauthner's work, which gave rise to the Viennese challenge to language that became the devastating explosive used by the twentieth century against the conventions of philosophy. Without Stirner, we may not have known Nietzsche or Mauthner. Without them, we may not have known von Hofmanstahl, Freud, Wittgenstein or Musil. No one before Stirner had proposed that access to language was traumatic

259. Adorno, Theodor W. [1963]. Op. cit., p. 216.
260. Nietzsche, Friedrich [1873]. "On Truth and Lies in a Nonmoral Sense" (Chapter 10). Translated by Daniel Breazeale, in Breazeale (ed.), *Philosophy and Truth: Selections from Nietzsche's Notebooks of the Early 1870s*. Amherst, NY: Humanity Books, 1999, pp. 79–91.
261. Stirner, Max [1844]. *The Ego and His Own: The Case of the Individual Against Authority*. Translated by Steven T. Byington. New York: Libertarian Book Club, 1963.

in terms that anticipated Leiris's painful experience when he learnt that he could not say "*. . . reusement*":

> He who cannot get rid of a thought is so far *only* man, is a thrall of *language*, this human institution, this treasury of *human* thoughts. Language or "the word" tyrannizes hardest over us, because it brings up against us a whole army of *fixed ideas.*[262]

Everyone who exists is a self that is convinced of its own being: "I" and is also an other. There is no self that persists over time. Identity is a deception produced by memory that aspires to continuity, which is believed to be permanent and is not recognized as perforated and conditioned by repression and forgetting. All speakers appear to be motivated by an existential imperative: that of maintaining the phantasy of a continuous and homogenous identity. Autobiographers also suffer this commandment but find—if their testimony is to be acceptable—a command to the contrary: the need to present what is discontinuous, broken, zigzagging, all of which is the essence of their history. Insofar as they are poets and creators, they are attracted by the magnetic temptation of producing their own past, giving it a novelized form, inventing themselves as protagonists of the ups and downs that tossed them about like toys. Furthermore, they need to believe that, by writing about the past, they are in some way recovering it and fixing it for all eternity, that their memories contain the keys to their personalities. "Life is not what one lived, but what one remembers and how one remembers it in order to tell it" (García Márquez, cit.). Even if the memories were "genuine," they could not express the identity of the subject or guarantee the continuity of the subject's existence. The composition and the scaffolding necessary, the selection that one has to make in the process, is a task of artifice, of cutting and pasting together the disperse pages of the book of one's life. Baudelaire wrote at the beginning

262. Op. cit., pp. 345–346.

of *Spleen*: "I have more memories than if I had lived a thousand years" (*"J'ai plus de souvenirs que si j'avais mille ans."*)[263] What book could possibly contain them?

263. Baudelaire, Charles. "Spleen," translated by Anthony Hecht. In *The Flowers of Evil*. Selected and Edited by Marthiel and Jackson Mathews. New York: New Directions, 1963, p. 91.

Bibliography

Adorno, Theodor W. [1962]. *Philosophische Terminologie. Zur Einleitung.* Frankfurt am Main: Suhrkamp, 1973. Not yet translated into English. *Terminología filosófica II.* Translated into Spanish by Ricardo Sánchez Ortiz. Madrid: Taurus, 1977.

Amat, Nuria. *La intimidad.* Madrid: Alfaguara, 1997.

André, Serge. *Flac, suivi de "L'écriture commence où finit la psychanalyse.* Bruxelles: Que, 2001.

Barthes, Roland [1980]. *La préparation du roman: de la vie à l'œuvre.* In: *Œuvres complètes.* Vol. V. Paris: Seuil, 2002.

Baudelaire, Charles [1860]. *Œuvres, completes.* Paris: Gallimard, La Pléiade, 1975.

Baudelaire, Charles. "Spleen," translated by Anthony Hecht. In *The Flowers of Evil.* Selected and Edited by Marthiel and Jackson Mathews. New York: New Directions, 1963.

Bayard, Pierre. *Demain est écrit.* Paris: Minuit, 2005.

Bellos, David. *Georges Perec: A Life in Words.* Boston: David R. Godine, 1993.

Bentham, Jeremy [1791]. *Le panoptique ou L'oeil du pouvoir.* Prologue by Michel Foucault. Paris: La Villette, 1977.

Bentham, Jeremy [1817]. *The Theory of Fictions.* Second Edition. London: Routledge, 1951.

Benveniste, Émile [1966]. *Problèmes de linguistique générale, I.* Paris: Gallimard, 1966. *Problems in General Linguistics.* Translated by Mary E. Meek. Coral Gables (Fla): Miami University Press, 1971.

Blanchot, Maurice. *The Last Man.* Translated by Lydia Davis. New York: Columbia University Press, 1987.

Borges el memorioso. Conversaciones de J.L. Borges con Antonio Carrizo. México: FCE, 1983.

Borges, Jorge Luis. [1977]. *"Blindness." In Seven Nights.* Translated by Eliot Weinberger. New York: New Directions, 1980.

Borges, Jorge Luis. *Obras completas.* Buenos Aires: Emecé, 1974.

Borges, Jorge Luis. *Veinticinco Agosto, 1983 y otros cuentos.* Madrid: Siruela, 1983.

Borges, Jorge Luis. "Funes the Memorious." Translated by James E. Irby in *Labyrinths.* Edited by Donald A. Yates & James E. Irby. New York: New Directions, 1964.

Borges, Jorge Luis. "The Mirror." Translated by Hoyt Rogers. In *Selected Poems.* Edited by Alexander Coleman. New York: Viking, 1999.

Borges, Jorge Luis. *Un ensayo autobiográfico.* Borges. Buenos Aires: Galaxia Gutenburg—Emecé, 1999.

Braunstein, Néstor A. "¿Conoce usted a Henri Boulard?" ("Do you know Henri Boulard?") In *Ficcionario de psicoanálisis.* Mexico: Siglo XXI, 2001.

Braunstein, Néstor A. "El amor en *La llama doble* de Octavio Paz y en los *Cahiers* de Paul Valéry." In *Ficcionario de psicoanálisis*. Mexico: Siglo XXI, 2001.

Braunstein, Néstor A. "Ficcionario." In *Excélsior*, México, May 2, 9, 16, 23, 26, and 30, 2001.

Braunstein, Néstor A. "Un recuerdo infantil de Julio Cortázar" ("A childhood memory from Julio Cortázar") pp. 1–6. In *Diccionario . . .* op. cit.

Braunstein, Néstor A. *El Goce. Un concepto lacaniano*. Buenos Aires: Siglo XXI, 2006.

Braunstein, Néstor A. *La memoria, la inventora*. México: Siglo Veintiuno, 2008.

Bringuier, Jean-Claude. *Conversations with Jean Piaget*. Translated by Basia Miller Gulati. Chicago and London: The University of Chicago Press, 1980.

Broch, Hermann. *Autobiographie psychique*. Translated into the French by Laurent Cassagnau. Paris: L'Arche, 2001.

Brodsky, Joseph. *Less Than One: Selected Essays*. New York: Farrar, Straus, Giroux, 1988.

Buonarotti, Michelangelo. *Poesie*. Milan: Adelphi, 1996.

Canetti, Elias [1976]. *The Conscience of Words*. Translated from the German by Joachim Neugroschel. New York: The Seabury Press, 1979.

Canetti, Elias. *The Torch in My Ear* (1921–1931). Translated by Joachim Neugroschel. New York: Farrar Straus Giroux, 1982.

Canetti, Elias. *The Tongue Set Free: Remembrance of a European Childhood* [1977] (*Die gerettete Zunge—Geschichte einer Jugend*). Translated from the German by Joachim Neugroschel. New York: Continuum, 1983.

Carotenuto, Aldo. *A Secret Symmetry: Sabina Spielrein Between Jung and Freud*. Translated by Arno Pomerans, John Shepley and Krishna Winston. New York: Pantheon 1982, pp. xix, 250.

Carroll, Lewis [1872]. *Through the Looking-Glass*, Chapter 5.

Chateaubriand, François-René, vicomte de. *Mémoires d'outre-tombe*. [Nouvelle édition critique, établie, présentée et annotée par Jean-Claude Berchet.] Paris: Classiques Garnier, 1989.

Cortázar, Julio. *El perseguidor y otro textos: Antología II*. Buenos Aires: Ediciones Colihue, 1996.

Cortázar, Julio. "Conservación de los recuerdos." In *Historias de cronopios y famas*. Buenos Aires: Minotauro, 1962.

Cortázar, Julio. *Hopscotch*. Translated by Gregory Rabassa. New York: Pantheon Books, 1966.

de Man, Paul [1983]. Quoted in Derrida, Jacques. *Memoires for Paul de Man: The Wellek Library Lectures at the University of California, Irvine*. Translated by Cecile Lindsay, Jonathan Culler, and Eduardo Codava. New York: Columbia University Press, 1986.

de Man, Paul. "Autobiography as defacement." In: *The Rhetoric of Romanticism*. New York: Columbia University Press, 1984.

Derrida, Jacques. "Être juste avec Freud." *Penser la folie: essais sur Michel Foucault*. Paris, Galilée, 1992.

Derrida, Jacques. *Memoires for Paul de Man*. Translated by Cecile Lindsay, Jonathan Culler, and Eduardo Codava. New York: Columbia University Press, 1986.

Derrida, Jacques. *Memoirs of the Blind: The Self-Portrait and Other Ruins*. Translated by Pascale-Anne Brault and Michael Naas. Chicago and London: The University of Chicago Press, 1993.

Derrida, Jacques. *Parages*. Paris: Galilée, 1986. "The law of genre." In Jacques Derrida, *Acts of Literarure*. Derek Attridge (ed.), translated by Avital Ronell. New York and London: Routledge, 1992.

Derrida, Jacques. *The Ear of the Other: Otobiography, Transference, Translations*. Translated by Kamuf and Avital Ronell. Lincoln and London: University of Nebraska Press, 1988.

Des Forêts, Louis-René. "Une mémoire démentielle." In *La chambre des enfants*. Paris: Gallimard, L'imaginaire, 1960.

Diccionario panhispánico de dudas. Asociación de Academias de la Lengua Española. Bogotá: Santillana, 2005.

Doubrovsky, Serge. *Fils*. Paris: Galilée, 1977.

Draaisma, Douwe. *Metaphors of memory: A History of Ideas about the Mind*. Translated by Paul Vincent. Cambridge; New York: Cambridge University Press, 2000.

Ferenczi, Sandor and Otto Rank [1923]. *The Development of Psychoanalysis*. Translated by C. Newton. New York: Dover, 1956.

Freud, Sigmund [1899]. "Screen Memories," *The Standard Edition of the Complete Psychological Works of Sigmund Freud*. Vol. III (1893–1899). Trans. James Strachey with Anna Freud. London: The Hogarth Press and The Institute of Psycho-Analysis, 1950.

Freud, S. [1901], *Psychopathology of Everyday Life*. Translated by Alan Tyson. New York: W.W. Norton & Company, 1960.

Freud, Sigmund. *The Complete Letters of Sigmund Freud to Wilhelm Fliess: 1887–1904*. Trans. & Ed., Jeffrey Moussaieff Masson. Cambridge, MA & London: Belknap Press of Harvard University Press, 1985.

Freud, Sigmund [1908]. "Neurotics' family romance" *Standard Edition*, cit., vol. IX.

Freud Sigmund. [1910] *Leonardo da Vinci: A Memory of his Childhood* , St. Ed. cit., vol XI.

Freud, Sigmund [1916]. "On Transience," in *Character and Culture: Psychoanalysis applied to anthropology, mythology, folklore, literature, and culture in general*. Editor, Philip Rieff. New York: Collier Books, 1963.

Freud, Sigmund [1917]. "A Childhood Recollection from '*Dichtung und Wahrheit*' (1917)" in *Character and Culture: Psychoanalysis applied to anthropology, mythology, folklore, literature, and culture in general*. Editor, Philip Rieff. New York: Collier Books, 1963.

Freud, Sigmund. *Beyond the pleasure principle*. Translated by James Strachey. New York: Liveright, 1950.

García Márquez, Gabriel, *Living to Tell the Tale*. Translated by Edith Grossman. New York: Alfred A. Knopf, 2003.

Goethe, Johann Wolfgang von [1811]. *The Autobiography of Goethe: (truth and fiction: relating to my life)*. Translated by John Oxenford. Boston: Dana Estes & Company Publishers, 1848.

Gorostiza, José. *Death without End*. Austin (Tx): Harry Ransom
Humanities Center. Translated by Laura Villaseñor. 1971.
http://www.geocities.com/poesiamsigloxx/gorostiz/gorosti2.html#Death

Halbwachs, Maurice [1877–1945]. *Les cadres sociaux de la mémoire*, Paris:
Presses Universitaires de France, 1952. English translation by Lewis
Coser: *On collective Memory*. Chicago: The Chicago University Press.
1992.

Halbwachs, Maurice. *La mémoire collective*, Paris: Presses Universitaires
de France, 1950. *The Collective Memory*. Edited by Mary Douglas. New
York: Harper and Row Colophon Books, 1980.

Hartley, L.P. [1953]. *The Go-Between*. London: H. Hamilton, 1953.

Hegel, Georg Wilhelm Friedrich. *The Philosophy of History*, "Introduction"
Translated by J. Sibree, 1900, p. 9.

Hegel, Georg Wilhelm Friedrich [1830]. *Philosophy of Nature:Encyclopæædia
of the Philosophical Sciences*. Translated by A.V. Miller. Cambridge (Ma):
Oxford University Press. 1971.

Hobbes, Thomas [1651]. *Leviathan*. Edited by Richard Tuck. Great Britain:
Cambridge University Press, 1991.

Hoffmanstahl, H. von [1903] *The Lord Chandos Letter*. Translated by Russell
Stockman. Marlboro, Vt.: Marlboro Press, 1986.

Horace. *The Complete Odes and Satires of Horace*. Translated by Sidney
Alexander. Princeton: Princeton Univ. Press, 1999.

Joyce, James. *Ulysses*. London: Egoist Press, 1922.

Joyce, James. *Finnegans Wake*. London: Faber and Faber Limited, 1939.

Joyce, James. *Stephen Hero*. New York: New Directions Publishing Co., 1963.

Kandel, E.R. *In Search of Memory. The Emergence of a New Science of Mind*.
New York: Norton, 2006.

Lacan, Jacques [1936–1949]. *"Le stade du miroir . . ." In Écrits*, Paris: Seuil,
1966.

Lacan, Jacques [1945]. "Logical Time and the Assertion of Anticipated
Certainty: A New Sophism." In *Écrits: the first complete edition in English*.
Translated by Bruce Fink in collaboration with Héloïse Fink and Russell
Grigg. New York: W.W. Norton & Co., 2006.

Lacan, Jacques [1948]. "Presentation on psychical causality." *Ibid*.

Lacan, Jacques [1953]. "Le mythe individual du névrosé ou poésie et vérité
dans la névrose." *Ornicar?*, no. 17–18, 1979, pp. 289–307.

Lacan, Jacques [1956]. "Le séminaire sur *La lettre volée*." In *Écrits*. Paris:
Seuil, 1966.

Lacan, Jacques [1958]. "Jeunesse de Gide, ou la lettre et le désir." In *Écrits*.
Paris: Seuil, 1966.

Le Robert: *Dictionnaire historique de la langue française*. Paris: Le Robert,
1994.

Leiris, Michel [1939]. *L'Âge d'homme*. Paris: Gallimard, Folio (435), 1973.
Manhood: A Journey from Childhood into the Fierce Order of Virility.
Translated by Richard Howard.Chicago: University of Chicago Press,
1992.

Leiris, Michel [1926]. *Aurora*. Paris: Gallimard, 1973, first published in 1940.
Aurora. Translated by Anna Warby. London: Atlas Press, 1990.

Leiris, Michel. *La règle du jeu.* Paris: Gallimard, La Pléiade, 2003. *The Rules of the Game.* Translated by Lydia Davis. New York: Johns Hopkins University Press, 1997.

Leiris, Michel. [1948]. ". . . reusement," *"Biffures. La règle du jeu."* Paris: Gallimard, La Pléide, 2003. *Biffures. Scratches (Rules of the Game: Volume 1).* Translated by Lydia Davis. New York: Paragon House, 1991.

Leiris, Michel [1938]. *Miroir de la Tauromachie.* Illustrated by André Masson. Paris: Fata Morgana, 1981. *Mirror of Tauromachy.* Translated by Paul Hammond. London: Atlas Press, 2007.

Leiris, Michel. *Fourbis. Scraps (Rules of the Game: Volume 2).*Translated by Lydia Davis. Baltimore and London: The Johns Hopkins University Press, 1997.

Lejeune, Philippe. [1975]. *Le pacte autobiographique.* Paris: Seuil. Points (326). *Nouvelle édition augmentée.* 1996. *On Autobiography.* Translated by Paul J. Eakin. Minneapolis: University of Minesotta Press, 1989.

Lejeune, Philippe. *La mémoire et l'oblique. Georges Perec autobiographe.* Paris: Hachette, 1991.

Levinas, Emmanuel. *Totality and Infinity: An Essay on Exteriority.* Translated by Alfonso Lingis. Pittsburgh, PA: Duquesne University Press, 1969.

Loti, Pierre [1890]. *Roman d'un Enfant.* Paris: Flammarion, 1998, p. 39.

Magris, Claudio. *Danube.* Translated from the Italian by Patrick Creagh. New York: Farrar, Straus, Giroux, 1989.

Marx and Engels, *The Communist Manifesto*, introduction by Martin Malia. New York: Penguin, 1998.

Markson, David. *Wittgenstein's Mistress.* Chicago: Dalkey Archive Press, 1988.

Michaux, Henri [1927]. *Œuvres completes.* Paris: Gallimard, La Pléide, 1998, p. 73.

Nabokov, Vladimir, *Speak, Memory: An Autobiography Revisited.* With Introduction by Brian Boyd. New York: Alfred A. Knopf, Inc., 1999.

Nassif, Jacques. *En Face. Confessions d'un Psychanalyste.* Paris: Aubier, 2001.

Nietzsche, Friedrich. [1874]. *Untimely Meditations.* Edited by Daniel Breazeale. Translated by R.J. Hollingdale. Cambridge; New York: Cambridge University Press: 1997.

Nietzsche, Friedrich [1873]. "On Truth and Lies in a Nonmoral Sense." Translated by Daniel Breazeale, in Breazeale (ed.), *Philosophy and Truth: Selections from Nietzsche's Notebooks of the Early 1870s.* Amherst, NY: Humanity Books, 1999.

Nietzsche, Friedrich [1886]. *The Will to Power.* Translated by R.J. Hollingdale. New York: Random House. Vintage.

Nietzsche, Friedrich [1888]. *Twilight of the Idols; or, How to Philosophize with a Hammer.* Translated by Duncan Large. London: Oxford University Press, 1998. In *The Nietzsche Reader.* Malden, MA: Blackwell Publishing, 2006.

Onetti, Juan C. *Cuando entonces.* Mexico: Diana, 1988.

Ozick, Cynthia. *Metaphor & Memory: Essays.* New York: Alfred A. Knopf, 1989.

Pascal, Blaise [1670]. *Pensées.* Translated by A.J. Kreilsheimer. New York: Penguin (USA), 1995.

Perec, Georges. *A Man Asleep*. Translated from the French by Andrew Leak. London: Collins Harvill, 1990.

Perec, Georges [1967]. *Things: A Story of the Sixties*. Translated from the French by David Bellos.

Perec, Georges [1969]. *La disparition*. Paris: Denoël, Gallimard, L'imaginaire. 1987. English translation: *A Void*. Translated by Gilbert Adair. London: Harvill, 1994.

Perec, Georges [1972]. "Les revenentes. Texte," in *Romans & Récits*. Paris: Le livre de Poche, La pochothèque, 2002. English translation: "The Exeter Text: Jewels, Secrets, Sex," translated by Ian Monk in *Three by Perec* (Harvill Press, 1996).

Perec, Georges [1975]. *W, or the Memory of Childhood*. Translated by David Bellos. Boston: David R. Godine, 1988.

Perec, Georges. *La vie mode d'emploi*. Paris: Hachette, 1978. *Life: A User's Manual*. Translated by David Bellos. London: Vintage, 2002.

Perec, Georges. "Ellis Island: Description of a Project" ("Récits d'Ellis Island") in *Species of Spaces and Other Pieces*, from *I Was Born* (*Je suis né*). Translated by John Sturrock. London: Penguin Books, 1997.

Perec, Georges. "I Was Born" ("Je suis né") in *Species of Spaces and Other Pieces*, from *I Was Born* (*Je suis né*). Translated by John Sturrock. London: Penguin Books, 1997.

Perec, Georges. "Les lieux d'une ruse" in *Penser/classer*. Paris: Hachette, 1985.

Perec, Georges. "The gnocchi of Autumn" ("Les gnocchis de l'automne") in *Species of Spaces and Other Pieces*, from *I Was Born* (*Je suis né*). Translated by John Sturrock. London: Penguin Books, 1997.

Perec, Georges. *Je me souviens*. Paris: Hachette, 1978.

Perec, Georges. *Le voyage d'hiver*. Paris: Denoël-Seuil, 1979.

Perec, Georges. *Un cabinet d'amateur. Histoire d'un tableau* [1979]. Paris: Seuil, 1994.

Piaget, Jean [1945]. *Play, Dreams and Imitation in Childhood*. Translated by C. Gattegno and F.M. Hodgson. New York: The Norton Library, 1962.

Pontalis, Jean-Baptiste with Jean Laplanche. *Vocabulaire de la psychanalyse*. Paris: PUF, 1968.

Pontalis, Jean-Baptiste [1955]. *Après Freud*. Paris: Gallimard, NRF (237), 1968.

Pontalis, Jean-Baptiste [1977]. *Frontiers in Psycho-Analysis: Between the Dream and Psychic Pain*. Translated by Catherine Cullen and Philip Cullen. New York: International Universities Press, Inc., 1981.

Pontalis, Jean-Baptiste [1986]. *L'amour des commencements*. France: Éditions Gallimard, 1986.

Proust, Marcel [1913–1927]. *À la recherche du temps perdu*. Paris: La Pléiade, Gallimard, 1969. *Remembrance of Things Past*. Translated by C.K. Scott Moncrieff and Terence Kilmartin; and Andreas Mayor. New York: Random House, 1981.

Proust, Marcel. *Jean Santeuil*. Translated by Gerard Hopkins. London: Weidenfeld and Nicolson, 1955.

Rank. O. [1924]. *The Double: A Psychoanalytic Study*. Translated by Karen Christenfeld. London: Karnac, 2000.

Reik, Theodor. *The Search Within*. New York: Grove Press, 1956.

Ricoeur, Paul. "Narrative Identity." *Philosophy Today*. 35:1 (1991–Spring), pp. 73–90.

Rimbaud, Arthur [May 13, 1871], letter to Georges Izambard, Paris, Gallimard (nrf), 1984.

Robles, Martha, "El primer recuerdo. Su doble espejo" ["The First Memory. Its Mirror Double"]. *Arena*, literary supplement of *Excélsior*. Mexico, Sunday, June 3, 2001.

Robles, Martha. *La condena*. México: FCE, 1996.

Robles, Martha. *La ley del padre*. México: FCE, 1998.

Roth, Joseph. *Flight Without End*. Translated by David Le Vay in collaboration with Beatrice Musgrave. London: Peter Owen, 1977.

Roudinesco, E. and M. Plon. *Dictionnaire de la psychanalyse*. Paris, Fayard, 1997. Article: Spielrein, Sabina.

Rousseau, Jean-Jacques. *The Confessions of Jean-Jacques Rousseau*. Translated by J.M. Cohen. London: Penguin Books, 1953.

Sartre, Jean-Paul [1964]. *Les mots*. Paris: Gallimard, Folio, 1974.

Sartre, Jean-Paul [1964]. *The Words*. Translated by Bernard Frechtman. New York: George Braziller, 1964.

Sartre, Jean-Paul. *Nausea*. Translated by Lloyd Alexander. New York: New Directions, 1959.

Schacter, D.L. *Searching for Memory: the brain, the mind, and the past*. New York: Basic Books, 1996.

Sebald, W.G. *Campo Santo*. Translated by Anthea Bell. New York: Random House, 2005.

Shakespeare, William. Sonnet LXXVII.

Shakespeare, William. *All's Well That Ends Well* [1602–1603].

Sheridan, Alan. *André Gide. A life in the present*. Cambridge (Ma): Harvard University Press, 1999, p. 148.

Simon, Claude. *The Wind*. Translated by Richard Howard. New York: George Braziller, 1986.

Spence, Donald. *Narrative Truth and Historical Truth*. New York: Norton, 1982.

Spence, Donald. "The Rhetorical Voice of Psychoanalysis," *J. Amer. Psychoanal. Assn.* 38: 579–603, 1990. Stendhal (Henri Beyle). *The Life of Henri Brulard*. Translated by Catherine Alison Phillips. New York: Alfred A. Knopf, 1939.

Stephen, Leslie. [1881]. *Hours in a Library*, "Autobiography." New York and London: G.P. Putnam's Sons, 1904. (Republished: Grosse Pointe, Michigan: Scholarly Press, 1968.)

Sterne, Laurence. *The Life and Opinions of Tristram Shandy, Gentleman*. Oxford-New York: Oxford University Press, 1983.

Stirner, Max [1844]. *The Ego and His Own: The Case of the Individual Against Authority*. Translated by Steven T. Byington. New York: Libertarian Book Club, 1963.

The Holy Bible. King James Version.

Tolstoy, Count Lev N. *The Complete Works of Count Tolstoy. Volume XXIII. Miscellaneous Letters and Essays*. "First Recollections (1878)." Translated from the Russian by Leo Wiener. Boston: Dana Estes & Company, 1905.

Tomkins, Calvin. *Duchamp: A Biography*. New York: Holt & Co., 1996.

Trotsky, Leon. *My Life: An Attempt at an Autobiography*. Mineola, New York: Dover Publications, Inc., 2007.

Valéry, Paul. [1936]. *Cahiers*. Paris: La Pléiade, Gallimard, 1994.

Weinrich, Harald, Weinrich, Harald. *Lete. The art and critic of forgetting*. Translation by Stephen Randall. Ithaca (NY): Cornell University Press, 2004.

S. Wetzler: "The Historical Truth of Psychoanalytical Reconstructions," *Int. R. of Psychoanal.* 12: 187–197, 1985.

Winnicott, D.W. [1967]. *Playing & Reality*, "Mirror-role of Mother and Family in Child Development." London and New York: Tavistock/ Routledge, 1989.

Woolf, Virginia [1937]. "A Sketch of the Past" in *Moments of Being*. New York: Harvest / Harcourt Brace & Co., 1985.

Woolf, Virginia [1927]. *To the Lighthouse*. London: Wordsworth Classics. 1994.

Woolf, Virginia [1929]. *Orlando: A Biography*. New York: Harcourt, Brace and Company, 1929.

Yourcenar, Marguerite. *Dear Departed: A Memoir* [Souvenirs pieux]. Translated by Maria Louise Ascher. New York: Farrar Straus Giroux, 1991.

Yourcenar, Marguerite. *How Many Years: A Memoir* [Archives du Nord]. Translated by Maria Louise Ascher. New York: Farrar Straus Giroux, 1995.

Yourcenar, Marguerite. *Archives du Nord*. Paris: Gallimard, 1977.

Yourcenar, Marguerite. *Souvenirs pieux*. Paris: Gallimard, 1974.

Yourcenar, Marguerite. *Quoi? L'Éternité*. Paris: Gallimard, 1988.

INDEX

LaVergne, TN USA
09 June 2010
185534LV00003B/4/P